P9-CCJ-650

The complete book of

Greek Cooking

The complete book of
Greek Cooking

Explore this classic Mediterranean cuisine, with over 160 step-by-step recipes and over 700 stunning photographs

Rena Salaman & Jan Cutler

NOTES
Bracketed terms are intended for American readers.

For all recipes, quantities are given in both metric and imperial measures and, where appropriate, measures are also given in standard cups and spoons. Follow one set, but not a mixture, because they are not interchangeable.

Standard spoon and cup measures are level: 1 tsp = 5ml, 1 tbsp = 15ml, 1 cup = 250ml/8fl oz

Australian standard tablespoons are 20ml. Australian readers should use 3 tsp in place of 1 tbsp for measuring small quantities of gelatine, cornflour, salt, etc.

Medium (US large) eggs are used unless otherwise stated.

This edition is published by Hermes House

Hermes House is an imprint of Anness Publishing Ltd
Hermes House, 88–89 Blackfriars Road, London SE1 8HA; tel. 020 7401 2077
fax 020 7633 9499; www.hermeshouse.com; www.annesspublishing.com

If you like the images in this book and would like to investigate using them for publishing, promotions or advertising, please visit our website www.practicalpictures.com for more information.

ETHICAL TRADING POLICY
Because of our ongoing ecological investment programme, you, as our customer, can have the pleasure and reassurance of knowing that a tree is being cultivated on your behalf to naturally replace the materials used to make the book you are holding. For further information about this scheme, go to www.annesspublishing.com/trees

A CIP catalogue record for this book is available from the British Library.

Publisher: Joanna Lorenz
Editorial Director: Judith Simons
Project Editor: Jennifer Mussett
Editorial Reader: Rosanna Fairhead
Photographers: Tim Auty, Martin Brigdale, Nicky Dowey, Gus Filgate, Michelle Garrett, John Heseltine, Janine Hosegood, William Lingwood, Craig Robertson
Stylist: Helen Trent
Food Stylists: Jacqueline Clark, Joanna Farrow, Carole Handslip, Lucy McKelvie, Emma Patmore, Annabel Ford, Bridget Sargeson, Jennie Shapter, Carol Tenant, Linda Tubby, Sunil Vijayakar, Jenny White
Designer: Graham Webb
Cover Designer: Chloe Steers
Recipes: Rena Salaman, Catherine Atkinson, Jacqueline Clark, Trish Davies, Roz Denny, Joanna Farrow, Jenni Fleetwood, Christine Ingram, Lucy Knox, Maggie Mayhew, Keith Richmond, Jennie Shapter, Jenny White, Kate Whiteman

Much of the material in this book has been previously published in *The Greek Cook*, by Rena Salaman

The nutritional analysis given for each recipe is calculated per portion (i.e. serving or item), unless otherwise stated. If the recipe gives a range, such as Serves 4–6, then the nutritional analysis will be for the smaller portion size, i.e. 6 servings. Measurements for sodium do not include salt added to taste.

American pints are 16fl oz/2 cups. American readers should use 20fl oz/2.5 cups in place of 1 pint when measuring liquids.

Electric oven temperatures in this book are for conventional ovens. When using a fan oven, the temperature will probably need to be reduced by about 10–20°C/20–40°F. Since ovens vary, you should check with your manufacturer's instruction book for guidance.

Contents

INTRODUCTION

Think Greek, and your mouth positively waters: all those wonderful and diverse flavours, served individually or combined so skilfully in a cuisine that is good for your heart, body and soul. From the mountainous and harsh terrain that covers most of mainland Greece and its islands, a flavoursome diet has developed, centred on vegetables and other fresh ingredients, and with quality seasonal produce at its heart. Greek food is healthy: it's the classic Mediterranean diet, rich in fruit and vegetables, with a little meat and fish, olives and olive oil, home-made bread, and home-produced cheeses.

The olive is the backbone of this healthy diet, adding richness and developing the flavours of the simplest of ingredients; it is grown almost everywhere and processed into the finest extra virgin olive oil in the world. Indeed, butter is never eaten in most parts of Greece. Lemons, too, grow all over the country and give that quintessentially Greek flavour to many dishes. A plethora of wild leaves grow throughout most of the year and feature prominently in the diet, eaten every day in salads, lightly cooked as a vegetable or as a filling for pies.

Below: Greece, in south-east Europe, occupies the southern part of the Balkan Peninsula and many islands in the Ionian and Aegean Seas.

A CUISINE SHAPED BY GEOGRAPHY

The majority of the country is covered with mountains and hills, and most of the land is exceptionally dry. Many people work on their own hill farms, growing sufficient for their needs, as well as using wild plants.

In the north, the pine forests give way to coastal plains with orchards and cattle pastures. The cuisine here is flavoured with spices and ingredients brought over from Turkey, such as cinnamon, aubergines (eggplants) and rice. Central Greece is mountainous, good for goat shepherding, game hunting, beekeeping, and cheese and dairy products. East of the Pindus Mountains, the fertile plains of Thessaly produce plentiful grains and fruit, with some cattle grazing too. The Peloponnese to the south of the mainland is a mountainous region with shepherding and cheese-making.

Above: Colourful religious festivals are accompanied by dancing, feasting and special cakes and sweets.

Greece has over 170 inhabited islands, which are mostly mountainous. Fruit and vegetables can be grown in small areas, with the odd pocket of fertile land going to grazing, vineyards and olive groves. Fish and shellfish are the mainstay, featuring in many specialities, such as the spectacular fried squid with feta cheese.

INFLUENCES FROM THE PAST

No study of Greek cuisine could ignore its history, not only that of the ancient Greeks, but also the variety of cooking techniques and flavours inherited from those Greeks who returned from Asia Minor in the early 20th century. They brought with them an array of spices and flavourings as well as new and different ways of cooking dishes. These distinctions have remained to this day and give a noticeable regional flavour to food from northern Greece.

On the western edge of Greece, the food of the Ionian Islands reflects hundreds of years of Venetian rule, with plenty of tantalizing pasta dishes. Corfu was a British protectorate for half a century and the cuisine retains a few British favourites, such as beef or lamb stew and ginger beer.

EVERYDAY FARE

Throughout history the Greeks have been mostly vegetarian, partly because of the various rules of the Greek Orthodox Church but also from necessity. As pasture land in Greece is sparse large herds of animals are rare, so meat is typically eaten only on Sundays, and at Easter and Christmas. Many Greek recipes have two versions: one with meat and one without.

Above: The familiar sight of octopus fresh from the sea drying in the afternoon sun on the island of Mykonos.

With its many islands, Greece actually has more boats per capita than cars. There are few areas of Greece that are more than 80km/50 miles from the sea and so fish is generally easily available. Coastal markets overflow with a wide diversity of sea creatures that, having been caught that day, are superbly fresh. Fish is widely enjoyed both as a main course and as mezedes.

Most rural families keep sheep and goats, but it is not economically viable to kill the animals for their meat except occasionally, so they are kept mainly for their wool, which may be sold on, and milk, which is made into some very good quality regional cheeses. These are used in a variety of tasty dishes and salads.

Other culinary specialities have grown from the rural culture. Pies are the traditional fare in shepherding communities: they make for an easily transportable meal, ideal for the shepherds' nomadic lifestyle. In these areas you will find an extensive tradition of pie-making, mostly using filo pastry.

The need to preserve food in the mountainous interiors has led to notable specialities, such as pickled and salted fish, cured meats and sausages. These are often served as mezedes, and may also feature in some main dishes.

Left: Fresh seafood is delivered straight off the boats to the waterside cafés and restaurants.

The Mainland

Greek cuisine is the product of the country's landscape: the mountains and rugged hillsides, the lowlands and the sea. Approximately 80 per cent of the country is mountainous terrain: the Pindus range dominates central and western Greece, extending down through the Peloponnese. No wonder the Greek legend describes the country as the work of a god who sifted all the available soil through a sieve and used just the stones to create Greece. But from this harsh terrain comes a diet rich in vegetables and olive oil, and on the grassy lowland plains orchards, citrus groves, wheat and other crops grow.

CLIMATE

Summer temperatures on mainland Greece are hot – up to 40°C/104°F. Spring, autumn and winter bring rain to all regions, especially the coastal plains. Although the winters are generally mild, there are heavy snowfalls in the mountains of the Peloponnese and, to the delight of skiers, the Pindus.

Although more than a quarter of the arable land requires irrigation during the extremely dry summers, other crops thrive in the hot, dry atmosphere: the ubiquitous olive tree grows all over Greece, and fig trees with their hand-shaped leaves and bulbous fruits grow wild by the roadside.

Many herbs and edible leaves grow wild, even in dry areas. They are eaten with every meal, sometimes becoming the main feature. Mushrooms are gathered in the wetter areas, and game is also found.

Below: Olive trees clothe the parched landscape, covering extensive areas of mainland Greece.

THE NORTH

Black-pine forests clothe the mountainous areas of Thrace to the east and Macedonia to the west. Here the brown bear, wildcat and roe deer have their homes. Even wolf, wild boar and lynx are occasionally seen. Rainfall is spread evenly throughout the year, making a wetter climate than further south – perfect for the orchards and crops of wheat, corn and barley grown here. Orchard fruits ripen in the autumn, and grapes grow widely. These all appear in savoury northern cooking, even the unripe juice of grape, the verjuice, which is added to a delicious piquant aubergine (eggplant) salad called *agourida*.

The misty climate encourages mushrooms as well as a wide variety of wild leaves – *horta* – to grow, which are traditionally picked after the day's work in the fields has finished, and eaten in salads or as a vegetable. *Horta* is also made into a popular tasty pie called *hortopita*.

Above: Goats are essential to the northern smallholding, providing milk, cheese and meat.

Preserving food is essential to ensure that there will be enough for the winter months. Cabbage and other vegetables are pickled and used in mezedes, pies and stews. Wild greens and herbs are dried, to be crumbled into winter stews. Fruit is also dried and used in savoury dishes; prunes, made from the local plums, are especially flavoursome in rich meat and vegetable stews. Preserved fish include *politiki lakerda* (brine-cured bonito), smoked eels and trout. There are excellent cured meats, and the sausages are spicy: lamb and pork flavoured with hot pepper flakes and leeks, or beef with cumin and garlic.

Preserved foods make a marked appearance at the meze table. Air-dried, smoked and pickled fish, cured meats and pickled vegetables are all popular dishes from the store cupboard.

Macedonia

When the Greeks from Asia Minor returned to Greece early in the 20th century, most made their homes in

Right: Farmers in the north enjoy an ideal soil and climate for orchard fruits and fruit vegetables.

Macedonia. They brought back with them new spices, ingredients and recipes from Turkey and Anatolia. Cinnamon, allspice and cloves became popular, and aubergines and rice were also introduced. Little pastas filled with cheese or meat, and pickled vegetables, grains cooked with milk, and yogurt dishes were eaten. Grilled (broiled) rather than air-dried pasta dough, such as *siron*, was also brought back from Turkey and Asia Minor.

Butter features in the northern diet and is sometimes used instead of olive oil. The Macedonian filo pastry, for example, is made with butter and not olive oil, giving it a different flavour. The area has many of Greece's favourite cheeses, and the local specialities include a *kefalotiri* cheese called *batsos* that has been aged in brine and is usually served pan-fried.

Peppers grow well in Macedonia, from sweet (bell) to fiery hot, and they feature in many local dishes, relishes and spreads. They are also powdered and dried as flakes, called *boukovo*. In September you can see them drying outside before they are oven-dried and powdered. In October giant beans, or *fasolia gigantes,* are harvested and often slowly casseroled with red peppers to make a local speciality dish.

Below: Fresh vegetables abound in Macedonia, notably (bell) peppers and aubergines (eggplants).

Even though Macedonia is cooler and moister than most parts of Greece, olives still grow here: the thick-skinned and wrinkled *halkidiki* is one of the most popular varieties, and there are many more besides.

Thrace

Apples, plums and cherries are all grown in the picturesque eastern province of Thrace, making beautiful preserves and spoon sweets, which are always offered to guests and presented as gifts at celebrations. The plums from here are often dried to make succulent prunes for home consumption and for export.

Right: Cherries are grown in Thrace, where they are used to make delicious local preserves and spoon sweets.

Beef and pork farming is popular and the region has many meat stews in its repertoire, many with peppers.

A rich, golden-brown *tahini* is made here from locally grown sesame seeds. It is eaten mixed with grape-must molasses, called *petimezi*, as a spread.

Left: Shepherds in the Pindus Mountains traditionally eat local pies, some made from feta cheese, cornmeal and buttermilk.

In Thrace, recipes often hint at a Balkan influence from the North. Bulgur wheat, paprika and sesame seeds, for example, are regularly found; the regional dish is a delicious sausage called *babo*, which contains beef and pork, bulgur wheat and leeks.

WESTERN AND CENTRAL GREECE

The snow-covered peaks of the Pindus Mountains run down the centre of the mainland. They separate the wide, lush plains of Thessaly on the east from the forested mountains of Epirus and Roumeli on the west. Attica lies on the eastern lowlands.

Thessaly

The fertile plain of Thessaly, rich with wheat, corn, barley and sugar beets, bears down to the east coast of the central mainland. Cattle graze on the pastures, and the local diet reflects plentiful supplies of beef, lamb and pork: as a stuffing for slices of aubergine (eggplant), in the local sausages to be eaten with *spetzofai*, or as a slow-cooked dish with tomatoes and red (bell) peppers. Orchard fruits grow well, and are made into a wide range of spoon sweets or are dried and used to flavour dishes.

Thessaly also boasts a fine cheese-making tradition and there are a wealth of local specialities. The *graviera* cheese here is renowned for its sweet and fresh flavour, and Thessaly produces the bulk of Greece's *kasseri* cheese.

A visitor here might be astonished at the variety of pies found in the region, traditionally made as a portable meal for shepherds. Some are simple, with cornmeal, feta or buttermilk mixed together and baked. Others contain *trahana* – a small, round pasta frequently made with bulgur wheat – mixed with feta cheese and eggs, and encased in filo pastry. Yet others are more elaborate and include meat and locally grown leeks.

The range of mezedes is one of the joys of visiting the area, and seafood features very prominently, often accompanied by pickled vegetables such as red peppers. Freshwater trout and carp caught from Thessaly's lakes, rivers and streams are also enjoyed to the full.

Epirus

West of the Pindus Mountains lies the region of Epirus. Most of the land is mountainous, and its peaks are snow-capped in winter and spring, but olives, oranges and corn grow on its northern plains. Game birds, deer and wild

Right: Orchard fruits such as plums grow well in Thessaly; many are dried to make prunes for export.

boar live in the forested areas, and chanterelles and other wild mushrooms thrive there. The lower slopes of the mountains are also rich with wild greens, herbs and flowers. Bees produce an especially fine honey from the wild flowers and herbs that grow profusely, a speciality of the region, and rivers rush down the mountainsides into lakes where freshwater fish were once plentiful. Now, however, trout and salmon are mostly farmed, and often enjoyed simply pan-fried. Other fish and seafood also enrich the diet, and include prawns (shrimp), crayfish and eels.

At the foot of the mountains there is enough rich pastureland to support a thriving shepherding community and dairy production. The region's food reflects this, with all kinds of pies for the shepherds to take with them on their jouneys into the mountains. Some contain cheese, wild greens and perhaps meat; others are simply made with a base or topping of cornmeal or a batter of egg, olive oil and water enclosing a flavourful filling of cheese, mint and wild greens.

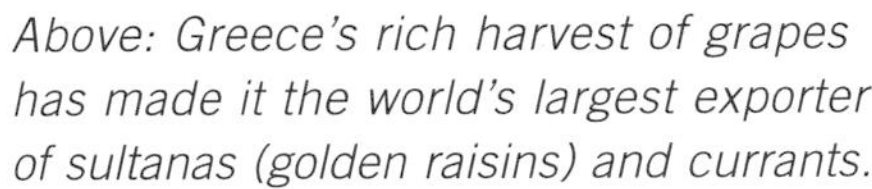

Above: Greece's rich harvest of grapes has made it the world's largest exporter of sultanas (golden raisins) and currants.

Below: Beehives dot the landscape, collecting fine honeys oozing with the flavours of wild flowers.

Meat recipes from the region revolve around lamb or game such as rabbit, with a number of good poultry dishes. Among the most frequently used vegetables are leeks, and spinach, which is found in pies or as a bed for baked fish.

Epirus also has an established cheese-making tradition and produces feta, the soft *ghalotiri* and the hard *kefalotiri*, as well as a whey cheese, *manouri*. Milk is cooked in pies with cheese, and simmered with greens.

Cherries, apples, apricots, peaches and plums grow along the Epirot coastline, and almonds and walnuts also thrive there. Nuts and honey are included in the regional pastry, *yianniotiki*, which is enclosed in a shredded-wheat crust. There are many other nut and honey-based cakes and spoon sweets that have crept into the region from the north of Greece and from Turkey and the Middle East.

Unlike most regions that originally grew corn and then turned to wheat production, Epirus remains a corn-growing area and its bread reflects this, with cornbreads eaten daily. However, special occasions call for wheat breads, and specialities are made during Easter, at Christmas and for weddings.

Roumeli

In the south of central Greece is Roumeli, an extremely mountainous region, where sheep and goats roam. Meat is eaten more often here than in other parts of Greece. Lamb dishes feature prominently, as well as pork, poultry and occasionally beef. Vegetables are varied, with wild greens and aubergines (eggplants) plentiful. Local dishes include the locally grown *fasolia gigantes*, and there are several noteworthy cheeses, including the mild and slightly chewy *formaella*, which is delicious when served pan-fried or used for a filling in traditional pies.

Fresh fish is abundant on the coast, but inland the need for preservation has led to many specialities. Salted fish, such as anchovies and bream, are split down the centre and opened out, and are commonly prepared for mezedes.

Attica

The area around Athens is known as Attica. Rich in archaeology, it attracts vast numbers of visitors each year. Market towns thrive on the coast selling luscious fruits and vegetables, and freshly caught fish is sold from the harbourside. Citrus trees and grapes grow on the hot surrounding Attic plain, and the finest retsina, a wine flavoured with pine-tree resin, is produced in the Mesogeia region.

Above: Eating in Athens is more cosmopolitan. Here young people enjoy afternoon refreshments outside at a café in Plaka Old Quarter, Athens.

Left: Most of the country's artichokes are grown in the Peloponnese.

Athens

The capital of Greece, Athens is home to stunning classical and neoclassical architecture. Restaurants and open-air tavernas provide food for locals and tourists alike. Every food imaginable is available at the central market in Athens, from fresh food, to preserves, olives, and canned and dried goods.

Athens is a melting pot where all the tastes of Greece come together. The fresh seafood dishes from the coast and the islands feature alongside the regional cheeses and preserved meats and fish from northern Greece. The quintessentially Greek sauce, lemony *avgolemono*, originated from Athens.

THE PELOPONNESE

South of Attica, the narrow Isthmus of Corinth joins the huge peninsula of the Peloponnese to mainland Greece. Almost an island, it is mountainous and has a mainly rural economy.

In the south lies the city of Kalamata, the main marketplace for the well-known *Kalamata* olives – smooth-skinned tapered olives of high quality – as well as currants, figs and other fruit crops grown on the fertile Messinian plain on the south-eastern corner of the Peloponnese. Vinegar and raisins feature in many of the local dishes.

Wheat grows plentifully on the plains and is made into breads and pastries. Pasta, too, is eaten regularly and might

Above: Wild rabbits and other game are used in the traditional stew, stifado, *enjoyed throughout mainland Greece.*

simply be tossed in garlic and olive oil. An array of local cheeses is produced, including *sfela* made with sheep's milk and aged in cans. The region is well known for sesame seeds, enjoyed as a brittle sweet made with honey.

East of the Messinian plain are the Taygetos Mountains, their lower slopes clothed with grapes, olives and citrus fruits. The mountains create a barrier between the rural communities and the sea, so traditionally the majority of fish eaten here is preserved. Salt cod recipes abound, often using raisins or wild greens. For the coastal communities, however, there is a greater variety, with fish such as octopus and bonito cooked wrapped in paper and flavoured with herbs.

Most of the artichokes sold in Greece are grown in the Peloponnese and are cooked in myriad ways, such as fried or stuffed with oregano-and-fennel-flavoured rice. Aubergines (eggplants) are also plentiful, as is garlic which, unusually for Greek cooking, features strongly in many local recipes. Sweet and flavoursome plum tomatoes are grown here, and often made into a rich, cinnamon-flavoured sauce.

Meat is seasonal, with pork usually eaten as a winter meat, either roasted or stewed with vegetables. In the mountain villages it is cured in salt then wine, seasoned with allspice and cinnamon, and stored in clay vessels to last until the spring.

Above: Olives and excellent olive oils are a speciality of the Peloponnese, with the Kalamata olives renowned for their particularly high quality.

Below: The rugged mountains of the Peloponnese contain little farmland, leaving the population reliant on seafood and small harvests of local fruit and vegetables.

THE ISLANDS

Of over 2,000 Greek islands only about 170 are inhabited, and most can be reached only by boat. The islands are mostly rugged and mountainous, and although some have fertile valleys and plains there are others that cannot support much agriculture. For these islands, fresh supplies of fruit and vegetables arriving by boat are eagerly anticipated by the locals. Plenty of fish and shellfish dishes are found on all the islands, and octopus and squid are common. Nevertheless, the islanders still have fresh vegetables and olive oil at the centre of their cuisine.

THE IONIAN ISLANDS

Off the western coast of Greece lie the fertile Ionian Islands, which include Corfu, Ithaca, Lefkada, Kefallinia and Zakynthos. Five hundred years ago the islands were ruled by the Venetians, whose presence is seen in the many pasta dishes eaten here. A lovely thick tubular pasta is most often used in Corfu, and makes a delicious dish called *pastitsatha*, with chicken and tomatoes. For *pastitsio Venetsianiko*, a crisp pastry encloses a mixture of pasta, cheese and various meats in a rich white sauce. Pies are a speciality of the island of Kefallinia, and often contain the creamy local feta cheese.

The Ionian Islands were also protectorates of Britain for 50 years in the 19th century and a British influence is evident in some of the dishes. An example is the traditional Christmas meal of roast turkey. Many locals even enjoy a type of ginger beer, called *tzitzibeera*. But for more traditional tastes the island is rich in olives and wild greens, and these are found in many of the dishes.

Above: Courgette (zucchini) flowers are a favourite on Corfu, where they are stuffed with garlic and celeriac to make a local speciality.

Left: The harbour is at the centre of island life, with cafés and restaurants awaiting the fisherman's return.

Rose-water vinegar is a speciality of Lefkada and is used in *riganatha* – a meze made with toasted and moistened bread dressed with olive oil and served with fish. Vegetables are in abundance, and an attractive dish is courgette (zucchini) flowers stuffed with garlic and celeriac. The island boasts all types of seafood: tiny shrimps, clams and mussels, and dried octopus are specialities. The two best-known fish dishes of the Ionian Islands are a peppery stew called *Corfiot bourtheto* from Corfu, and a garlicky fish stew called *bianco*.

THE ARGO-SARONIC ISLANDS

From the south coast of Attica and down the east coast of the Peloponnese run the Argo-Saronic Islands. Although most of them are rugged, Poros and Spetses are lush with pine forests and olive groves. Aigina is a popular island for Athenians on a city break as it is quick and easy to get to by hydrofoil from Piraeus. Apart from the fabulous seafood dishes served in the tavernas

Above: Fishing boats set out at sunrise from the harbour and capital of Poros, one of the Argo-Saronic islands.

and ouzeries by the fish markets and harbours, Aigina is well known for its excellent pistachio nuts, which are sold the world over.

THE DODECANESE ISLANDS

Along the coast of Turkey lie the Greek Dodecanese, which include Rhodes with its wealth of grapes and olives, Nisyros, Kalymnos and Kos. The landscapes are frequently barren and mountainous although there are also some fecund valleys.

The cos lettuce and an assortment of other vegetables and herbs grow in the flat and fertile land of the island of Kos. Pasta dishes from the region, such as the yogurt and *kefalotiri* cheese sauce from Kassos, are frequently topped with caramelized onions. Chickpea fritters are found all over the Dodecanese, flavoured with the locally grown herbs or favourite spices, such as mint and cumin. They are eaten as part of a meze table or make a wonderful snack.

The leaves of cyclamen take the place of vine leaves to wrap around fillings on the islands of Rhodes and Nisyros, and the bulbs are made into a preserve that is used to flavour savoury meals. Dishes that have a fragrant sweet sauce are also popular in the region. They include an unusual sweet tahini sauce for pasta and a sweet wheat soup from the island of Kastellorizo. This latter dish is traditionally prepared by a married woman to present to her mother-in-law at Christmas time. It also contains sprouted wheat, cinnamon, cloves, raisins and sugar.

Kabourma is a cured beef found on board fishing boats from the island of Kalymnos, as it is an easily stored food for taking on voyages. The beef is preserved in butter, which melts when the beef is cooked.

Fish dishes from the islands include whole grouper baked on a bed of vegetables with a tahini and wine sauce. The island of Kalymnos specializes in garlicky octopus patties. Sea urchins are eaten as a salad mixed with onion, tomatoes and broken barley rusks.

EVVOIA AND THE SPORADES ISLANDS

The large and forested island of Evvoia lies just off the north-east coast of Attica, and the islands in the Sporades are found a little further out into the Aegean Sea. A common sight in Evvoia and the Sporades is the profusion of dried octopus hanging out to dry on lines on the harboursides. It is served as part of a mezedes or combined with pasta or potatoes as a main dish. Lobster is also popular, often served with pasta, and enormous prawns (shrimp). They are baked with cheese, local herbs and fresh tomatoes to make a local dish. Cheese or garlic and parsley are a filling for filleted sardines.

THE NORTH-EAST AEGEAN ISLANDS

The islands of the north-east Aegean include Limnos, Lesvos, Samos, Thassos and Chios, and are just off the coast of Thrace. They have a rich and active fishing industry, making fresh seafood a firm favourite both for locals and for tourists. Sea urchins are a particular speciality, eaten raw with a little lemon juice. Snapper, bass and bream are also regularly found on menus, as is the distinctive speciality, carp roe and fennel patties. On Samos, the smallest fish from the catch are tossed in flour and then cooked together in a pan, to form a kind of savoury cake that can be cut into slices and served as part of a meze table. Another speciality is a sweet ravioli made with cinnamon-flavoured pumpkin drizzled with honey.

On Lesvos, freshly caught langoustine is prepared in a herby tomato sauce, and sardines, either smoked or salted, make popular mezedes. Fish is used as a stuffing with rice to fill cabbage, washed down with Lesvos ouzo, considered among the best in Greece.

Above: Oranges abound on the island of Chios, where sweet orange-blossom water is made.

Wild greens grow profusely and are cooked with pulses, and sometimes snails. Fresh broad (fava) beans are tossed in batter and fried until crisp and served with *skordalia*, a garlic sauce.

Cheeses from the region are varied, and some highlights include the basket-shaped *kalathaki* cheeses from Limnos, and *melipasto*, which is matured and then washed in the sea, giving a slightly salty edge to its sweet taste.

Oranges, lemons and tangerines grow on Chios, as well as olives and figs, even though there is no permanent watercourse, so irrigation is necessary. Sweet orange-blossom water is made here, and the island is famous for its mastic, an aromatic tree resin, which is used as a flavouring. Tomatoes dry in the sun, providing richness to stews.

Thassos prides itself on the superb quality and strong flavour of its small black and wrinkled dry-cured olives.

From the tourist island of Samos comes a fine dessert wine produced from muscat grapes; it is so delicious that biscuits are flavoured with it.

THE CYCLADES ISLANDS

There are 56 islands in the Cyclades including Naxos, with its lush groves of olives, oranges and lemons, Mykonos, Santorini, Milos, Sifnos and Paros.

The region is well known for its variety of cheeses, and especially noteworthy is the *manoura* from Sifnos, which is preserved and matured in the dregs of

Left: Windmills once harnessed the force of nature on Santorini to grind locally grown grain.

Right: The beautiful island of Santorini at sunset as the locals and tourists alike seek out cafés for aperitifs and mezedes.

wine at the bottom of the barrel, making it pungent and hard. *Kefalysio spilias milou* is another unusual cheese, which is rubbed with the pulp that remains after pressing olives for oil. It has a dark coating and is aged for up to a year to develop the flavour. The Easter speciality from Sifnos is tartlets filled with an interesting mix of honey and fresh soft *mizithra* cheese.

Thyme grows plentifully on the fertile island of Paros and is used in meat and vegetable dishes. The sun also dries the small fish, *gavros*, on Paros, which are popular as a meze. On the island of Syros capers can be seen drying in the sun. As well as complementing fish in a stew, capers are added to a tomato spread that is eaten on bread.

The volcanic island of Santorini feeds not only the locals but also the many tourists who visit every year. The island is famed for its yellow split peas, which are made into fava, often served with fried squid. Delicious tomato rissoles are also popular fare with both locals and tourists. Nothing beats the local specialities *brandada Santorinis* – salt cod served with a thick sauce made from garlic, potatoes and tomato – and squid stuffed with rice and olives.

Below: Terraces are cut into the hillside to provide strips of land for growing vegetables on Milos.

CRETE

The climate and soil of Crete are ideal for growing olives and grapes, and approximately 20 per cent of all Greek wines are produced here. The Cretans have always believed that they have the healthiest diet, as many of them have lived well beyond 100 years. Their diet consists of little meat but lots of fresh fruit and vegetables, pulses, cereals, olives and olive oil; indeed, Cretans consume the most olive oil per head in the world.

Among the vegetables grown here are artichokes and a huge selection of wild greens. Crete also produces a wide variety of local hard and soft cheeses. Local dishes include *pallikaria* – pulses casseroled with wheat grains – and squid cooked with olives and fennel. Olive trees grow in abundance, providing excellent black varieties. The island also abounds with orchards of citrus fruit, especially lemons and oranges, that are used to flavour salads and to create spoon sweets.

History and Foreign Influences

It is from the Ancient Greeks that we have the word "gastronomy" – the art or science of good eating – taken from the very first cookbook, *Gastronomia*, written by Archestratus in the 5th century BC. For the ancient Athenians, mealtimes were sumptuous and pleasurable affairs where the spirit as well as the body was nourished. Greeks today have continued this mealtime philosophy of relaxation and enjoyment amongst family and friends.

THE ANCIENT GREEKS

Beef, lamb, pork, goat and fish were favourite foods of wealthy ancient Athenians, although the poorer urban Greeks had less variety in their food. In the countryside, however, fruit, vegetables and pulses were plentiful. Honey was the main sweetener and olives and olive oil were eaten by all. And then, of course, there were grapes and the renowned wine. Barley and wheat were the most commonly grown cereals, and bread was a staple food. Cheese-making has a long history; feta, the best known of all Greek cheeses, and *kasseri* cheese may have been first produced more than 6,000 years ago and are probably the oldest cheeses in the world.

By the 5th century BC Greeks had travelled to and settled in Sicily, southern Italy and the coast of Asia Minor (now Turkey), all around the edge of the Black Sea and in areas of North Africa, taking olives, chickpeas and grapes with them.

FOOD FROM DISTANT LANDS

Philip of Macedon defeated the ancient Greek city states by 338BC, and his son, Alexander the Great, incorporated Greece into a vast empire that stretched as far as India. Spices were bought back by the conquering army, including saffron, nutmeg and cinnamon, as well as rice from India. In AD168, Greece was conquered by the Romans and absorbed into the Roman Empire. A spice trade was developed with Sri Lanka (Ceylon) and India.

By AD323 the emperor Constantine divided the Roman Empire into the Latin-speaking west and the Greek-speaking east, with its capital at Constantinople, and this had developed into the Byzantine Empire by the end of the 4th century AD.

Travel, trade and migration brought new products and foodstuffs back to Greece, for example Black Sea salt roe and caviar (*tarama*, used in *taramasalata*). From other parts of the Middle East came aubergines (eggplants), melons and oranges, and the distilling process from which the Greeks were able to develop ouzo. Also introduced were cane sugar and confectionery, which began to develop into what we now know as spoon sweets – an essential element of Greek hospitality. Okra, a native of West Africa, also appeared at this time.

Above: Aubergine (eggplant) dishes were introduced from the Middle East during the Byzantine period.

THE OTTOMAN EMPIRE

In 1453 the Muslim Ottoman Turks captured Constantinople, ending the Byzantine Empire. Greece was then a part of the Ottoman Empire for nearly four centuries. The Ottomans brought with them beans, spinach, coffee and the many small dishes that are now known as mezedes. *Imam bayaldi* – stuffed aubergine – is a Turkish dish too. They also introduced the *kafeneion* (coffee shop), where coffee and mezedes are taken. Rice became part of the staple diet during this period.

During the Turkish occupation all Greek dishes had to have Turkish names. As a result it is often wrongly thought that many dishes have a Turkish origin, when in fact much of Greek cuisine developed independently.

Left: The Athenians built the Parthenon on the hill of the Acropolis as a celebration of life and their city.

ITALIAN INFLUENCES

The Venetians held Crete from the 13th to the 17th century, and seized the Ionian Islands and part of the Cyclades in the mid-15th century, remaining for approximately 400 years. They introduced crops from the Americas: (bell) peppers, green beans, corn, potatoes, pumpkins (still called Venetian squash on Zakynthos), and introduced many pasta dishes.

THE BRITISH ON THE IONIAN ISLANDS

During the 19th century, the Ionian Islands were protectorates of Britain for 50 years. British influences can still be seen in many of the dishes. A sweet mustard sauce is made to accompany their traditional Christmas meal of roast turkey, and a type of ginger beer, called *tzitzibeera*, is also popular.

Below: Restaurants at the waterfront in the old Venetian town of Chania on Crete, seen complete with gondolas.

Above: Kebabs, among other Middle Eastern favourites, were brought back by the Greeks returning from Asia Minor in the early 20th century.

THE GREEKS RETURN

The Ottomans were expelled from mainland Greece in the Greek War of Independence (1821). The following century, the Greeks tried to recapture control over Asia Minor, but in 1922 this ended in disaster and defeat by Turkey. Millions of Greeks were expelled from Smyrna in Turkish Anatolia, where there had been a considerable Greek population, ending thousands of years of Greek presence in Asia Minor.

The Asia Minor Greeks, or *Mikrasiates*, returned mainly to Macedonia and Thrace, bringing with them two millennia of culinary experience from Asia Minor and the shores of the Black Sea. Over the course of this period a cosmopolitan and complex cuisine had developed for city dwellers and rural farmers alike. They brought back *tzatsiki*, stuffed vegetables, smoked fish, kebabs, *pastourma* and much more – including the iconic moussaka.

Food, Culture and Hospitality

The Greeks are hospitable people who enjoy socializing and sharing their food. The family unit is strong, with the majority of young people living at home until they marry. The love of food and enjoying it in relaxed surroundings is integral to the way they live.

Their social lives and even many businesses revolve around the family. Although there are now many Greek women in professions, such as medicine and law, and there are other women who have their own businesses, many still choose to remain in the home with their young children, especially outside the main towns.

Above: Central to life in Greece is the big family meal, complete with a spread of dishes and plenty of ouzo.

SMALLHOLDINGS

Many people in Greece still make their living from farming, and family-owned smallholdings are the norm, growing what the family needs. Goats are hardy enough to survive in the rugged landscape on limited food resources, and are frequently kept, although sheep are also common, and their milk is made into a variety of cheeses. Olives are grown for family use and sale.

Many people are required to work on the land, and almost a third of the Greek labour force is employed in agricultural work. However, the young find it increasingly difficult to make a living from it and continue to migrate to the larger cities. About a third of the population of over 10 million now live in and around Athens.

HOMELY FOOD

Whenever possible, people who have moved to the cities return to their family home to relax in comfortable surroundings and enjoy the good, homely food that, although humble, is wholesome and never plain. Greek food is mostly based on a rural tradition – the recipes have been passed down from mother to daughter, by word of mouth. Although in many parts of Greece the Greeks love to eat out, there are some places where there is no real restaurant culture, and festivities and feasts are all enjoyed at home.

Traditional cooking and eating is central to family life. One of the most evocative images we have of the Greek lifestyle is a long wooden table outside a white-painted house in bright summer sun, with the extended family seated around it enjoying a convivial meal together. For many Greek families this country scene remains unchanged. Eating outdoors is a great pleasure during the summer months and, because the cooking traditionally took place outdoors, it was an easy and straightforward way to eat.

Left: Local fishermen bring in their catch every evening, keeping some aside for their families.

Right: Using a long-handled wooden paddle, bakers make bread in the traditional way in an outside oven.

Most family meals start with a meze table, filled with local specialities and *tzatsiki*, *hummus*, *taramasalata*, fried shellfish and seafood, marinated or cured meats or fish, rissoles, aubergine (eggplant) salads, pitta and crusty white bread, and so on. A large meze table may constitute a whole meal by itself. A main meal is often barbecued outside in the spring and summer, served with salads and breads. During the colder months, pots of chicken with *avgolemono* sauce, moussaka or pork stewed with orange and chickpeas are prepared over the stove or in an oven.

Traditional country homes have their ovens outside to keep the house cool. These external ovens are lit only once a day, for bread and meat or pies. In some villages and towns, it is still quite common for traditional homes not to own an oven at all, but to have a simple, small cooking hearth built into the external wall.

In more basic households, a pot will be raised or lowered over a fire to regulate the heat for cooking a stewed dish or soup. For these families, the local baker is extremely useful: the women prepare their bread and meals that need to be oven-cooked and then carry them in their dishes to the baker to be put in the oven after the bread has been baked. A little later, when the mouth-watering smells of roasting meat and baking vegetables fill the air, the village women collect their lunches and take them back to the family tables.

Cooking outside the home keeps the heat of an oven out of the house, and even today, in places where almost every home possesses an electric oven, you will still see women taking their meals to the baker, especially on hot summer days. It's a good opportunity for chatting and gossiping along the way – and socializing in all its many forms is an essential part of everyday life for Greek people.

Left: Barbecued seafood and meats are popular both for family celebrations and for outdoor entertaining.

ENTERTAINING

There is a superstition in Greece that a guest could be a god in disguise. The Greeks will therefore extend their hospitality even to strangers who call in, and will offer them spoon sweets: these are home-made fruit preserves offered to the visitor on a spoon as a sign of welcome.

Entertaining at home is something that the Greeks enjoy wholeheartedly, even if times are lean. If necessary they will live exceptionally frugally for days beforehand so that they are able to offer a good spread to their guests. The cooking will be imaginative and creative, often including luxuries, fresh seafood and the best cuts of meat, with a selection of bright fruit to finish.

DAILY LIFE

The day starts with a light breakfast, and may be simply a small cup of Greek coffee or tea with lemon. By mid-morning many Greeks enjoy a snack such as *koulouri*, covered with sesame seeds, or a hot cheese pie, called *tyropitta*, bought from a street seller. Lunch is traditionally served late – around 2 p.m. – although many of the younger generation have adopted the western European lifestyle and eat at about midday. Cakes and pastries are an afternoon treat taken with coffee.

Above: A classic scene: two men sitting outside a café in the late afternoon, passing the time.

PASSING THE TIME OF DAY

In the small towns and villages, the day will usually include enjoying a drink of Greek coffee and a snack – meze – in a small coffee shop or *kafeneion*. Traditionally, these are largely male preserves, where the men will gather with their friends to smoke or discuss politics. However, the atmosphere has now relaxed and women, too, can enjoy a drink and a chat there. The *kafeneion* is also a centre of communication where people can collect mail or use the telephone.

EATING OUT

Because of the long afternoon siesta, the evening meal will also be served late, at about 9 or 10 p.m. In many parts of Greece – especially more cosmopolitan areas – dining out at a local restaurant or *estiatorion* is very popular. Although home cooking is still enjoyed, the Greeks may go out for a meal two or three times a week.

The local restaurant will be friendly and noisy, selling local food and wines. When visitors from other countries dine there, they will often be invited into the kitchen to see the food that has been prepared so that they can make their choice from the array of large pans containing various dishes. Raw meats and fish ready for barbecuing and vegetable dishes will be laid out on the stove top, the crisp salads nearby.

Tavernas are a more relaxed setting for a drink and a meal, and are usually open only in the evenings. Quite often, a taverna menu will be fairly small, offering perhaps eight mezedes and just four main courses, with salads and vegetables to accompany.

Fish dishes are the speciality of *psarotavernas*, whereas spit roasts and chargrilled meat, including game, are specialities of the *psistaria*. The atmosphere in an *ouzeri* is more gregarious. Although it is essentially a drinking establishment, small savouries are usually served to accompany the glasses of ouzo, served with water.

To start their meal, Greeks accompany their pre-dinner drinks – perhaps some ouzo – with simple mezedes: shiny olives and feta cheese or, if the restaurant or taverna is by the sea, fried baby squid, whitebait or clams. The main meal might be a combination of different mezedes shared by everyone and washed down with wine, perhaps retsina or, more recently, non-resinated wines.

Below: Cakes are enjoyed as an afternoon snack with coffee, or as part of a celebration. Guests often arrive with cakes for their hosts.

Alternatively, vegetables stuffed with lamb or rice might be chosen. A salad of wild leaves is always served and expected, as it is a vital part of the spread; it might even constitute the main dish served with some grilled (broiled) or fried fish. The meal always finishes with fruit, sometimes served with honey, nuts and pastries.

Above: Snacks, such as sweet pastries and cakes, can always be picked up from street vendors. This one in Athens is selling sweet breads.

Below: Guests come together to dance during a traditional wedding feast on the beautiful island of Sikinos in the Cyclades.

Weddings
Food is symbolic in the Greek wedding, and for good luck and happiness certain strict culinary traditions need to be followed. Before the wedding day, relatives or unmarried girls stuff the mattress of the marriage bed with lamb's wool and lay sugared almonds and sesame sweets on the linen to symbolize fertility. A pomegranate – a fertility symbol – will be smashed against the front door and the seeds left to dry.

On the big day, the celebrations begin with eating bread; a special sourdough bread is made and gifts are sometimes hidden inside. The celebrations continue with a spit-roast lamb, and pear- or star-shaped almond cakes, called *amygthalota*, are always served. Later, a spoonful of sugar will be given to the bride at her new mother-in-law's home to ensure that she will be a "sweet wife".

Feast Days and Festivals

In Greece 98 per cent of the population follow the Greek Orthodox faith, and Greeks celebrate numerous saints' days and festivals throughout the year.

The highlight of the Greek Orthodox calendar is Easter Sunday when Christians celebrate the day Christ rose from the dead, ending the 40 days of fasting during Lent. Meat plays a very central role in celebrations, as it will have been avoided during Lent. Probably the most important meal of meat to be enjoyed during the festival year is the roast lamb that is cooked as part of the Easter celebration.

CARNIVAL

Three weeks before Lent is Carnival, or *apokries*, when the Greeks eat meat in preparation for the Lenten fasts. During the first week of Carnival a pig is slaughtered, and people can eat as much meat as they like in the second week. "Burnt Thursday" takes place during this week, when food is allowed to char or burn, and during the third week cheese is eaten. Music and dancing, and brightly coloured costumes, add to the merrymaking in the Carnival evenings. On the island of Skiros, the men will dress as half men and half beasts by wearing goatskin masks and furry jackets.

CLEAN MONDAY, THE START OF LENT

The sixth Monday before Easter Sunday is the first day of Lent. It is known in Greece as Clean Monday, the day on which to clean all pots and pans to make sure that no trace of animal produce remains.

The feast, where no meat, butter, eggs or cheese are present, ushers in 40 days of fasting, which most Greeks, even the non-religious, observe.

Far from being a solemn occasion, Clean Monday is dedicated to picnics of fasting food and kite-flying, washed down with plenty of wine. Families picnic on shellfish, *taramasalata*, octopus, salads, pickles and loaves of unleavened bread.

Above: Spring lamb provides the most important celebration meal of the year, on Easter Sunday.

HOLY WEEK

During the week before Easter there will be fasting and little entertainment. Families who have moved away to the cities always return home to take part in the Easter celebrations. In preparation for the big day, special breads are made from ingredients that have been

Below: Midnight celebrations in Crete: candles and fireworks mark the end of Lent and the beginning of Easter Day.

Above: This Easter bread from the island of Ios is traditionally made from ingredients blessed by the local priest.

previously blessed by the priest. The traditional red-dyed eggs are made on the Thursday before Easter – the red dye symbolizing the blood that was shed by Christ. Scarlet dye is added to water and vinegar in which brown-shelled eggs are boiled. Once cooked, the eggs are polished with olive oil and then arranged in mounds for Easter Sunday. These brightly coloured eggs are displayed in cake shops and the windows of homes, and presented as gifts. They are also added to the traditional Easter bread made from braided sweet dough formed into a circle – a tradition that harks back to the Byzantine era.

GOOD FRIDAY

A national holiday in Greece, Good Friday is a day of mourning with funeral services held in churches. There are restrictions on what can be eaten to reflect the importance of the day on which Christ was crucified. No food that has to be prepared by crushing or deforming in any way is eaten. Therefore, no olive oil or lemon juice is served on Good Friday, although vinegar is allowed, as a reminder of the vinegar offered to Christ on the cross. In the church, Christ's effigy, known as the Sacred Icon of Christ, will be laid on a bier, highly decorated with flowers and garlands made by the young girls of the parish. After the evening service the bier is carried through the streets, followed by a candlelit procession.

THE FAST ENDS

Late on the Saturday evening before Easter Sunday, all the family attend a church service, each carrying an unlit candle. At midnight the lights will be turned off and the priest will invite the whole congregation to receive the holy light from his candle and each person will light a candle within the church. The end of Lent and beginning of Easter Sunday is celebrated with the words "Christ is risen". Outside, fireworks light the sky and street parties begin.

The first meal to mark the end of fasting can be eaten after midnight, and is traditionally *mageritsa* soup made from the offal (variety meats) of the lamb that was slaughtered that day.

There are some regional differences in the Easter celebrations throughout Greece. In Corfu ceramic pots are tossed out of people's windows to throw away evil, whereas in Crete and the Peloponnese a doll is dressed in old clothes and burned, to represent the burning of Judas. Young women in Thrace and Macedonia, called the *Lazarins*, sing traditional Easter songs around the villages.

EASTER SUNDAY

On Easter Sunday the red-dyed eggs are cracked open to celebrate the new life symbolized by Christ's death and his resurrection. They are also used for Easter games.

The meal, of course, will be the highlight of the day, with lines of whole lambs gently roasting outside on spits. Sometimes, in the villages, *lambriotis* – stuffed lamb or goat that has been cooked overnight – will be brought to the feast instead of spit-roast lamb. The tables are set outside and laid with white tablecloths and spring flowers. The men drink retsina and ouzo while they watch the lambs roasting, and the occasion is celebrated with traditional drinks and ouzo to accompany the festive meal.

Afterwards, there will be sweets made with the first cheeses of the season as well as cinnamon-flavoured pastries and special Easter biscuits to celebrate the end of Lent. The day concludes with dancing and bouzouki music. Even visitors are most welcome to join in the fun and celebrations.

Below: Brightly coloured and patterned eggs are displayed with red-dyed eggs that symbolize Christ's blood.

Left: Members of the Rhodes State Dancers perform traditional dance during the celebration of a saint's day in the summer.

CHRISTMAS

In Greece, Christmas is less significant than Easter, although it is a national holiday and still involves plenty of feasting, dancing and celebrations, including the giving of presents. The Christmas table is filled with all sorts of food. Traditionally, roast piglet or another pork dish is eaten for the main meal. There is always meat (pork mainly, or turkey) and *Christopsomo* (Christ's bread). The meal is followed by a range of traditional sweets, such as *kourambiethes* (nut cookies dusted with powdered sugar), *diples* (fried dough cookies dipped in honey) and *melomakarona* (honey-dipped cookies, often stuffed with nuts).

Sweets, cakes and Christmas cookies are all given out as gifts throughout the festive period. On Christmas Eve morning, children holding small metallic triangles or other musical instruments knock on people's doors and sing Christmas carols for cakes or sweets.

NEW YEAR

The national holiday of Saint Basil is on 1 January. As it coincides with New Year, the holiday is celebrated by eating the traditional Basil cake. This is actually a glazed bread, called *vasilopita*, with a coin hidden inside; whoever finds the coin will enjoy good fortune in the coming year.

To celebrate fertility in the New Year, Greeks eat symbolic foods, including pomegranates, almonds, honey and sesame seeds.

INDEPENDENCE DAY

To commemorate the revolt against the Ottoman Empire in 1821, a national holiday is celebrated on 25 March with parades and dancing. The religious festival of the Annunciation of the Virgin Mary is also celebrated on the same day. As this takes place during Lent it is a good opportunity for Greeks to break their fast: the Church allows fish and seafood to be eaten on this day.

MAY DAY

Families celebrate the national holiday on 1 May with picnic feasts and outdoor games. They also gather wild flowers from the countryside and make them into wreaths, which they hang outside their houses, on cars and on boats to ward off evil.

ASSUMPTION OF THE VIRGIN

The icon of the Madonna, bedecked with ribbons, is paraded and kissed for the national holiday on 15 August in celebration of the Virgin. Festivities might last for days and include music and dancing, with brightly coloured ceremonial costumes.

OTHER FESTIVALS

Each town has its own saint's day, and festivities always include a small procession with music, dancing and feasting often carrying on long into the night. Street vendors sell special cakes and snacks for each occasion. There are also several national holidays that

Below: Christopsomo*, or "Christ's bread", is baked specially for the Christmas period.*

Name days
Traditionally, Greek children do not celebrate their birthdays after the age of 12. Instead they celebrate the saint after whom they were named. Each saint has a special day and celebrations take place all over the country. Friends and relatives call on the home of the named person, bringing all kinds of cakes and pastries. It's a busy day for the cake shops, *zaharoplastia*, especially on days that have popular names. Nowadays children celebrate their birthdays as well.

are celebrated in Greece. For rural communities, important days include 23 April to mark the feast of Saint George, the patron saint of shepherds, and 17 July, which is the special day for Saint Marina who protects crops. Boats and icons are paraded on the beaches on 6 December, with celebrations taking place in harbourside churches to mark the day of Saint Nicholas, the patron saint of sailors. There is wild revelry on the island of Halki in the Cyclades to celebrate the Transfiguration of the Saviour on 6 August, when people have messy food fights, throwing eggs, flour, yogurt and squid ink at each other.

Above: Church leaders head a colourful pilgrimage through the island of Kos to celebrate a saint's day festival.

Below: Greek traditional dress is extravagantly decorated, and people of all ages enjoy dressing up on saints' days.

THE GREEK KITCHEN

Fresh vegetables hold centre stage in the Greek kitchen, transformed by rich and fruity olive oil into wonderful dishes. The Greek pantry also contains pulses, nuts and seeds, fresh fish and meat, and home-produced cheeses and dairy products.

Olives and Olive Oil

Greeks sometimes describe their friends as people they share bread and olives with – so essential are these foods to their lives. A vital asset to the Greek economy, the olive is a staple of the Greek diet with each person consuming on average 20 litres (35 pints) of olive oil in a year.

Greek olives have a history dating back to at least the third millennium BC when the Cretans traded their olive oil around the eastern Mediterranean, creating great wealth. By the sixth century BC, the Greeks had become major exporters of oil. The olive was regarded as sacred, and even today the olive is tied to folk and religious rituals, and is used at christenings to anoint the child's head.

Above: Thassos throumba from Macedonia are matured on the tree and cured in dry salt.

Above: A crunchy green olive with a mild flavour is produced on the Ionian Islands.

Today, there are around 137 million olive trees in Greece, and over 60 per cent of the cultivated land in Crete is planted with them. Most rural families own trees, which sustain them in olives and oil each year. The fruity, green oil used lavishly in food adds a depth of flavour that is especially noticeable in the richness it contributes to vegetable and vegetarian dishes.

Some of the best olive oils are from the Peloponnese and western Crete, where olives grow on the high and arid mountains. Perfect conditions for growing olives are found in most parts of Greece and this is why the country is the largest producer of olives and olive oil in the Mediterranean.

THE OLIVE YEAR

In late spring the tiny olive flowers appear. If conditions are perfect and a dry spring is followed by a long, hot summer, a fine crop of green fruits will form. These green olives eventually fully ripen, becoming black approximately six months after fertilization, when their oil content will have reached its maximum. However, the finest oil is taken from the fruit when it is just beginning to ripen.

Harvesting by hand begins in the autumn, but may continue through the winter. It is a social event for rural communities, with everyone helping to pick their neighbours' crops; civil servants are officially allowed time off work to help on the family farms.

Left: Pimiento-stuffed Halkidiki olives are a popular choice for mezedes all over Greece.

Below: Olives are preserved in a variety of ways, including curing, drying and canning in oil.

An average yield from a mature tree is 15–20kg/33–44lb, which will produce 3–4 litres/5–7 pints of oil. The olives are transported to the presses where the first cold pressing will produce the finest liquid.

PROCESSING THE OIL

The quality of Greece's olives is exceptional, and three-quarters of the oil produced here is finest extra virgin.

Extra virgin olive oil is the liquid that is first extracted from the fruit, known as the "first cold pressing", and has very low acidity at under 1 per cent. The dark green oil will have a distinctive aroma and strong, fruity flavour, which will depend on the local climate and olive variety. It contains no additives. This oil is not used for frying, as its subtle qualities are lost once it is heated. It is perfect for salad dressings or using unheated to add flavour to dishes. The Coroneiki olive is grown all over Greece particularly for its oil, and large crops are found in the Peloponnese. Two other top-quality oils are Karyatis, pressed from Coroneiki olives, and Iliada, pressed from the Kalamata olive.

Virgin olive oil also comes from the first pressing but will have a slightly higher acidity level at 1.5 per cent. It is a good oil to use for salad dressings.

Olive oil has a milder taste and darker colour than virgin oils and is best for frying. It is refined and its high acidity level is lowered by blending with extra virgin oil.

Right: On average a Greek person consumes 20 litres (35 pints) of olive oil every year.

Right: Extra virgin olive oil flavoured with freshly chopped herbs is used as a dressing for salads.

OLIVES

Eaten as mezedes, made into bread and cooked with many dishes, olives are abundantly used in Greek cuisine. The best-quality olives are marinated in extra virgin olive oil with fresh and dried herbs, notably oregano, and served with drinks or as a meze. These may be pitted and stuffed with pimiento for extra flavour.

There are several types of olive grown in Greece and many areas have specialities in both variety and preparation. Some appear in traditional regional dishes, often combined with locally produced cheeses, fresh fruit and vegetables, and fresh and dried herbs for a fuller, richer flavour.

The principal varieties are black, green and cracked. The island of Thassos produces small, black, wrinkled, dry-cured olives with a strong flavour, whereas the Ionian Islands produce a variety of large and crunchy green olives with a mild flavour. Tasty cracked green olives are produced by cracking unripe green olives, and then placing them in water for several weeks to remove their bitterness, before they are stored in brine.

Types of olive

Kalamata Probably the most famous Greek olive is the purple-brown Kalamata olive from the southern Peloponnese. The shape is elongated, with a tapered base. The skin is perfectly smooth and regular and it has a superior, rich flavour.

Amfissa This round and black olive from central Greece has a lovely nutty, sweet taste.

Halkidiki A large and succulent pale-green olive, Halkidiki is harvested when young, and brine-cured. It is suitable for stuffing with pimientos.

Maonias These dark olives are grown throughout Macedonia and are usually cured in brine.

Thassos throumba is a black, wrinkled olive that is matured on the tree. It is cured in dry salt.

Below: Olives can be marinated in oil with lemon and herbs to give extra flavour.

Fruit

In Greece a meal always ends with fresh fruit, leaving sticky pastries and cakes to be enjoyed during the afternoon. Fruit grows abundantly in Greece and many kinds are available for eating fresh, cooking or making into preserves to be served as spoon sweets.

Above: The flavour of lemon is a favourite with the Greeks.

CITRUS FRUIT

Orange groves are found in the more fertile areas of Greece, such as Epirus, and the fruit is used in savoury as well as sweet dishes. On the Aegean coast, chickpeas are cooked with oranges, and the juice of bitter oranges is used to cure olives from the Dodecanese. Oranges and nectarines are also made into preserves. Kumquats are grown on Corfu and are candied as well as being used to make a richly coloured and flavoured liqueur.

The lemon originated in South-east Asia and reached Greece at about the end of the third century BC. Now, however, the lemon tree is found everywhere and its fruit is used widely. It is a familiar combination with olive oil as a dressing for salads, and with eggs in the sauce *avgolemono*, which is traditionally served with plain meats or vegetable dishes. The lemon blossom can also be made into a preserve.

Above: Grapes are used in many Greek dishes, as well as for wine. Grapevines are found throughout Greece.

QUINCES

The quince ripens in October and is delicious baked with lamb or beef in casseroles or made into preserves. Quince also makes a delicious sauce with olive oil, garlic and onion to serve with pork, and it can even be hollowed out and stuffed with lamb spiced with cinnamon and cloves.

GRAPES

Grapevines are a familiar sight throughout the Greek countryside, clothing the landscape of many islands. Apart from their use in wine, grapes are eaten fresh to follow a meal, and their must – the crushed fruit after it has been pressed for winemaking – can be made into a dessert called *moustalevria*, which is made with semolina flavoured with cinnamon and nuts. In Macedonia a sweet sauce called *meli* is also made from the must of the native *xinomavro* grape and used in an aubergine (eggplant) preserve. The verjuice, which is the juice from unripe grapes, is also used in various ways, mostly to add to dishes to provide a sour taste when lemons are unavailable.

FIGS

From dark purple to green to a golden yellow, there are many different varieties of fig available. They probably came originally from Asia Minor, but now grow wild in Greece and can be seen

Above: Quinces may be elongated or large like melons, and when cooked the golden flesh turns pink.

Left: Fresh figs may be served simply, cut open with a generous dollop of yogurt.

everywhere, with many households having their own tree for home cooking and to eat as a dessert with honey and yogurt. As well as being eaten after a meal, figs are baked, cooked with savoury foods and made into preserves. To the ancient Greeks the fig tree was erotic, but it was also said to be hallucinatory, so no one would sleep beneath it for fear of it sending them mad.

WILD BERRIES

Blackberries are collected from the hedgerows in late summer and early autumn. They make tasty preserves. In Roumeli, the sweet Cornelian cherry is also gathered. Called *krana*, it is usually made into a spoon sweet.

ORCHARD FRUIT

Greece is fortunate in having so many orchard fruits: apples, pears, plums, peaches, apricots, cherries and mulberries grow in profusion and are eaten fresh or used for compotes and preserves. Stewed orchard fruits are also served with yogurt and they find their way into savoury dishes, too, such as prunes with beef in a hearty *stifado* from Macedonia.

OTHER FRUITS

Succulent strawberries, melons and pomegranates are grown and enjoyed in Greece. Melons will sometimes be served with mezedes, sliced and lightly spiced. Associated with fertility, pomegranates have special significance at weddings and for New Year. As well as eaten to follow a meal they are cooked with savoury foods, and are especially delicious with duck.

The *oleaster* is a small, oval fruit that has a date-like flavour. The trees are grown in Corfu where the fruit is eaten fresh as well as sun-dried and preserved in ouzo.

DRIED FRUIT

Prunes, raisins, sultanas (golden raisins), currants and dried apricots are used in many Greek dishes, both sweet and savoury. In Macedonia and Thrace a staple dish is prunes cooked with a variety of savoury dishes, such as stewed with leeks, cherry plums, tomatoes and wine as an accompaniment to roasted meat. In areas where raisins and currants are plentiful they will often be included in breads, cakes and pastries, as well as stuffings for fish, meat or vegetables. In Thessaly, they are even combined with chickpeas, then flavoured with lemon to make a sweet.

Left: Apples will be served at the end of a meal, or used in cooked dishes.

Spoon sweets

As the different fruits ripen during the year they are made into sweet preserves known as spoon sweets, so called because they are eaten from a spoon. Any sweet food is usually eaten in the afternoon with a glass of water and, perhaps, a cup of tea or coffee. Spoon sweets are also offered as a welcome to unexpected visitors. Even dried fruits, such as apricots, sultanas and prunes, can be used. Some preserves are especially delicious: kumquats with their exquisite oil are excellent. Cherry tomatoes, although a vegetable fruit, make a delicious preserve combined with quince, and many fruit preserves make a luscious topping for yogurt and honey.

VEGETABLES

In Greece the diet is centred on seasonal vegetables, and every meal will celebrate the different flavours and textures of the wide variety available. Visiting the local market to choose fresh produce is part of the regular routine for Greek women. Vegetables are served in separate small dishes in the same way as mezedes. They are also stuffed, baked, grilled (broiled), added to stews and casseroles or made into wholesome soups; and no meal is complete without a salad of fresh leaves. Olive oil is the essential ingredient when cooking vegetables in Greece.

Below: Rocket (arugula) is found throughout Greece, both cultivated and growing wild.

LEAVES

Known as *horta*, wild or cultivated green leaves are used for salads or served hot with a lemon and oil dressing. Many *horta* are prolific in the autumn especially when the weather is wetter. Wild leaves include asparagus, nettle, chicory, young poppies, dandelion, amaranth, curly endive and milk thistle. They are also served sautéed with cheese or pasta to make a substantial dish, made into pies, or mixed with a batter and fried in patties. *Horta* are dried in the late summer or autumn to be eaten in pies during the winter.

Purslane This herb-like plant grows prolifically all over Greece and is one of the most popular *horta* leaves. Wild purslane is slender and has small, crunchy leaves, whereas the cultivated variety has silvery, furry leaves and thick stems. Purslane, with its light, lemony taste, is frequently used in salads as well as on its own or with cucumber, tomatoes or other *horta*.

Lettuce Abundant in summer and used in the salads so loved by the Greeks, lettuce is often served simply dressed with oil. Cos lettuce is often grown and it is eaten as part of the Easter fare in a fricassée with lamb.

Rocket (arugula) With its peppery taste and bright green leaves, rocket grows wild in Greece. As it quickly goes to seed it must be harvested while young. The tender leaves are succulent served with red radishes or slices of feta cheese. It also makes a good salad with cos lettuce, or is delicious added to a potato salad. Cheese and fish also go well with rocket. The young leaves have a milder taste; use them whole but trim the stems from older leaves.

Vine leaves Tangy-flavoured fresh vine leaves are used to wrap food in Greece. Rice is the base for the most well-known stuffing for vine leaves, to which is added a mixture of herbs, onions, nuts and perhaps meat, making the dish *dolmades*. Vine leaves also make a tasty wrapper for fish that will be baked or grilled, imparting a lemony flavour. The leaves are best when picked fresh while young in early summer, but vine leaves preserved in brine are a good substitute and can even be eaten as they are with a little lemon juice or vinegar. If using preserved vine leaves for stuffing, rinse thoroughly a few times to ensure that the preserving salt is properly removed.

Grapevines often grow over the walls of Greek houses and the leaves will be picked, rinsed and then blanched briefly in boiling water before use. They can

Salad with every meal

The Greeks enjoy a salad with every meal. It can be simply *horta* – wild or cultivated leaves – dressed with oil and lemon juice or it can include a variety of other vegetables. Whatever the time of year, the Greeks will create a salad using seasonal ingredients. When tomatoes are used in a salad, the dressing is always simply olive oil and not a vinaigrette.

Horiatiki salata is a peasant-style salad, which is perfect with grilled fish or as a light lunch. It includes tomatoes, onion, pepper, olives, feta cheese and fresh oregano.

Below: Fresh, luscious tomatoes are used widely in the Greek kitchen.

also be used or packed raw and frozen. When ready to use, the frozen leaves are quickly plunged into boiling water for 1–2 minutes then drained. They are often as good as fresh leaves, although sometimes the texture can be damaged and they are not strong enough to hold large amounts of stuffing.

VEGETABLE FRUITS

Tasty vegetable fruits feature prominently in the Greek diet.

Aubergines (eggplants) In Greece, aubergines will be taut and plump and come in a number of varieties, shapes and sizes – they are not the uniformly shaped vegetables that so often fill our supermarket shelves. Aubergines originally came from the East, probably India. The earlier varieties were inclined to be bitter and needed to be salted and then left to drain for an hour to release their bitter juices. Modern aubergines, however, have lost their bitterness and no longer need to be soaked. If a recipe calls for frying aubergines, it is important to cook them carefully, as they will readily soak up oil; baking is a healthier way to cook them. They are often served stuffed or braised, or might be sliced and rolled with a stuffing such as minced (ground) beef flavoured with mint and served with a tomato and chilli sauce. Aubergines are the essential ingredient in the famous dish moussaka, where they are layered with minced lamb and a rich cheese sauce. The herbs basil and oregano particularly complement their flavour. Aubergines can also be made into a spoon sweet.

Courgettes (zucchini) The courgettes found in Greece are pale green with white stripes. They are usually smooth-skinned and may be short and rounded. Their sweet taste makes them useful in many dishes. They are a popular summer vegetable, often coated in seasoned flour and fried or stuffed as a meze. They are also frequently included in pies and salads. Their attractive yellow blossoms are delicious stuffed.

Tomatoes Although used in many dishes, the tomato arrived in Greece only in 1815 and it was some time before they became an integral part of Greek cooking. The Greek tomatoes grown today are the large and very tasty varieties, ripened specially in the sun. They add flavour to salads and sauces, and make a delicious soup. They can also be fried. Rice, wheat or minced (ground) meat is used as a stuffing for tomatoes. They are also traditionally preserved whole in jars, and made into tomato paste. At the end of the summer they will be left to dry in the sun – cut from the plant in bunches and hung in a sunny spot. When dried they will be stored to use in winter cooking or boiled down to a pulp, sieved and stored in oil. Small and tasty cherry tomatoes can be made into a sweet preserve that is eaten as a spoon sweet. Tomatoes are now available in winter, grown in polytunnels, but these are inferior in quality.

Cucumber Crisp cucumber is added to summer salads. It is an essential ingredient of the well-known *tzatsiki,* combined with yogurt, garlic, oil and mint and served with vegetables, fish or meat, or with pitta bread and salad as a delicious meze.

Pumpkins The smaller varieties of pumpkin are sweeter and are often made into pies, sweet tarts and soups. Pumpkin is also eaten raw, finely sliced in salads with cheese, red (bell) pepper, mint and spring onions (scallions).

Below: Cucumbers, peeled, cut into chunks and then cored, form one of the main ingredients of the popular traditional Greek salad.

Below: Found in many savoury Greek dishes, red, yellow, orange and green (bell) peppers add a lovely sweet flavour.

Preparing okra
Okra is a familar sight in dishes from Greece and the Middle East, adding texture and flavour.

1 When preparing okra for cooking whole, pare off the conical head from each pod, either making a straight cut or angling the knife.

2 Take care not to cut so deep that you expose the seeds as this will affect the cooking. Remove the black tip at the other end.

3 Rinse the pods quickly under cold water and drain them well. Don't slice the pods unless you need the mucilaginous liquid to thicken the dish.

Peppers Introduced from the New World, (bell) peppers form an integral part of Mediterranean food. There are several hundred varieties, in many shapes, sizes and colours, and their flavours vary from sweet to hot. Stuffed peppers might have a rice and lamb filling. They are served with garlic sausages to form the Pelion speciality called *spetzofai*, and are also eaten pickled. The dish *briami* includes peppers, courgettes (zucchini), potatoes, garlic and tomatoes.
Okra Originally from West Africa, okra is often cooked with tomatoes and onions in Greek cuisine. The smaller varieties are popular in Greece as they are less slimy. To remove any remaining sliminess, they will often be dried in the sun for a little while before they are cooked. When sliced, the sticky liquid oozes from the vegetable and this is good for thickening stews. Okra is delicious with meat and chicken, or with fresh tomatoes in the casserole *bamies*, and can be dusted with flour and fried.

BEANS AND PEAS

Fresh beans and peas are always welcomed when in season and make imaginative combinations with other vegetables and meat.
Green beans There are several varieties. The thin, long *ambellofasoula* is picked in early summer and served as a salad with olive oil and lemon juice. *Tsaoulia* are shorter beans, and *bourounia* is a flat variety. In August the scarlet-lined pods of *handres* appear. These are similar to fresh Italian borlotti beans and are always used shelled. The bean insides make a robust and hearty addition to casseroles.
Broad (fava) beans Tender broad beans first appear in April and are eaten with young artichokes in a variety of combinations. In some recipes the pale green skin is removed to reveal the rich bean.
Peas When peas are available in spring they will be made into casseroles, or combined with artichokes and cooked with dill. They are excellent with spring lamb and baby courgettes (zucchini).

ROOT VEGETABLES

In wintertime especially, root vegetables come into their own.
Potatoes Introduced from the New World, potatoes are now eaten all over Greece. They are fried, mashed or baked or can be sliced or cubed for bakes and casseroles. They also form part of the garlic sauce, *skordalia*.

Below: The sweetness of peas in spring is a delight. Podding them can be a family affair.

Beetroot (beet) Eaten during the winter, both the root and green leafy tops of beetroot will be eaten. The root is also delicious roasted and served with the garlic sauce, *skordalia*.
Fennel This white bulb has a delicate aniseed flavour and is eaten cooked or raw in salads. It goes particularly well with fish and chicken.
Leeks A flavoursome winter vegetable, leeks are baked into pies and are a traditional flavouring for sausages, especially in the north.
Onions An essential ingredient in Greek cooking, onions impart their rich flavour to many dishes: casseroles, stuffings, pies and tarts. They are also enjoyed raw with bread and cheese. Purple onions are traditionally grated before they are added to dishes. Small, pickling-size onions are added to stews.
Spring onions (scallions) Pungently flavoured spring onions are used in many dishes. They add a sweet flavour to meatballs and fava, and are an essential ingredient when combined with onions to flavour *dolmades*.
Radishes Bright red and also white radishes are useful salad ingredients.

Below: Spring onions (scallions) are used to add a fresh flavour to rissoles, salads and other Greek dishes.

CRUCIFEROUS VEGETABLES

Leafy greens, such as cabbage and spinach, feature in many Greek dishes.
Cabbage An essential and tasty winter ingredient, cabbage can be shredded and made into a crunchy salad. Lahano is a big, flat-headed white cabbage with large leaves, which are useful for stuffing like vine leaves.
Cauliflower A useful winter vegetable, cauliflower can be made into a *stifado*, a thickened stew with onions, garlic and bay, or braised with other vegetables. It is also popular in an *avgolemono* egg and lemon sauce, served as a side vegetable or as part of a larger feast. It can also be lightly boiled so that it is still slightly crunchy for use in a winter salad.
Spinach Crisp, bright-green spinach can be briefly cooked as a vegetable, but it is also combined with feta cheese in the well-known winter dish *spanakopita*, a pie made with filo pastry. Young, baby spinach can be made into a salad and is particularly tasty with feta cheese, artichokes and walnuts. It is also cooked with rice and dill or added to squid to make a tasty dish.

OTHER VEGETABLES

The Greek repertoire of dishes uses every kind of vegetable available, especially those native to Greece.
Globe artichokes Originally introduced by the Venetians, globe artichokes are cooked in various ways. The hearts are used in casseroles or omelettes, or thinly sliced and eaten raw in salads. They are also delicious fried in oil or grilled (broiled), and the whole artichoke can be stuffed. In spring, baby artichokes are eaten whole, as the hairy choke has not yet formed and is tender to eat. The hearts of young artichokes are delicious braised with baby onions and baby carrots. The artichokes ripen in March, and a traditional spring dish called *anginares me koukia* combines young artichokes with broad beans. Also enjoyed in the spring alongside the artichokes are the season's young lambs, a speciality dish for the Easter festive period, taking advantage of the artichoke season.
Celery Although rarely used in Greek cookery celery sticks can be pickled and the leaves and stalks are used to add flavour to soups.
Mushrooms Not widely used in Greek cuisine, however wild mushrooms will be picked in woods and forest slopes by people who live near them, and added to dishes for extra flavour.

Preparing artichokes
Artichokes are frequently used and need quick preparation.

1 Cut artichokes discolour readily, so prepare some acidulated water. Fill a bowl with cold water and add the juice of half a lemon.

2 Remove the outer leaves until you reach the tender ones. Cut off the head halfway down, leaving the heart with a short collar of tender leaves.

3 Slice the artichoke in half lengthways, using a sharp knife, so that you can see the hairy choke in the middle of the heart, surrounded by small, hard purple leaves. Scoop this out with a teaspoon and throw it away.

4 Cut off the stalk, leaving about 4cm/1½in attached to the artichoke. Peel away the woody green outer surface and pull away any small base leaves. Drop the artichoke into the bowl of acidulated water until you are ready to cook it.

Beans, Pulses, Nuts and Seeds

Because the Greek diet is largely vegetarian, beans, peas and lentils, nuts and seeds are an important source of protein for everyone, and the Greeks are masters at producing delicious dishes using a wide variety.

BEANS, PEAS AND LENTILS

Popular in the vegetarian-style dishes, all kinds of beans and pulses are used, both fresh when in season, and dried added to winter fare. During Lent, when no meat may be eaten, pulses really come into their own, providing a tasty, nutritious meal. Herbs and rich flavourings such as tomatoes and onions are often used to complement the individual qualities of the beans. Good-quality olive oil is always used to cook them – it brings out a robust flavour. Most dried pulses must be soaked overnight before they are cooked, although some Greek households use canned pulses.

Fasolia gigantes are fleshy beans with a sweet taste. Grown in the north of Greece in Macedonia and Epirus, they are available in the markets from September and are used in soups, salads, as purées, in slow-cooked casseroles and to accompany meat. A delicious baked dish using them contains a rich sauce made with tomatoes, garlic, oregano and thyme, and lots of olive oil. Pork will sometimes be added.

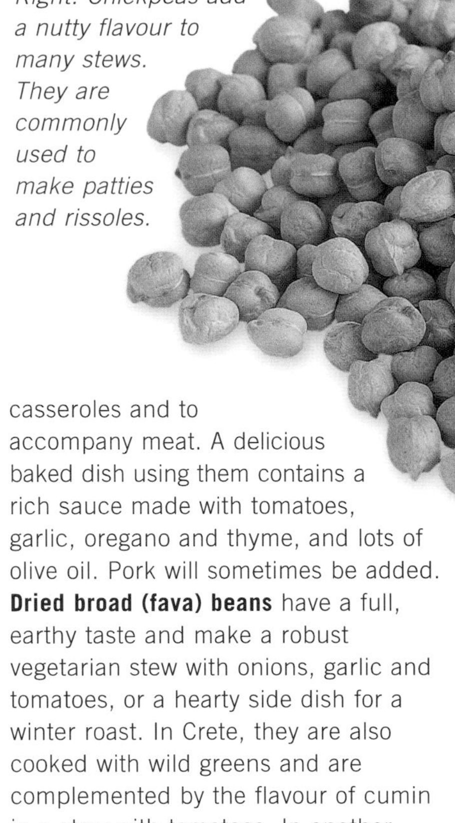

Right: Chickpeas add a nutty flavour to many stews. They are commonly used to make patties and rissoles.

Dried broad (fava) beans have a full, earthy taste and make a robust vegetarian stew with onions, garlic and tomatoes, or a hearty side dish for a winter roast. In Crete, they are also cooked with wild greens and are complemented by the flavour of cumin in a stew with tomatoes. In another Cretan dish, the dried beans are grilled (broiled) and then softened in salted water. Once soft they are served as a meze. Cooked and mashed with lots of olive oil, dried broad beans make a rich, creamy accompaniment for fish.

Above: Cannellini beans are used in slow-cooked meat and vegetarian stews and also in soups.

Above: Split peas form the base for fava, *a dip that includes onion, lemon, salt and olive oil.*

Lentils Native to the Mediterranean, lentils are available in many shapes, sizes and colours. The small green-brown varieties are the most frequently used and have the best flavour; they do not need to be soaked before cooking. Lentils make good soups, and can make a substantial meal cooked with *kritharaki*, a rice-shaped pasta, and flavoured with oregano and bay.

Cannellini beans Imported from Argentina, cannellini beans are popular in Greek cooking, especially during autumn and winter. They can be cooked with lamb or pork in stews, and make a hearty soup called *fasolatha*, which is richly flavoured with carrots, celery, onion, tomatoes and plenty of oregano.

Split peas In Greece, small yellow split peas are used for the dish *fava*. These are smaller than the ones familiar to cooks in other countries. Split peas are also cooked with tomatoes and aubergines (eggplants), and made into tasty bitesize patties.

Chickpeas Native to the Mediterranean region, chickpeas have a nutty flavour that is perfect for casseroles. They are cooked with pork or lamb and are puréed with olive oil to make hummus. Lemon complements their flavour and, combined with olive oil, gives chickpea soup a robust savoury taste. Chickpeas

Above: Tahini, shown here with black and white sesame seeds, is a smooth, rich paste used to flavour stews and casseroles.

are also used to make spicy rissoles and as a stuffing for *dolmades*. Skinned and roasted, they are eaten as a meze with raisins and nuts. Fresh chickpeas are eaten in the pod when in season.

Haricot beans Small haricot (navy) beans are used in stews and added to salads. They make good soups; a recipe from Crete flavours them with orange.

Black-eyed beans These nutty-flavoured beans (peas) are quick-cooking and good in stews and soups. They are delicious when combined with wild greens and tomatoes, or simply boiled and served with *skordalia*, the garlic sauce. Caramelized onions are used as a topping for a dish from the Dodecanese where the cooked beans are tossed in a dressing of red wine vinegar, onions and parsley.

NUTS

A wide variety of nuts is grown and used in Greek cooking, and nuts are most frequently found in the delicious cakes and pastries.

Almonds are used for pastries, such as *kourebiedes*, where they are ground and combined with eggs and honey. Fresh green almonds are also eaten.

Pine nuts are the seeds from the pine tree *Pinus pinea*, and grow all over Greece. They have a subtle and sweet flavour that goes well with rice and other dishes. They are often toasted or lightly fried in a non-stick pan and added to salads, snacks, cakes and baked goods.

Walnuts are used in island cooking especially. They are added to *skordalia*, the garlic sauce, and are delicious cooked with braised chicken, as well as pastries and sweet pies.

Hazelnuts are grown in Zagora, Thessaly, and are often added to pastries and tarts.

Sweet chestnuts are grown all over Greece and are roasted and sold by street sellers as a snack during the winter months in Athens and other large cities.

Pistachio nuts often appear in pastries. The high-quality cakes and desserts, such as baklava, often use prime pistachio nuts for the filling. The best-quality pistachio nuts come from the island of Aigina.

SEEDS

Sesame seeds are the most frequently used seed and can be found topping breads and cakes and sprinkled over savoury dishes. They are also ground to make tahini, a common flavouring for sauces and stews.

Sunflower seeds are a recent crop to be grown in Greece and are eaten in the north as a meze.

Left: Pistachio nuts are used in many pastries, as well as making an excellent meze or snack.

Rice and Pasta

All over Greece, rice and pasta are found in a variety of dishes. Long grain, short grain and brown rice are used in casseroles, stews, soups, stuffings and pilaffs. Short grain rice also features in desserts and sweet tarts.

The tradition of making pasta goes back to ancient times, and different regions and islands produce their own varieties, using egg, wheat, semolina and sheep's milk.

Rice and pasta are important sources of carbohydrate in the Greek diet.

Below: Long grain white rice (right) and brown rice (left) are commonly used to bring substance to casseroles and soups.

RICE

During the period of Ottoman Turk rule, rice became a staple part of the Greek cuisine, used to thicken stews and soups. There are two main varieties: short grain, which is similar to Italian risotto rice, and long grain.

Long grain rice is used in pilaffs and added to casseroles for the final 15 minutes. Soups can be thickened with it; *avgolemono* chicken soup is just one example. It is also ideal for absorbing the juices of cuttlefish, squid, mussels and other shellfish when they are cooked together.

Both short and long grain rice are used for stuffing vegetables and meat. To stuff vegetables, rice is always rinsed and drained but uncooked when it is mixed with the raw stuffing ingredients. Plenty of olive oil is then added, making the mixture moist enough to cook the rice. The filled vegetable will then be baked for 1½ hours.

Short grain rice is used for creamy puddings, such as Greek rice pudding with fruit, and as a filling for sweet pies.

Above: Rice is often used in Greek dishes, flavoured with a variety of fresh herbs and spices.

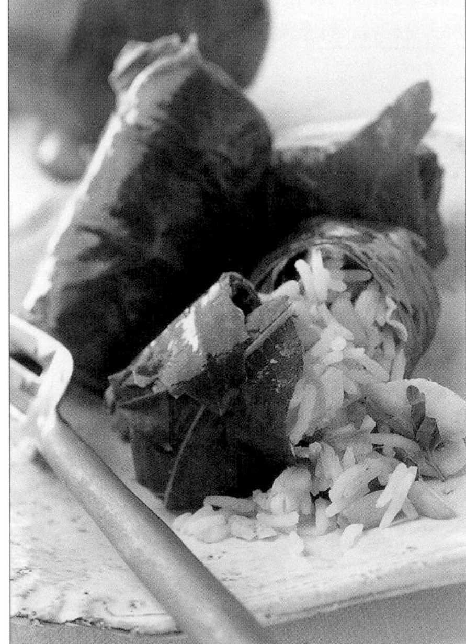

Above: Stuffed vine leaves, or dolmades, *are filled with rice, herbs and small amounts of vegetables.*

PASTA

Pasta-making probably goes back to ancient Greece, when laganum – an early kind of pasta dough – was dried by grilling (broiling) to preserve it. The Venetians also introduced several kinds of pasta to the Ionian Islands as well as the Dodecanese. Pasta is traditionally made at the end of the summer and left to dry in the air. It is then stored for use as a hearty winter staple. Traditionally hand-made pasta is available all over Greece and some of the islands specialize in producing several different kinds. On the Ionian Islands pasta is eaten with almost every meal, and pasta of all shapes and sizes is produced. The Greeks prefer it to be well cooked, and it is frequently added to a sauce or stew so that it will cook in the liquid until it is soft.

There are also stuffed pastas, such as *varenika*, which might be filled with meat, cheese or vegetables. Vegetarian dishes feature strongly in the Greek diet, and there are several pasta dishes that use pulses or dairy products. *Kritharaki* is a pasta dish from Rhodes, cooked with a black-eyed bean (pea) and vegetable stew in a filling dish. On the same island, noodles are cooked with lentils and topped with crisp caramelized onions. In Kassos, small,

Right: Pilaff dishes are popular in Greece. Here mussels are combined with garlic, dill, oregano and white wine.

curl-shaped pasta called *makarounes* are tossed in cheese or yogurt for a Greek macaroni cheese.

Pies, also, will often contain pasta, which may be partnered with cheese and meat; *passa makarouna* from Kos is an example. Pasta is also used for sweet dishes and may be cooked in a fruit syrup or sauce, such as the thick pasta, *moustokoulika*, from Limnos, which is boiled in grape syrup.

Types of pasta

Aftoudia Meaning "ears", this simple pasta from Chios and Limnos is made with flour and water and shaped into small ear shapes.
Avgohilos is a long, thin pasta from Crete, made with egg.
Evriste Similar to tagliatelle, *evriste* originated from the Black Sea area and is made with flour and water.
Flomaria Made on Limnos, *flomaria* are available as round strands or long flat strands similar to linguine.
Gongides From the southern Peloponnese, *gongides* is a shell-shaped pasta popular with meat.
Hilofta From Crete, *hilofta* is a thin, short pasta, which is often sweetened with honey and is traditionally served to women who have just given birth.
Hipolites Made from egg and wheat, this pasta is made into two types: noodle-shaped, long and thin; and small even squares.
Kofto makaronaki is a short, thick macaroni-shaped pasta.
Kouskousi Made with semolina, wheat, egg and milk, *kouskousi* comes from Thrace. It is shaped into tiny balls and used to thicken meat, poultry and vegetarian casseroles.
Kritharaki is a small, tear-shaped pasta made with wheat and egg. It is usually added to stews so that it becomes well cooked and soft in the sauce.
Mangiri This Cretan pasta is shaped into evenly sized squares.
Moustokoulika is a small, heart-shaped pasta popular throughout Greece.
Niokos is similar to *kritharaki*, and is also known as *birbiloni*. It comes from the Ionian Islands.
Pastitsatha From Corfu, this pasta is thick and tubular.
Petoura Made in Macedonia, this rich egg pasta contains sheep's milk and is used in aubergine (eggplant) dishes.
Schioufichta Made with flour and water, this Cretan pasta is shaped into curls.
Siron Shaped into short tubular spirals, siron is grilled and not air-dried. It is usually served with cheese.
Striftades These are small spirals of pasta from the Peloponnese.
Toutoumakia These tasty egg noodles come from the Peloponnese.
Trahana is tiny pasta made with buttermilk, and is either sour or sweet. It is most often used in soups.
Triftoudia Similar to *kritharaki*, this rice-shaped pasta comes from Crete.
Valanes Known widely as *makarounes*, this is a small, curl-shaped pasta from Chios. It features widely in ground meat and vegetarian dishes.

Right: Gongides *are a shell-shaped pasta from the Peloponnese, popular with minced (ground) meat, aubergines (eggplants) and cheese.*

Bread and Pastries

Every meal is accompanied by bread in Greece, and special breads have an important significance in rituals. Sweet pastries are often rich and delicious, enjoyed with coffee and presented as gifts when visiting friends.

Left: Daktyla *is a Greek village bread covered with seeds.*

BREAD

There are two basic essentials in Greek food: bread and olive oil. Bread has always been a major staple in Greece. It is used to scoop olive oil from the plate, as well as mopping up rich sauces cooked around roasted meat, or it is dipped into soups, casseroles or mezedes such as the aubergine (eggplant) dip called *melitzanosalata*.

In earlier times all bread was made with barley. Nowadays, most bread is made from wheat, much of it grown in Thessaly, although some is still made with barley and occasionally corn. Local breads might be quickly pan-fried and some fried breads contain a soft, creamy cheese, such as *mizithra*, in the centre. Celebrations and festivals will be marked with their own special bread; and every locality will have its own Easter, Christmas and New Year breads as well as a myriad of variations for saints' days, birthdays, christenings and weddings. Sweet breads for special occasions are sometimes decorated with designs or a person's name.

Herbs and spices, such as cinnamon and cloves, flavour some savoury loaves, whereas sweet breads may be flavoured with citrus peel and glazed with honey. Olives are added to savoury breads and rolls, and some will be stuffed with cheese and vegetables; spinach and cheese is a favourite combination. Sesame seeds and nuts make tasty toppings, and salt or caraway seeds cover crisp, irregularly

Below: Greek pitta bread can be eaten on its own or used to wrap other foods.

Below: Many savoury country breads have olives and herbs to add extra flavour, especially for mezedes.

shaped bread sticks. Raisins add flavour to sweet breads, and more unusual flavourings such as wine are also included.

Types of bread

Psomi horiatiko The most commonly found bread is *psomi horiatiko*, meaning peasant or village bread, and each village will have its own recipe. All are made from a sour dough, called *psomi*, using a starter that is continually refreshed and grown for the next batch of loaves. *Psomi horiatiko* is usually made with wheat, although some villages will add a little cornmeal. Sesame seeds or nuts might be sprinkled over the top.
Daktyla This is a traditional shaped loaf also made in Greek villages and covered in sesame seeds. The name *daktyla* means fingers: it is slashed across the top before baking so that it can be broken into finger-like pieces.
Paximadia This hard, rusk bread has been baked twice. The loaf is first baked until golden and then cut into thick slices, which are then baked once more. *Paximadia* is one of the earliest breads and is made from barley flour, although wholemeal (whole-wheat) flour is also occasionally used. Cheese or spices can be added to the dough. The bread is often eaten dunked into wine or coffee.

Above: Melopitta *is a delicious cake made with* mizithra *cheese. It comes from the island of Sifnos.*

Pitta Unlike the pitta breads bought from supermarkets, Greek pitta is thick, unleavened and made with wholemeal flour. It is often wrapped around pieces of meat, cheese or vegetables.
Kolyva Made with whole wheat berries and a rich combination of dried fruit and nuts flavoured with spices, *kolyva* is a sweet bread. It is baked especially for funerals and to be given to neighbours 40 days after a death. It is also eaten during Lent and at other times in remembrance of the dead.

PASTRIES

The afternoon is the traditional time for indulging in sweet cakes and pastries. Wherever you are in a Greek town or village you are sure to find a *zaharoplastio*, a cake shop, which will announce itself by its sweet aroma of scented honey cakes. As well as selling confectionery, a *zaharoplastio* will sell ice creams and other frozen desserts, and it usually has an area where you eat the cakes, which are sold with a glass of water to drink.

Left: These crescent-shaped pastries come from the island of Tinos.

Above: Melomakarona *are delicious honey-coated bread cookies served throughout the Christmas season.*

Greek confectionery tends to be very sweet with plenty of flavour; nuts, spices, dried fruit, lemon and other citrus fruits are commonly used. Occasionally, savoury ingredients are used. For example, sweet potato is combined with a walnut filling for pastry crescents flavoured with honey from the island of Tinos.
Baklava is the most well-known cake, and must be the epitome of Greek confectionery: filo pastry layered with chopped nuts and sticky with lemon-scented honey.
Greek halva is another familiar cake, made with semolina and almonds. After baking, the cake is soaked with a sugar and lemon syrup.
Kourabiedes are almond shortbreads that are served at weddings, with brandy as a key ingredient.
Melopitta is a tart from the island of Sifnos, combining soft *mizithra* cheese with thyme-scented honey and eggs.
Melomakarona are bread cookies steeped in orange and honey and packed with walnuts and cinnamon. They are a special treat for Christmas.
Bougatsa is a cream-filled filo pastry from Thessalonika.

Herbs, Spices and Flavourings

In Greece several varieties of herbs can be gathered wild from the hillsides and taken home to use in cooking. Spices, too, are used in cakes, breads and pastries, as well as enhancing savoury dishes.

HERBS

Parsley and oregano are the most commonly used herbs but there is a wide selection available.

Dill Whole bunches of dill might be used by Greek cooks in just one casserole, so much do they love its flavour. Native to the Mediterranean, it grows wild on the hillsides. A typical Greek dish flavoured with dill is a leg of lamb, cubed and cooked with cos lettuce, dill and *avgolemono.*

Fennel grows wild in the countryside and on the islands of Greece and is used to flavour stews.

Oregano A herb native to the Mediterranean, oregano is closely identified with Greek cooking. Its tiny aromatic leaves are borne on woody stems and it can be found wild on hillsides and fallow fields in summer. Oregano adds flavour to soups, casseroles and meatballs.

Left: Thyme is used to flavour meat, fish and vegetarian dishes, as well as salads. It partners very well with oregano.

Above: Oregano is widely used in Greek cooking, adding flavour to many dishes.

Thyme Indigenous to Greece, thyme grows wild on the hillsides. It is added to roasted and grilled (broiled) fish and meat, and is especially fragrant when partnered with oregano.

Flat leaf parsley Used extensively in Greek cooking, flat leaf parsley is an all-year herb. Coarsely chopped, it is added to shredded cabbage and tomato salads. Parsley is also added to bean and lentil soups and *dolmades*, and can be made into a salad with garlic, olives and hard-boiled eggs.

Above: Bowlfuls of flat leaf parsley are often added to vegetable dishes to give a gloriously rich flavour.

Coriander (cilantro) The leaves of coriander impart a distinctive flavour to soups, stews, sauces and spicy dishes. They are also used in salads.

Bay Both fresh and dried leaves of the bay tree are used widely in Greek cooking for their subtle flavour.

Rosemary is often used to flavour olives and vinegar. Lamb will sometimes be flavoured with rosemary. It is also added to the Greek fish sauce *sovari.*

Sage Although not used a great deal, grey-green sage is occasionally added to dishes to give a special flavour. For example, it is combined with parsley and spices to flavour chickpea rissoles.

Mint is added to meat and vegetable dishes. Spearmint is the variety preferred by most people.

Basil Often grown on the windowsills of houses in Greece, basil is used for flavouring chicken, preserves and stuffed vegetables.

Garlic Used widely in Greek cooking, garlic is added to braised dishes, casseroles and stuffings. It is also made

Above: Fresh, chopped herbs such as oregano, mint and parsley are frequently used to flavour olive oil for marinades and sauces.

into a sauce, called *skordalia*, where raw, chopped garlic is pounded with mashed potatoes or bread, some olive oil, herbs and nuts.

Capers are the immature flower buds of a shrub called *Capparis spinosa*, which grows wild in Greece. They make a tasty garnish for fish, especially crayfish and octopus, and can be pickled in brine or dry-salted. The islanders of Santorini pickle the young caper shoots and serve them with olive oil as a meze. Large capers can also be served as a meze.

SPICES

Sweet cakes and pastries and savoury dishes such as stews and roasts can be flavoured with spices.

Cumin Although cumin seeds are not widely used, they are added to some sausages and *stifado*, a stew from northern areas that have been influenced by Turkish cuisine.

Allspice lends itself especially to savoury foods. It is used for flavouring *voliotika* sausages, and is added with cinnamon to give a rich flavour to braised octopus.

Cinnamon is used in savoury dishes, such as sausages and bean casseroles, but mostly it is very popular for flavouring pastries and sweet pies.

Cloves are used in cakes, sweets and pastries. They are also included, with cinnamon, in some of the beef *stifado* recipes from the islands.

Saffron Although it is cultivated in Macedonia, saffron is not often used in Greek cooking, except sometimes it is used in pilaffs. Most of the saffron grown in Greece today is exported.

FLAVOURINGS

Other natural flavourings are used in all kinds of Greek recipes, both in sweet and savoury dishes.

Mastic is a solid gum or resin from the bark of the tree *Pistacia lentiscus*, grown on the island of Chios. It is used in Greek breads and cakes as well as ice creams and *masticha*, a liqueur.

Honey is plentiful in Greece because of the long flowering period. It is intensely scented and flavoured with flowers or herbs, such as thyme. Used in sweets and pastries, it is also served with thick yogurt and topped with walnuts.

Rose water is added to cakes and to the coating of sugared almonds, a speciality of Lesvos. It is also traditionally added to baked halva made with semolina and almonds.

Partnered with orange, rose water adds a delicate flavour to pastries and cakes.

Above: Garlic enhances the flavour of many Greek dishes, and is included in skordalia *sauce.*

Vanilla is used to flavour sweet pies and pastries as well as preserves.

Aniseed is used in ouzo for its distinctive flavour and is also added to a variety of breads. It can sometimes be added to robust soups and stews.

Vinegar is made organically and aged. It has a rich flavour and is used when cooking rabbit and hare.

Below: Greek honey is intensely flavoured because of the long flowering season. Different regions and islands have specialites, such as the clear thyme honey from Rhodes (far right).

Fish and Shellfish

Greece is on a peninsula with many islands, and seafood has a special place in its cuisine. Around 90 per cent of the population lives close to or by the sea, making seafood a reliable local source of food, especially in areas where the terrain is poor. The emphasis on seafood is also partly for religious reasons, as it is one of the foods the Greek Orthodox Church allows during the Lent fast, when all meats are avoided. Also, for many years the Greeks complied with the strict religious rule, now waived, that fish should be eaten on a Friday; and because old habits die hard, fish is still a popular dish eaten that day.

COOKING METHODS

Vegetables, herbs and spices enhance many Greek fish dishes, but the favoured cooking methods are simply baking, frying or grilling (broiling) with olive oil and lemon juice, and sometimes a few herbs. Barbecued fish is usually flavoured with thyme or oregano, and some fish will be wrapped in vine leaves before barbecuing to seal in the flavour and protect the outside from burning. Small, oily fish, such as sardines and mackerel, are particularly suitable for cooking by this method.

In Greece fish are never deep-fried. The whole fish, including the head, will simply be tossed in a little flour and shallow-fried in olive oil. Batter will sometimes be used, and if very small fish are to be battered they will be gathered into groups and dipped and then fried together, making more of a patty that can be cut into slices. The smaller varieties of fish are almost always fried. Larger fish might be baked, as in fish *plaki*, on a bed of seasonal vegetables.

Salt cod

Traditionally, salt cod is eaten on 25 March, the day of the Annunciation of the Virgin Mary. It is soaked well and then dipped in batter and fried, and served with the garlic sauce, *skordalia*. Salt cod is also baked with potatoes and garlic or made into croquettes, fried and then served with *skordalia*.

SMALL FISH

Sardines and sarthelles (very small sardines) are tasty wrapped in vine leaves and grilled or barbecued, or they can be oven baked with parsley and oregano. Sardines can also be filleted, salted and then sprinkled with fresh coriander (cilantro) and pepper and left to cure for about 48 hours. Delicious brown picarel are favourite small island fish. *Bourtheto* are small fish that are often baked whole in a rich spicy tomato sauce.

Left: Fresh sardines are a popular choice – grilled (broiled) or baked whole, or filleted and cured.

POPULAR FISH

These readily available fish are frequently eaten and can be mezedes or a main course.

Conger eel is sometimes slit along the belly, salted and dried, to be eaten sliced and grilled (broiled). The thickest section of the eel, behind the head, is the best part, as the lower parts are very bony. Smoked eel is served as a meze.

Mackerel This oily fish is eaten in August when it is plentiful around the coasts. Smaller mackerel are usually grilled (broiled); larger ones can be baked and stuffed with onions, (bell) peppers and herbs.

Red mullet is commonly found in the Mediterranean. It is usually fried, or sometimes wrapped in paper and baked. Red mullet is a traditional dish for the Sunday before Easter, marinated

Below: Whitebait and other small fish are fried in batter and served with lemon as a popular meze.

Anchovies
These are especially popular in Greece, and are eaten fresh as well as salted or marinated in flavoured olive oil. Small anchovies, called gavros, are often baked with garlic, olive oil, lemon and oregano, or fried until crisp. The heads of gavros are always removed first, as they can be bitter. Anchovies can also be made into a pâté and then served with toasted pitta bread.

Above: Sea bass may be cooked with herbs and citrus fruits to bring out its delicate flavour.

in oil, red wine, vinegar, garlic, currants and rosemary. It is also delicious baked with slices of orange.
Grey mullet is fished from Rhodes. The well-known meze, *taramasalata*, is made with its roe mixed with olive oil and lemon juice, although sometimes a cheaper version is made using smoked cod's roe. Grey mullet roe is also smoked and salted, and eaten as the dish *avgotaraho*.
Tuna September is the time when tuna is at its best and cheapest throughout the Mediterranean. The large fish has dense, dark-coloured flesh, which is usually sold in steaks. In Greece it is enjoyed baked with potatoes, tomatoes and garlic or pan-fried with vegetables. White tuna is pickled, and is called *lakerda*; it makes a wonderful addition to a meze table and is much loved by all the Greek people.

Swordfish One of the largest fish, the swordfish is eaten as brochettes or grilled in steaks, liberally brushed with olive oil flavoured with garlic, dried oregano and lemon. It is fished from the Greek islands.
Scorpion fish is a rockfish with poisonous spines, which needs to be prepared with care. It is always boiled and has delicious white flesh. It is excellent served in a soup.

LUXURY FISH

A selection of less common and more expensive fish is also enjoyed.
Cod is imported and cooked simply. The roe is sometimes used for *taramasalata*.
Bream The firm flesh of black bream and saddled bream is excellent grilled (broiled) or baked.
Dover sole is best simply grilled; it has an excellent flavour.

Dentex (Mediterranean sea bream) is usually cut into steaks and fried or grilled. It is also sometimes baked and served with a mayonnaise sauce.
John Dory Fished off Crete, this is a popular fish and is best grilled or fried.
Grouper is a large fish, often fished off the island of Mykonos. It has a fine flavour and dense white flesh. The steaks are ideal for grilling or baking. Smaller grouper can be baked whole with garlic and served with herb-flavoured olive oil and lemon.
Sea bass has delicately flavoured soft flesh, and is usually cooked whole without overpowering flavourings or herbs. It is often baked in a little red wine vinegar with fresh rosemary.

Left: Swordfish from the day's catch can be seen at the harbourside, awaiting transport to the cities.

Left: *Larger octopus should be tenderized before cooking, perhaps with vinegar, onions and tomatoes.*

RARE FISH

Some fish are rarely caught, mainly owing to the overfishing that occurs throughout the Mediterranean. They include bonito, enjoyed eaten fried or grilled (broiled) with garlic and lemon. The small garfish, when found, are eaten fried, whereas larger ones are delicious grilled or baked with onions, garlic and tomatoes.

Once, when the Caspian Sea was full of sturgeon, caviar was used in Greek salads. Now, because of overfishing, it is substituted with imported black lumpfish roe.

Fish soup

Kakavia is a famous fish soup made by the fishermen of the Greek islands, using the tiny fish that are too small to sell. The Aegean fish soup, *psarosoupa*, uses a variety of fish, such as scorpion fish, red gurnard (pictured below), grey mullet and sea bass, to which are added mussels and prawns (shrimp). Leeks and herbs give the soup flavour, and it is a meal in itself.

FRESHWATER FISH

Trout is more frequently farmed than found in the lakes and rivers of central and northern Greece these days. It is usually grilled or fried, but can also be stuffed with dill and parsley and baked. Carp live in streams and ponds, so they are inclined to taste muddy. Their flavour is enhanced by a rich tomato and red (bell) pepper sauce.

CEPHALOPODS

These are eaten regularly, especially on the islands.

Octopus Baby octopus might be marinated in olive oil and oregano. Older octopus is often tenderized before sale, by being beaten against a rock. It is then cut into cubes and cooked in red wine, which also helps to tenderize it. Octopus can be braised with vinegar, onions and tomatoes and flavoured with allspice and cinnamon. Octopus will often be found served raw in tavernas, where it is served in slices with olive oil and lemon juice as a meze. Skinned slices of cooked octopus can be made into a salad with dill. It is also pickled in white wine vinegar.

Squid There are several varieties of squid in the Mediterranean. With its sweet, aniseedy flavour, squid is a popular food in Greece, especially during the winter, when it is often fried and served with cannellini bean soup for a filling dish. Tiny squid are sweet and tender and usually eaten whole. Larger squid can be sliced and then grilled or stewed, or they can be left whole and stuffed. Squid is also added to pilaffs.

Cuttlefish The flesh of cuttlefish is sweet-tasting and tender. It is usually fried, but it can also be casseroled with white wine and onions, or cooked in a pilaff. Spinach also goes well with it. There is more ink in its sac than is found in octopus or squid, although Greeks do not use the ink when cuttlefish is used in pilaffs.

SHELLFISH

In Greece, shellfish and crustaceans are traditionally chargrilled or pan-fried with herbs, olive oil and lemon juice.

Below: Mussels are very versatile and may be added to soups, stews or pilaffs, or served on their own.

Above: Squid may be cooked whole or sliced before grilling (broiling). Larger squid can also be stuffed.

Mussels Available in the winter, flavourful mussels make an inexpensive meal. They are added to pilaffs and can also be briefly cooked and then coated with batter and quickly fried.
Cockles (small clams) are tasty in pilaffs.
Mediterranean prawns can reach about 20cm/8in in length and are always bought uncooked. The cooking liquid is sometimes made into a sauce. Prawns (shrimp) are delicious simply served in a salad with extra virgin olive oil and lemon juice. For the dish *yiouvetsia*, they are baked in a tomato, oregano and wine sauce, and served with feta cheese on top. They are rarely peeled before cooking, and dishes are accompanied with lemon wedges.
Langoustines or spiny lobster are delicious in tomato and saffron sauce.
Lobsters, crayfish and crabs are eaten simply with olive oil and lemon juice.
Dark purple sea urchins and their roes are a popular dish, eaten raw.
Oysters are simply eaten fresh and raw with a squeeze of lemon juice.

Below: Prawns are a firm favourite with the Greeks and are often served simply fried with garlic and fresh lemon juice.

Preparing squid and cuttlefish
The cleaning and preparation of squid and cuttlefish can take a few minutes, so set aside some time.

1 Wash the squid or cuttlefish carefully. If there is any ink on the body, rinse it off so that you can clearly see what you are doing.

2 Holding the body firmly, pull away the head and tentacles. If the ink sac is still intact, remove it. Either keep it for cooking or discard it if you prefer.

3 Keeping the squid or cuttlefish intact, gently pull out all the innards, including the long transparent stick or "pen".

4 Peel off and discard the thin purple skin, but leave the two small fins on the sides.

5 Slice the head across just under the eyes, severing the tentacles. Discard the rest of the head. Squeeze the tentacles at the head end to push out the round beak in the centre. Throw this away.

6 Rinse the pouch and the tentacles. Drain well and pat dry.

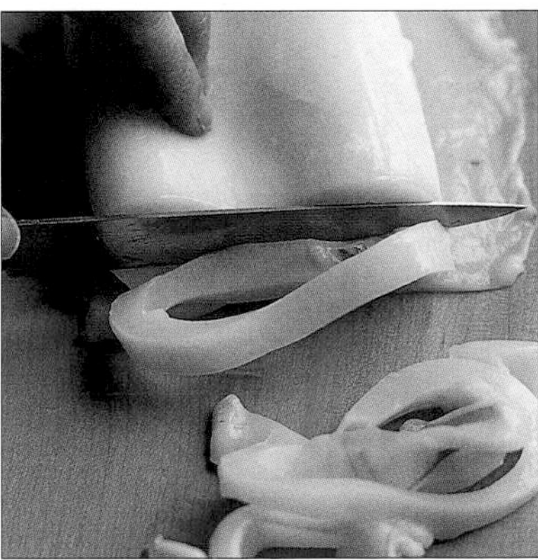

7 If the squid or cuttlefish is to be stuffed, leave the pouch whole. Alternatively, slice it into rings. The tentacles are often left whole for frying, but they can be chopped into shorter lengths if you prefer.

POULTRY AND GAME

In Greece, most poultry is free-range and full of flavour. Long, slow cooking methods are traditionally used so that the meat will be tender and moist.

Many migrating birds temporarily settle in Greece during September, so this is when most game is available. Hare is a favourite game animal, but when it is not available rabbit will be eaten. All the rabbit recipes are suitable for cooking with hare, and vice versa.

CHICKEN

Meats that are roasted are always accompanied by plenty of oil and water and usually vegetables to flavour the meat and keep it moist. Chicken will be roasted this way, often surrounded with potatoes, which will then cook in the juices. It can also be stuffed, and rice is a popular choice with the addition of nuts and herbs, such as peanuts, sultanas (golden raisins), oregano and thyme. For a spicy meat stuffing, minced (ground) lamb or beef can also be used, flavoured with allspice and cinnamon.

Chicken will also be pan-fried with basil and then simmered with some vegetables, or jointed and marinated in oil and herbs, such as oregano, before being spit-roasted or grilled (broiled).

Casseroled chicken with seasonal vegetables is popular. Okra makes a rich sauce, or alternatively onions, carrots and celery might be used. Lemon complements the flavour of chicken well and the lemon sauce, *avgolemono*, will often be served as an accompaniment to chicken that has been simply casseroled or fried. Chicken is also made into a soup, and a favourite cure for a hangover is chicken *avgolemono* soup.

A tasty chicken pie with filo pastry is also made, containing *kefalotiri* cheese and nutmeg.

Above: Roast chicken with vegetables is popular for Sundays and celebrations, served with an array of side dishes.

TURKEY

Introduced to Corfu by the French in the 19th century, turkey has become a popular meat for Christmas. Islanders there always accompany the roast bird with a sweet mustard, which grows on the island. Turkey can be stuffed with rice and nuts in the same way as chicken, or with a chestnut or minced (ground) meat stuffing. It is also roasted surrounded with vegetables.

QUAIL

Now no longer abundant in the wild, most quail bought from the markets will have been farmed. Quail does not have a strong gamey flavour and is usually cooked simply roasted with olive oil and wine. It is also delicious marinated in oregano and grilled, spit-roasted or barbecued. A traditional method of cooking is to wrap the bird in a dough made of red earth and water and then to bake it until the mud is hard. Another method is to put the bird inside a large aubergine (eggplant) that has had

Below: Chicken joints are commonly used for casseroles and bakes.

most of its flesh removed. It is then cooked in the oven until the aubergine is soft. Quail is also occasionally added to a *stifado*. Allow one per person.

WOODCOCK

These small birds weigh about 350g/12oz and serve one person each. They are usually roasted with oil, lemon juice and wine.

PIGEON

Wine and tomatoes make a tasty sauce for cooking pigeon. It is also suitable for barbecuing or grilling. Serve one for each person.

PARTRIDGES

First marinated in fresh lemon juice, partridges are then brushed with olive oil and roasted. Serve one per person.

DUCK

Wild duck can be found around the lakes of Macedonia, and they are traditionally pot-roasted. Because a wild duck feeds on fish, the cleaned bird is always seared inside before it is cooked, to remove the fishy taste. The bird might be packed with salt, bay leaves or rosemary and stored for a short period before cooking.

GUINEA FOWL

On Zakynthos, guinea fowl is cooked in a tomato sauce with cubes of melting cheese. It is also pot-roasted or even sometimes cooked in a *stifado*.

RABBIT AND HARE

The most common way to cook rabbit and hare is in a *stifado*, and recipes will differ slightly all over Greece. Wild rabbit has a strong flavour and is smaller than a hare, serving about three people each. A hare will serve five to six people. For rabbit or hare casserole, *kounelli stifado*, a dish that goes back to the ancient Greeks, honey and vinegar are added to give the meat a sweet-and-sour taste. Garlic, bay leaves, allspice, cloves, rosemary and wine might also be added. Both rabbit and hare are often marinated in vinegar before they are casseroled, and taste delicious simply cooked with lemon.

Above: Duck is traditionally pot-roasted in Greece. Pierce the skin with a knife to allow the fat to run out.

Below: Rabbit is often casseroled with baby onions, celery and rosemary.

Left, from top: Farmed rabbit, wild rabbit, saddle and leg joint – all popular with the Greeks for stews, roasting and grilling.

MEAT

Tender spring lamb or young goat roasted over a spit is the favourite with the Greeks. Indeed, most meat recipes are for lamb and few include beef. The reason for this is that there is insufficient suitable grazing land for cattle, so beef is scarcer than lamb. Sheep, and goats especially, are more suited to the rocky terrain that covers most of Greece. Where pastureland is particularly rich, such as Epirus, the meat will be especially flavoursome.

Traditionally, the Greek diet has included little meat, with most meat meals reserved for festivals and Sundays. However, over the years tourism has brought affluence to areas that were once poor and so meat is more affordable than it was in the past for many people.

The climate in Greece is not ideal for hanging meat for aging so most traditional recipes are based on long, slow cooking and casseroling, usually with wine, lemon juice or a tomato sauce added to tenderize it. Sometimes, meat that has been simmered will then be fried, as the Greeks believe it makes the flavour lighter than searing first and then simmering.

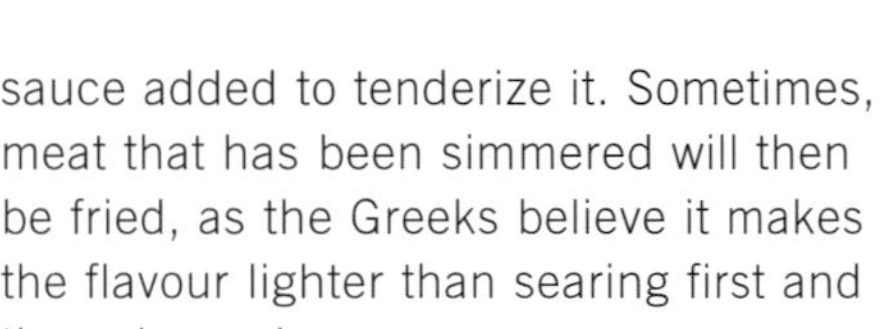

Above: Lamb leg (right) is among the most popular roasting meats for special occasions, and leg steaks (left) are commonly grilled (broiled).

Below: Leg of lamb can be roasted with thyme, potatoes and garlic for Sundays or a special occasion.

Pork is also enjoyed, although less frequently in the summer months when the heat makes for poor storage conditions. In some places pork is banned in August.

LAMB

A whole lamb will be auspiciously roasted on a spit over vine branches for Easter Sunday, the main festival day of the year. For Sunday roasts and other special occasions, a leg of lamb will usually be chosen over any other cut. The traditional lemon and egg sauce, *avgolemono*, will often be served to accompany the simply cooked lamb, and its sharp flavour is perfect to counteract the sweet richness of the meat.

Leg Greek roasting recipes for legs of lamb always include vegetables, such as potatoes, plenty of oil and some water, resulting in moist and succulent meat. Roasts are traditionally cooked very well – when a joint is left to cook in the baker's oven it is always well done – and so the addition of plenty of liquid ensures the meat does not dry out. Small, rice-shaped pasta and tomatoes are also cooked with lamb in this way.

Cut into cubes, leg of lamb can be simmered with vegetables in a casserole. It is the best cut to use for kebabs, where it might be flavoured with oregano, thyme and garlic. *Souvlaki* are kebabs that make tasty

Below: Minced (ground) lamb (top) is used for stuffings, and cubed lamb can be casseroled or baked with herbs.

street food, traditionally eaten at festival time, when they are sold in soft pitta bread with a yogurt, garlic and cucumber dressing.

Cutlets (US rib chops) make a great treat for special occasions. They are roasted with garlic and herbs or a thick tomato sauce, or can be grilled (broiled) or barbecued.

Shoulder Rarely roasted as a joint, shoulder of lamb is used for casseroles to which are added a variety of seasonal vegetables, such as okra and tomatoes. It is sometimes boned and cut into chunks to be simmered with vegetables, such as artichokes or broad (fava) beans, and then served with *avgolemono*. It can also be cooked in slices on the bone and casseroled with spring peas flavoured with dill.

Saddle For stuffing, saddle of lamb is the best cut of meat, and a stuffing might include rice, pine nuts, almonds, onions, cumin and basil.

Minced (ground) lamb is used for the traditional moussaka, where it is layered with aubergine (eggplant) slices and baked in a rich cheese sauce. It is also used for pie fillings, and is delicious mixed with courgettes (zucchini).

GOAT

Every rural family will keep a goat for milk. The meat from the kids will be reserved for festivals and special occasions. Young milk-fed goat is more popular than lamb. The dish *kleftiko*, where meat is cooked wrapped in paper, is frequently prepared using goat. Goat meat is also used to make meatballs. In some parts of the country the billy goat's meat is minced (ground) and used as a vegetable stuffing.

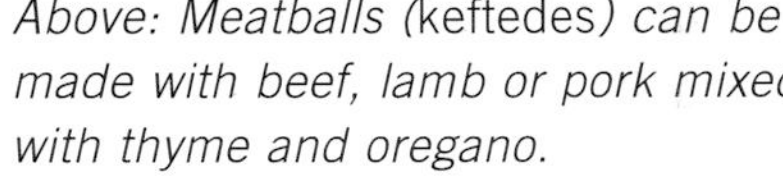

*Above: Meatballs (*keftedes*) can be made with beef, lamb or pork mixed with thyme and oregano.*

BEEF

Although traditionally little beef is eaten, dishes containing it are more common in Greece today. Steaks will be found in restaurants, but most traditional recipes use stewing cuts. Steaks will be simply grilled (broiled) with olive oil. Beef is called *moshari* in Greece, which is translated as "veal". This has caused some confusion with visitors to the country, as traditionally veal is not used in Greek cuisine.

Below: Beef steaks, simply grilled (broiled) with olive oil are often served in restaurants.

Chuck steak makes a delicious stew, which might include okra, tomatoes, garlic and parsley.

Rump steak, brisket and braising steak These are suitable cuts for stewing, and will be cubed for *stifado*. This dish is traditionally a thickened hare or rabbit stew, but it can contain beef, game and even snails instead. Tomatoes, garlic, olive oil and vinegar are added, and the other herbs and flavourings used will depend upon the region. On the islands, for example, cinnamon and other spices, such as allspice or cloves, will usually be included.

Capamas volou is a spicy, slow-cooked beef stew from Thessaly, which is flavoured with paprika and raisins. Also from the area comes a pepper-flavoured stew with melting cheese added at the last minute.

Minced (ground) beef will be used for rissoles, which might be flavoured with cumin. Minced beef can be substituted for lamb in moussaka.

Above: *Pork chops are a popular winter dish and can be grilled or cooked gently in a sauce with vegetables.*

PORK

Popular as a winter meat, pork is often roasted or casseroled, and roast sucking pig is a great favourite. Tender pork will be thickly sliced and cooked with cannellini beans or *fasolia gigantes* in a winter casserole that is cooked with tomato. In the northern areas pork is often combined with leeks and feta cheese in a pie of crisp filo pastry. A traditional food eaten on the Thursday before Lent, a pig's head is baked and the meat served as a meze.

Pork chops will be simmered with vegetables in a sauce, or marinated and grilled (broiled).

Below: Leg and shoulder of pork are often used for casseroles and go particularly well with olives.

Shoulder cuts and pork fillet are ideal for casseroles. The kebabs, *souvlaki*, are traditionally made with lamb but can also be made with pork fillet. They will be flavoured with lemon, herbs and olive oil. Thick pork cutlets are baked until tender in the Cretan dish *choirino kritiko*.

Leg will often be casseroled or baked and is particularly tasty cooked with garlic and olives.

Minced (ground) pork is used for meatballs, such as fried *keftedes*, with mint and cumin.

OFFAL/VARIETY MEATS

All parts of the animal are eaten in Greece. Lamb's offal especially is considered a delicacy and will be eaten in many ways. Young goat offal is particularly tasty and is preferred. The liver is sold with other organs attached, and so a "liver" dish will include the heart and other parts. For the dish *enthosthia lathorigani*, for example, lamb's liver, heart, kidneys and sweetbreads are cut into cubes and baked with oil and lemon juice. Liver on its own is also delicious cooked with wine and tomatoes or combined with olives, tomatoes, lemon and parsley, and cooked wrapped in paper to seal in the juices. Even lamb's feet will be cooked and eaten, often served with *avgolemono*.

Lamb's head will be roasted and is chargrilled with the testicles as a speciality in small countryside tavernas. The tongues will be boiled and then sliced and fried or cooked with a spicy tomato sauce. Lamb's, sheep's or calf's brains are poached and then fried whole or sliced thickly, and they are sometimes made into pastries.

Lamb intestines are made into *kokoretsi*, a favourite sausage that is eaten all over Greece at Easter. *Mageritsa* soup, made with lamb offal, is the first meal to break the fast on Easter Sunday, and *patsa* is a soup made from pig's or cow's intestines, stomach and feet. Tripe is also made into a soup or will be casseroled. The spleen is a traditional delicacy, which is sometimes cooked over charcoal and served as a meze, and sweetbreads will be dusted with flour and fried.

SAUSAGES AND CURED MEATS

Before modern methods of preserving, people cured meats and sausages so that they could use as much meat from an animal carcass as feasible. At the end of the year, the ancient ritual *hirosfagia* takes place all over Greece. Each family slaughters the pig that it has reared over the past year, and every piece of the carcass is used to give a variety of sausages and cured meats.

Sausages

There are regional differences in the way the sausages are prepared and the flavourings that are used. Leeks are a popular ingredient for sausages in Thessaly, for example, giving a very different flavour to that of the sausages found in the

Snails
On the island of Crete, snails are a delicacy and eaten as a meze or added to *stifado*. A summer dish, snails are gathered after there has been rain. As snails absorb the taste and smell of whatever they have eaten, rain cleanses them and refreshes their flavour. After collection they will often be fed on herbs and fresh water so that they have the best flavour prior to cooking. As a meze they might be cooked with tomatoes, grated onion and parsley, or with oil and vinegar.

Cyclades, where more herbs are used. Orange is favoured in sausages from the Peloponnese, whereas those from Andros contain aniseed and are smoked. Many sausages are fresh and not dried, especially those from the northern regions of Macedonia and Thrace.
Kokoretsi Made of lamb or goat offal, and flavoured with lemon juice, oregano, thyme and garlic, this fresh sausage is from Macedonia. It is eaten as a meze and also traditionally cooked at Easter on a spit with lamb.
Loukanika This fresh country sausage is made with coarse-cut lamb or pork, but sometimes beef is used. The sausage is flavoured with orange rind, marjoram, coriander and allspice, and sometimes chilli. It is usually sold coiled into a spiral. It will then be cut into chunks and pan-fried, roasted, barbecued or grilled. The dish *spetzofai* is a speciality of the region of Mount Pelion, where *loukanika* sausage is cooked in a spicy stew with green (bell) peppers.
Loukanika Nissiotika is a long, thin pork sausage made on a number of the Greek islands.
Maniatika From Mani in the Peloponnese, this sausage is made with pork and beef seasoned with oregano and mint.
Maties e saffathes is made with pork and rice flavoured with garlic, cumin and orange peel. It is first boiled and then fried, and is usually served with mezedes before the Christmas meal.
Soutzoukakia originated in Smyrna and was originally made with lamb. The Greek version contains beef and is flavoured with cumin, garlic and wine. There are many different types of *soutzoukakia*, which are usually formed into meatballs and cooked with a tomato sauce. The *soutzoukakia* from Crete is made from pork meat flavoured with orange and oregano.
Souzoukakia politiko A dried black sausage, *souzoukakia politiko* is sometimes flavoured with red chilli.
Thessalias Leeks give this pork sausage from Thessaly a rich flavour.
Voliotika This small, fat sausage from Volos is made from pork and beef and is seasoned with allspice.

Right: Fresh country sausages from Pelion are flavoured with orange rind, herbs and spices.

Left: Spicy sausage casserole from the Pelion region is flavoured with (bell) peppers and fresh oregano.

Cured meats

Although meats are cured all over the country, the north of Greece has the largest selection.
Kavourmas Traditionally made from beef, *kavourmas* is sometimes made from pork or lamb and is a delicacy from northern Greece. Large pieces of meat, including the fat, are boiled with leeks, onions and spices. The meat is then preserved with its layer of fat.
Pastourma This cured meat is a speciality of the regions that are near to Turkey, such as Thrace, the Dodecanese and the north-eastern Aegean islands. Beef is salted and covered by a layer of cumin, paprika and allspice. In the Dodecanese, goat meat is cured in this way. Slices of pastourma are often cooked in *Caesaria* pie, with *kasseri* cheese and tomato.
Apaki A speciality of Crete, *apaki* is made from pork that is salted and then marinated in vinegar. The meat is then smoked in aromatic herbs and wrapped in a layer of spices and flavourings, giving an aromatic taste.
Lountza This cured pork, produced in the Cyclades, is salted then marinated in red wine. It is smoked, covered in spices, and wrapped in intestine to mature. *Lountza* is eaten thinly sliced.
Noumboulo For this cured meat from Corfu, pork is marinated in red wine. It is then smoked, covered in aromatic herbs and wrapped in animal intestine.
Siglino Salted pork meat is boiled, sautéed and preserved in its own fat and a spice mix. The preserved meat is often sautéed with orange rind.
Liokafto comes from the Cyclades. Small pieces of meat are marinated in salt, vinegar and spices for a week and then left to dry in the air.

Dairy Produce

Goats and sheep provide most of the dairy produce in Greece, and their cheeses and yogurt are well known for their exceptional quality.

CHEESE

Greece is a major exporter of cheese and many of its varieties are world renowned. Cheese is still made in the traditional way and most of the cheese comes from northern Greece and especially the mountainous areas. Because the largely hilly terrain found in most parts of the mainland and islands is suitable for goats and sheep but not for cattle, the majority of Greek cheeses are made from these milks, although there are a few cow's-milk cheeses. Greek cheeses are eaten in many ways: as well as being enjoyed as table cheeses, they will be sliced and grilled (broiled) – called *saganaki* – to top a salad of wild leaves (known as *horta*), or used in stuffings for vegetables or pies. They will be used for pies and pastries and served alongside fresh fruit or fruit sauces. Firm cheeses, such as *kefalotiri*, will be sliced and fried, and then served with fresh lemon juice. Many of the cheeses are seasonal, and the traditional Easter sweets are made with the first creamy cheeses of the spring.

Soft cheeses

Greek feta cheese is enjoyed in many countries, but there are several other soft cheeses to be found.

Anthotiro There are two types of *anthotiro*; both are made from sheep's or goat's milk. The soft variety is similar to ricotta cheese.

Feta This popular Greek cheese is traditionally made from sheep's milk but goat's milk might also be added. It is stored in wooden barrels of brine and matured for at least two months. This method of preserving cheese was first discovered in ancient times and mentioned by Homer; feta may have been the first preserved cheese in Greece. Most feta comes from mountainous areas and its pure white colour comes from the milk of lean animals that roam the craggy slopes searching for food.

Goat's feta has a strong, gamey flavour, whereas sheep's has a richer taste. Both soft and firm feta are available. Soft feta is sweet and less salty than the firm variety, which has a crumbly texture. Feta is used in salads, such as the peasant salad *horiatiki*, where it is combined with tomatoes, cucumber, onion and olives. It is also baked in a variety of pies, including the well-known *spanakopita* with spinach.

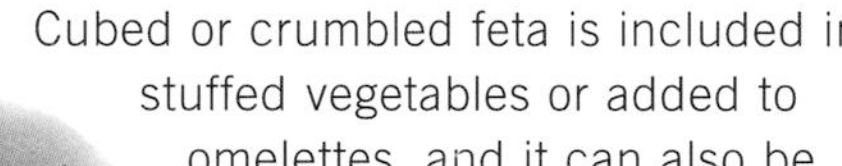

Cubed or crumbled feta is included in stuffed vegetables or added to omelettes, and it can also be used as a stuffing for fish. Feta is also served with fruit, such as watermelon. A piece is often enjoyed simply with olive oil poured over it and sprinkled with fresh oregano.

Above: Feta cheese is a staple in Greece, used in all forms of savoury and sweet dishes, salads and tarts, and making a favourite meze dish.

Ghalotiri Sharp-flavoured *ghalotiri* is a soft cheese made with goat's and sheep's milk.

Halloumi This firm cheese is made from goat's or sheep's milk. It can be cooked without melting, and so it is often used for frying or grilling (broiling).

Kalathaki From Limnos, *kalathaki* cheese is similar to feta and is made from sheep's milk.

Kopanisti Made from sheep's, goat's or cow's milk, *kopanisti* is produced in the Cyclades. It is a creamy soft cheese with a deeply rich flavour, and is matured for one year.

Manouri A traditionally prepared whey cheese, *manouri* is soft-textured, creamy and unsalted. It is made from sheep's or goat's whey, or a blend of both, and the milk curd. *Manouri* is produced in northern Greece, especially Macedonia. It is used in sweet pastries and pies, and is often served with fruit and honey as a dessert after a meal.

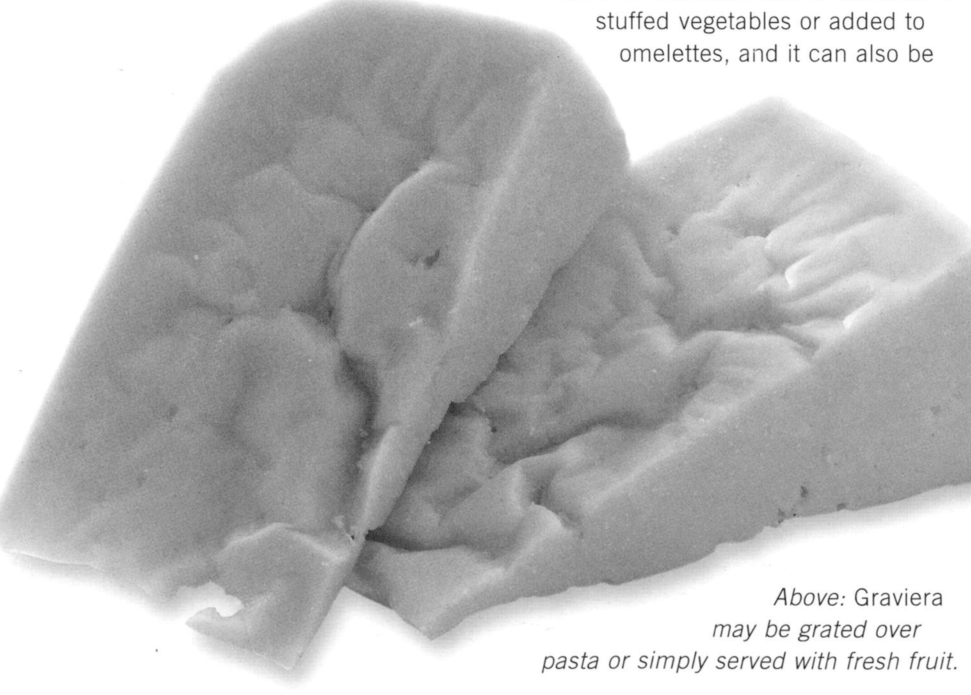

Above: Graviera *may be grated over pasta or simply served with fresh fruit.*

Below: Kasseri *is one of the oldest Greek cheeses and is usually eaten on its own.*

Mizithra
There are two types of *mizithra*; both made from sheep's or goat's milk whey, which remains after producing feta cheese. Fresh, soft *mizithra* is unsalted and has a texture similar to Italian ricotta cheese. It is often used for sweet pastries. There is also a hard variety of this cheese.
Telemes Similar in taste and texture to feta cheese, *telemes* is made from cow's milk and aged in cans.
Tirovolya is a soft, sweet-flavoured cheese from Mykonos.

Hard cheeses

Matured cheeses become hard and are perfect for grating or grilling (broiling).
Anthotiro Made from sheep's or goat's milk, the original soft *anthotiro* is aged until it hardens to form the matured hard variety.
Formaella arahovas parnasu This mellow-flavoured hard cheese is made from sheep's or goat's milk. It is left to mature for at least three months.
Graviera This hard cheese is made from goat's, sheep's or cow's milk or a blend, depending on the region or island in which it is produced. It has a mild flavour and is used for grating over pasta. A variety of *graviera* cheese is *aghrafon*, which is a pale cheese of high quality. A speciality of Zakynthos is the sharp-tasting *lathograviera Zakynthou*, which is stored in oil. *Graviera* is often served with fruit.

Kasseri There are several varieties of *kasseri*, and the flavours range from mild and creamy to sharp. *Kasseri* is an oily, pale-yellow, semi-hard cheese made from sheep's milk or a blend of sheep's and goat's milk. It is matured for three months. *Kasseri* is usually eaten on its own or with fruit. It is one of the oldest traditional Greek cheeses.
Kefalograviera This hard cheese is produced in areas of northern Greece, and particularly Macedonia. It is made from sheep's milk or a blend of sheep's and goat's milk and is allowed to mature for three months. Pale yellow in colour, *kefalograviera* has a distinctively sharp and slightly salty flavour. It is used grated, fried, and as a table cheese.

Above: Soft Greek cheeses, such as feta, are often added to salads – either diced or crumbled.

Below: Grilled halloumi makes a delicious appetizer served simply on a bed of salad leaves.

Left: Cheese pastries and pies are very popular as a snack, using a variety of cheeses, including feta cheese.

Kefalotiri This salty, sharp-tasting cheese is made with sheep's and goat's milk, and is matured for at least three months. It is an exceptionally hard cheese, which is used for grating, frying and cooking, and is delicious served with fruit. The savoury *saganaki* is made with *kefalotiri* cheese, dusted with flour then fried in olive oil and served with lemon.

Ladotyri Made from sheep's and goat's milk, rich-flavoured *ladotyri* is shaped into balls and sometimes called *kefalaki*, meaning "little head". The name *ladotyri*, however, refers to the olive oil in which the cheese is aged for about a year.

Mizithra Made from sheep's or goat's milk whey, dried *mizithra* is salted and aged until hard. It can be grated and is often used in cooking.

Smoked cheeses

A few smoked cheeses are also made in Greece. These two are very good.
Metsovone kapnisto is made mostly from cow's milk with the addition of some sheep's or goat's milk.
Touloumotiri is a white cheese with a sweet flavour. Made from sheep's or goat's milk, it is smoked and then stored in sheepskin or goatskin bags.

YOGURT

Thick and creamy Greek yogurt is made from sheep's and sometimes cow's milk. The yogurt is strained so that any remaining solids used for the yogurt are rich and creamy. Until the middle of the 20th century yogurt was delivered in clay pots to the door. Diluted with milk or water it was drunk by shepherds and labourers while they worked. Even today, traditional Greek yogurt has remained rich and creamy, made in the traditional way. Greeks enjoy it as a delicious snack or a tasty breakfast dish with

Above, clockwise from top: milk, yogurt cheese, thick cream, Greek yogurt, cream cheese and whey.

Right: Free-range (farm fresh) eggs are widely available.

honey and walnuts, and is often served this way in special milk shops, known as *galaktopoleia*. It is also added to savoury pies, such as *tyropitakia lefteritsas*, which contains feta cheese, dill or mint and onion. Yogurt will be served alongside vegetables and is especially delicious with stuffed vegetables, such as *dolmades*. It can also be made into a rich, chilled soup with cream, cucumber and mint, and makes a sweet yogurt cake flavoured with lemon, called *yiaourtopitta*. If Greek yogurt is unavailable, strained plain yogurt is a suitable alternative.

CREAM

Kaimaki is a very thick cream made by gently heating goat's or sheep's milk until a rich layer of cream forms on the surface. It is served with sweet pastries and puddings. *Kaimaki* is also used to fill small fruits such as prunes, which are then served with honey.

EGGS

Most country people keep hens for their eggs, as they are used in many Greek dishes. Omelettes are a favourite food and will often be filled with cheese, vegetables or *horta*. They might also be served with a sauce. In Thessalonika, the Greek Jewish community boils eggs with onion skins, to be eaten as a meze. Red-dyed eggs are a vital part of the Easter celebrations all over Greece, and are eaten on Easter morning.

Avgolemono is a sauce made with eggs and lemons that is added to almost any food that has been cooked in a simple way. The sauce adds body to casseroles and stews, because the eggs act as a thickener, and the lemons add their sharp citrus taste, which is so loved by the Greeks.

Left: Greek yogurt, creamy and rich, is used throughout Greece spooned into soups, casseroles and dips.

Avgolemono

This egg and lemon sauce is fundamental to Greek cooking, and gives an unforgettable flavour to all those dishes in which it is incorporated. The lemon brings out the natural flavours of meat, poultry and fish, whereas the egg provides consistency. Individual recipes give instructions for *avgolemono*, but here is a basic method for recipes to serve four.

1 Beat 2 large (US extra large) eggs, at room temperature, in a bowl, beat in the juice of 1–2 lemons, then add 5ml/1 tsp cornflour (cornstarch), mixed to a smooth cream with a little water.

2 Add a ladleful of the hot soup (or stock or cooking sauce) and beat for 1 or 2 minutes.

3 Continue to beat the egg mixture while adding a second ladleful of hot liquid, and then gradually add the remaining contents of the bowl to the soup, stock or cooking sauce, stirring vigorously all the time.

4 Warm the mixture over a gentle heat for about 1–2 minutes. If you cook for any longer the eggs may curdle, even though the cornflour mixture will have helped to stabilize the sauce. Season to taste with salt before serving.

DRINKS

Greek coffee is a favourite beverage, made strong and frothy. Amongst the alcoholic drinks produced in Greece are some excellent wines, as well as good spirits and beers.

COFFEE

Drinking frothy, thick coffee is part of daily life for Greeks, usually late in the afternoon. The coffee is made in a small, tall, cylindrical pan called a *briki*, which is heated on the stove. It is then poured into small, thick white cups. Greek coffee is always served black and never stirred once heated. There are several ways it can be drunk:

Sketos Strong and bitter, without sugar
Metrios Medium, with 5ml/1 tsp sugar
Ghlikos Very sweet
Ghlikivrastos Sweet, but it is reboiled so does not have any froth.

When making coffee for more than one person use the correct-sized *briki* and pour a little hot coffee into each cup before you distribute the froth.

FRAPPE

This cold and extremely sweet drink is made with instant coffee, sugar and condensed milk, whipped until frothy. Frappe is a popular drink, and is sold in cafés throughout Greece.

Right: Wine is produced from indigenous grapes in Greece, as well as from international varieties that have been introduced recently to the country.

WINE

From the drinking rites depicted on the decorated vases of ancient Greece we can see that wine has been enjoyed for centuries. However, all the invasions and occupations that occurred throughout history prevented the development of a Greek wine industry. Although the Ottoman Turks did not ban wine, it was heavily taxed, making it too expensive for most people to buy. By the time of Greek independence, in 1821, wine production was on a local basis with the wine kept in barrels.

Below: Strong and bitter coffee is often enjoyed in the morning or with sweets, cakes and pastries in the afternoon.

Today, the Greek wine industry has moved on, and in 1981 Greece joined the European Union and adopted the Appellation Control laws by which any wine sold under the AOC (Appellation d'Origine Controle) classification has to conform to certain strict criteria of quality control. There are also other classifications, including regional wines, that although good are not required to conform to all the AOC criteria, and some good table wines.

Wine regions of Greece

Throughout the mainland regions and the islands fine wines are now produced from the local classic indigenous grapes and also from the recently introduced international varieties that thrive in the various landscapes and climates.

How to make Greek coffee
Serves 1

1 Measure out 250ml/8fl oz/1 cup water into a one-cup sized briki. Add 5ml/1 tsp freshly ground coffee and 5ml/1 tsp sugar.
2 Put the briki over a low heat and stir until the coffee is diluted in the water. Hold on to the long handle of the briki while it heats.
3 As it starts to boil watch it rise until the foam reaches the lip of the briki. Immediately remove from the heat, and leave to stand for 1 minute. Do not stir. Pour the coffee into a small coffee cup.

Above: Salty pistachio nuts and olives go down a treat when accompanied by a glass of ouzo.

Macedonia is one of the oldest and finest winemaking regions, particularly the Naoussa area on the slopes of Mount Vermio, which produces delicious, full-bodied red wines from the xinomavro grape.

Epirus Despite the difficult growing conditions on the slopes of the Pindus Mountains, excellent wines are produced in the region, particularly Zitsa, a slightly sparkling dry or medium-dry white wine made from the debina grape.

Ionian Islands The dry, white Robola wine of Kefallinia is one of three AOC wines produced on the island. Also Zakynthos produces a traditional white wine, Verdea, which has a greenish colour because the grapes are picked early in the summer.

Attica is one of the oldest wine-producing areas, where the white savatiano grape dominates. It is probably most famous for the retsina produced here, but there are also some good wines produced from the cabernet sauvignon and merlot grapes.

Peloponnese Homer called the region *Ampeloessa* – full of vines – and the Nemea area, in the east of the region, is the most important. Higher up in the central mountains, the areas of Martinia and Patras also produce some excellent AOC wines.

North Aegean Islands The island of Samos has been famous for its sweet Muscat wine for centuries and now produces dry white table wines from the muscat grape. The volcanic soil on Limnos produces a dry white Muscat.

Santorini In about 1650BC a volcanic eruption covered the whole island with lava, pumice and ash, which have created the perfect conditions for making excellent AOC wines.

Crete The island is dominated by a mountainous spine running east to west, which protects the vineyards on the north of the island from the hot winds from Africa. Crete produces 20 per cent of all Greek wine including the AOC Archanes, Peza, Dafnes and Sitia wines, as well as a number of acceptable table wines.

Retsina

The resinated wine, retsina, goes particularly well with seafood. It is made from the native grape of Attica, the white savatiano, although red, rosé and champagne retsinas are also produced. The distinctive taste comes from resin from the Aleppo pine forests in Attica, which is added to the wine as it ferments. This method of preserving wine goes back to the ancient Greeks.

In the 19th century, retsina was available only in the tavernas of Athens, where it was poured into glasses direct from the barrel. It was not until the 1960s that bottled retsina was available, and the drink then became popular. Earlier types of retsina were extremely strong but modern drinks are scented rather than overpowered with the flavour of resin. Kourtaki is one of the main producers, making a popular medium to strong retsina. Other brands include the light and fruity Boutaris and the pungent Malamamatinas from northern Greece.

Right: Ouzo is the aperitif of choice in Greece, drunk while enjoying a selection of mezedes.

OUZO

Greeks like to start a meal with ouzo, distilled from grapes, as it is a good aperitif and goes well with the salty taste of mezedes. Although it is generally flavoured with aniseed, other flavourings are also used in some brands, such as mint or fennel. A good-quality ouzo is produced on Lesvos and its popular Mytilini brand can be found all over Greece. Other well-known brands are the mild Mini, the dry Aphrodite, and the smooth and herb-flavoured Metaxa.

TSIPURO

The liqueur *tsipuro* is distilled from the stems, pips (seeds) and skins of crushed grapes and is flavoured with herbs and spices, and sometimes with aniseed. It is an extremely strong drink, which is also known as *raki* and *tsikouda*. On the island of Chios, *tsipuro* is flavoured with mastic to make the liqueur *masticha*.

BRANDY

A popular drink in Greece, brandy is also used as a flavouring for cakes, such as *karythopitta*. Some makes of brandy are sweetened with the sweet grape *monemvasya*. Metaxa is the most popular brand made today.

BEER

Barley and hops are grown in Greece and there are several local beers, including Mythos and Alpha. Imported beers are in demand and many companies now brew international brands under licence.

Mezedes and Appetizers

The Greek word "mezedes" means "a tableful" and it comes from the Middle Eastern tradition of sharing small portions of savoury foods while relaxing with cool drinks. A selection of dishes will be shared to start a meal or a larger selection might be served for the main course itself.

YOGURT CHEESE IN OLIVE OIL

SHEEP'S MILK IS WIDELY USED IN CHEESE-MAKING IN THE EASTERN MEDITERRANEAN, PARTICULARLY IN GREECE WHERE SHEEP'S YOGURT IS HUNG IN MUSLIN (CHEESECLOTH) TO DRAIN OFF THE WHEY BEFORE PATTING INTO BALLS OF SOFT CHEESE. HERE IT'S BOTTLED IN EXTRA VIRGIN OLIVE OIL WITH CHILLI AND HERBS – AN APPROPRIATE GIFT FOR A FRIEND OR RELATIVE WHO ENJOYS GREEK CUISINE.

FILLS TWO 450G/1LB JARS

INGREDIENTS

- 750g/10oz/1¼ cups Greek sheep's yogurt
- 2.5ml/½ tsp salt
- 10ml/2 tsp crushed dried chillies or chilli powder
- 15ml/1 tbsp chopped fresh rosemary
- 15ml/1 tbsp chopped fresh thyme or oregano
- about 300ml/½ pint/1¼ cups olive oil, preferably garlic-flavoured

1 Sterilize a 30cm/12in square of muslin (cheesecloth) by steeping it in boiling water. Drain and lay over a large plate. Mix the yogurt with the salt and tip on to the centre of the muslin.

2 Bring up the sides of the muslin and tie firmly with string. You should now have a secured bag that can be hung. Use extra string and bag fixtures and fastenings if necessary.

3 Hang the bag on a kitchen cupboard handle or in a suitable position where it can be suspended with a bowl underneath to catch the whey as it drips. Leave for 2–3 days, or until the whey stops dripping.

4 Wash thoroughly and dry two 450g/1lb glass preserving jars or jam jars. Sterilize them by heating them in an oven preheated to 150°C/300°F/Gas 2 for 15 minutes.

5 Mix together the chilli and herbs. Take teaspoonfuls of the cheese and roll into balls with your hands. Lower into the jars, sprinkling each layer with the herb mixture.

6 Pour the olive oil over the soft cheese balls until they are completely covered. Mix gently with the handle end of a wooden spoon in order to blend the flavourings through the olive oil, making sure that you do not break up the cheese balls. Store in the refrigerator for up to 3 weeks.

7 To serve the cheese, spoon out of the jars with a little of the flavoured olive oil and spread on to lightly toasted bread.

COOK'S TIP

If your kitchen is particularly warm, find a cooler place, such as a cool cupboard or larder, to suspend the cheese. Alternatively, you can drain the cheese in the refrigerator, suspending the bag from one of the shelves.

Energy 1,331Kcal/5,485kJ; Protein 24g; Carbohydrate 7.5g, of which sugars 7.5g; Fat 138.2g, of which saturates 33.8g; Cholesterol 0mg; Calcium 563mg; Fibre 0g; Sodium 758mg.

TARAMASALATA

THIS DELICIOUS SPECIALITY MAKES AN EXCELLENT START TO ANY MEAL. IT IS PERHAPS ONE OF THE MOST FAMOUS GREEK DIPS, AND A CENTRAL PART OF ANY MEZE TABLE.

SERVES FOUR

INGREDIENTS

- 115g/4oz smoked mullet roe
- 2 garlic cloves, crushed
- 30ml/2 tbsp grated onion
- 60ml/4 tbsp olive oil
- 4 slices white bread, crusts removed
- juice of 2 lemons
- 30ml/2 tbsp milk or water
- freshly ground black pepper
- warm pitta bread, to serve

COOK'S TIP

Since the roe of grey mullet is expensive, smoked cod's roe is often used instead for this dish. It is paler than the burnt-orange colour of mullet roe but is still very good.

1 Place the smoked fish roe, garlic, grated onion, oil, bread and lemon juice in a blender or food processor and process until smooth.

2 Scrape down the edges of the food processor or blender to ensure that all the ingredients are properly incorporated. Blend quickly again.

3 Add the milk or water and process again for a few seconds. (This will give the *taramasalata* a creamier texture.)

4 Pour the *taramasalata* into a serving bowl, cover with clear film (plastic wrap) and chill for 1–2 hours before serving. Sprinkle the dip with black pepper and serve with warm pitta bread.

Energy 185Kcal/770kJ; Protein 8.4g; Carbohydrate 11.4g, of which sugars 1.7g; Fat 12.1g, of which saturates 1.8g; Cholesterol 95mg; Calcium 38mg; Fibre 0.5g; Sodium 139mg.

FETA AND ROAST PEPPER DIP WITH CHILLIES

THIS IS A FAMILIAR MEZE IN THE BEAUTIFUL CITY OF THESSALONIKA. IF YOU STOP FOR AN OUZO IN THE AREA CALLED LATHATHIKA YOU WILL INEVITABLY BE SERVED A SMALL PLATE OF HTIPITI.

SERVES FOUR

INGREDIENTS

- 1 yellow or green elongated or bell-shaped pepper
- 1–2 fresh green chillies
- 200g/7oz feta cheese, cubed
- 60ml/4 tbsp extra virgin olive oil
- juice of 1 lemon
- 45–60ml/3–4 tbsp milk
- ground black pepper
- finely chopped fresh flat leaf parsley, to garnish
- slices of toast or toasted pitta bread, to serve

VARIATION

The dip is also excellent served with a selection of vegetable crudités, such as carrot, cauliflower, green or red (bell) pepper and celery.

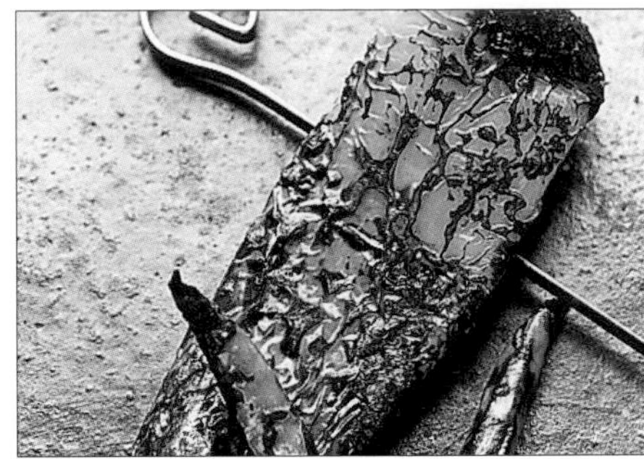

1 Scorch the pepper and chillies by threading them on to metal skewers and turning them over a flame or under the grill (broiler), until charred all over.

2 Set the pepper and chillies aside until cool enough to handle. Peel off as much of their skin as possible and wipe off the blackened parts with kitchen paper. Slit the pepper and chillies and discard the seeds and stems.

3 Put the pepper and chilli flesh into a food processor. Add the feta cheese, olive oil, lemon juice and milk, and blend well. Add a little more milk if the mixture is too stiff, and season with black pepper. Spread the dip on slices of toast, sprinkle a little fresh parsley over the top and serve.

Energy 245Kcal/1,014kJ; Protein 8.7g; Carbohydrate 4.5g, of which sugars 4.3g; Fat 21.5g, of which saturates 8.6g; Cholesterol 36mg; Calcium 198mg; Fibre 0.8g; Sodium 727mg.

TZATSIKI WITH COURGETTES AND AUBERGINES

TZATSIKI IS WELL SUITED TO THE HEAT OF THE SUMMER. IT CAN BE SERVED WITH GRILLED MEATS AND ROASTS, BUT IS PERFECT WITH FRESHLY FRIED SLICES OF COURGETTES AND AUBERGINES.

SERVES FOUR

INGREDIENTS

- 3 courgettes (zucchini)
- 1 aubergine (eggplant)
- 25g/1oz/¼ cup plain (all-purpose) flour
- sunflower oil, for frying
- salt and ground black pepper

For the *tzatsiki*

- 15cm/6in piece of cucumber
- 200g/7oz Greek (US strained plain) yogurt
- 1 or 2 garlic cloves, crushed
- 15ml/1 tbsp extra virgin olive oil
- 30ml/2 tbsp thinly sliced fresh mint leaves, plus extra to garnish

1 Start by making the *tzatsiki.* Peel the cucumber, grate it coarsely into a colander, and press out most of the liquid. Add the cucumber to the yogurt with the garlic, olive oil and mint. Stir in salt to taste, cover and chill.

2 Trim the courgettes and aubergine, then rinse them and pat them dry. Cut them lengthways into long, thin slices and coat them lightly with the flour.

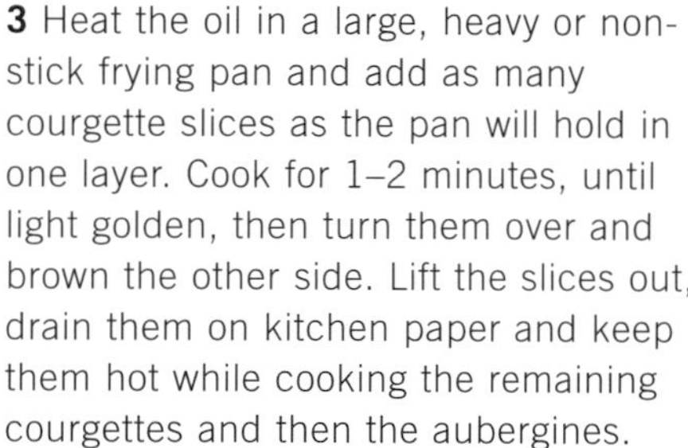

3 Heat the oil in a large, heavy or non-stick frying pan and add as many courgette slices as the pan will hold in one layer. Cook for 1–2 minutes, until light golden, then turn them over and brown the other side. Lift the slices out, drain them on kitchen paper and keep them hot while cooking the remaining courgettes and then the aubergines.

4 Pile the fried slices in a large warmed bowl, sprinkle with salt and pepper and serve immediately with the bowl of chilled *tzatsiki* garnished with a few mint leaves.

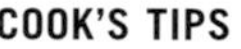

COOK'S TIPS

If you are making the *tzatsiki* several hours before serving, don't add the salt until later. If salt is added too far in advance, it will make the yogurt watery.

Energy 247Kcal/1,020kJ; Protein 7.6g; Carbohydrate 11g, of which sugars 5.5g; Fat 19.9g, of which saturates 4.6g; Cholesterol 0mg; Calcium 149mg; Fibre 3.2g; Sodium 41mg.

SALAD OF PURÉED AUBERGINES

In the heat of high summer, MELITZANOSALATA *makes a surprisingly refreshing meze. To be strictly authentic, the aubergines should be grilled over charcoal.*

SERVES FOUR

INGREDIENTS

- 3 large aubergines (eggplants), total weight about 900g/2lb
- 15ml/1 tbsp roughly chopped onion
- 2 garlic cloves, crushed
- juice of ½ lemon, or a little more
- 90–105ml/6–7 tbsp extra virgin olive oil
- 1 ripe tomato, peeled, seeded and finely diced
- salt and freshly ground black pepper
- finely chopped fresh flat leaf parsley, to garnish
- chicory (Belgian endive), and black and green olives, to serve

COOK'S TIP

You can barbecue the aubergines instead of using the oven. Prick them and barbecue over a low to medium heat for at least 1 hour.

1 Preheat the oven to 180°C/350°F/Gas 4. Prick the aubergines and lay them directly on the oven shelves. Roast them for 1 hour, or until soft, turning them over twice.

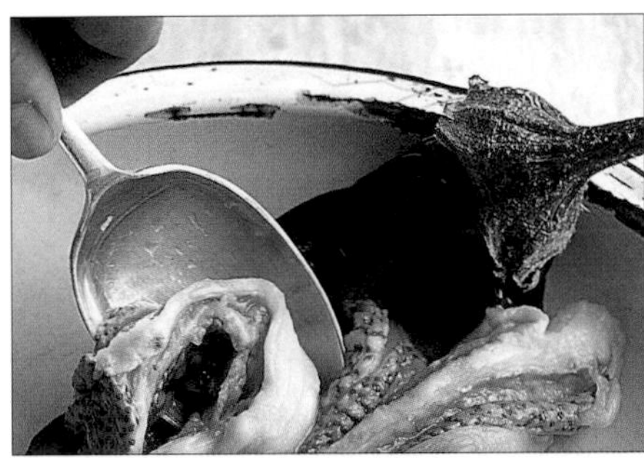

2 When the aubergines are cool enough to handle, cut them in half. Spoon the flesh into a food processor and add the onion, garlic and lemon juice. Season with salt and ground black pepper and process until smooth.

3 With the motor running, drizzle in the olive oil through the feeder tube, until the mixture forms a smooth paste. Taste the mixture and adjust the seasoning, then spoon the mixture into a bowl and stir in the diced tomato.

4 Cover and chill for 1 hour before serving. Garnish with chopped fresh flat leaf parsley and serve with fresh, washed chicory leaves and bowls of black and green olives.

Energy 190Kcal/788kJ; Protein 2.3g; Carbohydrate 6.7g, of which sugars 5.9g; Fat 17.5g, of which saturates 2.6g; Cholesterol 0mg; Calcium 28mg; Fibre 4.9g; Sodium 7mg.

Aubergine Dip

Adjust the amount of aubergine, garlic and lemon juice in this richly flavoured aubergine dip depending on how creamy, garlicky or tart you want it to be. The dip can be served with a garnish of chopped fresh coriander leaves, olives or pickled cucumbers. Hot pepper sauce or a little ground coriander can be added, too.

SERVES TWO TO FOUR

INGREDIENTS

- 1 large or 2 medium aubergines (eggplants)
- 2–4 garlic cloves, chopped
- 90–150ml/6–10 tbsp tahini
- juice of 1 lemon, or to taste
- salt and ground black pepper

COOK'S TIPS

You can grill or broil the aubergines instead of cooking them directly over a flame. Brush each side very lightly with extra virgin olive oil and then place under a hot grill (broiler), turning frequently, until charred all around.

1 Place the aubergine(s) directly over the flame of a gas stove or on the coals of a barbecue. Turn the aubergine(s) fairly frequently until deflated and the skin is evenly charred. Remove from the heat with tongs.

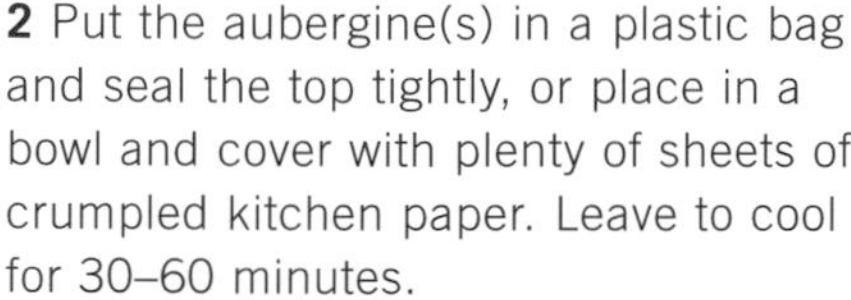

2 Put the aubergine(s) in a plastic bag and seal the top tightly, or place in a bowl and cover with plenty of sheets of crumpled kitchen paper. Leave to cool for 30–60 minutes.

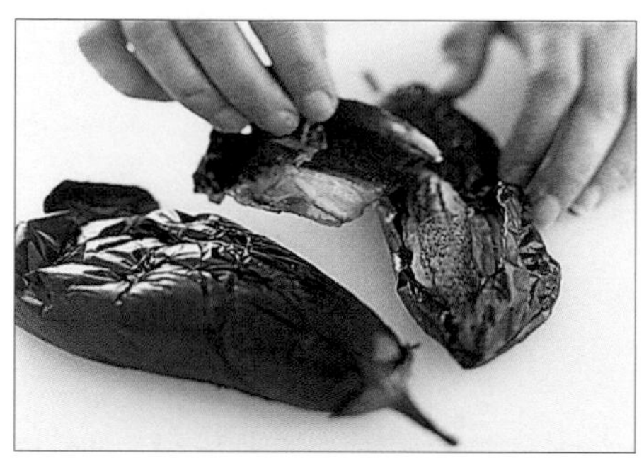

3 Peel off the blackened skin from the aubergine(s), reserving the juices. Chop the aubergine flesh, either by hand for a coarse texture or in a food processor or blender for a smooth purée. Put the aubergine in a bowl and stir in the reserved juices.

4 Add the chopped garlic and tahini to the aubergine and stir until smooth. You may prefer not to add all of the other ingredients all at once, but keep a little to one side to add after tasting.

5 Stir in the lemon juice. If the mixture becomes too thick, add 15–30ml/1–2 tbsp water. Season with salt and freshly ground black pepper to taste and spoon into a serving bowl. Serve at room temperature. Garnish with olives and a few sprigs of fresh coriander (cilantro) or fresh mint.

Energy 303Kcal/1256kJ; Protein 10.3g; Carbohydrate 5g, of which sugars 3.3g; Fat 27.2g, of which saturates 4g; Cholesterol 0mg; Calcium 323mg; Fibre 6.9g; Sodium 13mg.

HUMMUS

This classic Greek chickpea dip is flavoured with garlic and tahini – sesame seed paste. For extra flavour, a little ground cumin can be added, and olive oil can also be stirred in to enrich the hummus, if you like. It is delicious served with wedges of toasted pitta bread or with crudités as a delicious dip.

SERVES FOUR TO SIX

INGREDIENTS

- 400g/14oz can chickpeas, drained
- 60ml/4 tbsp tahini
- 2–3 garlic cloves, chopped
- juice of ½–1 lemon
- salt and ground black pepper
- whole chickpeas reserved, to garnish

VARIATION

Process 2 roasted red (bell) peppers with the chickpeas, then continue as above. Serve sprinkled with lightly toasted pine nuts and paprika mixed with a little extra virgin olive oil.

1 Reserving a few for garnish, coarsely mash the chickpeas in a mixing bowl with a fork. If you like a smoother purée, process the chickpeas in a food processor or blender until a smooth paste is formed.

2 Mix the tahini into the bowl of chickpeas, then stir in the chopped garlic cloves and lemon juice. Season to taste and garnish the top with the reserved chickpeas. Serve the hummus at room temperature.

Energy 210Kcal/880kJ; Protein 10.3g; Carbohydrate 16.9g, of which sugars 0.6g; Fat 11.8g, of which saturates 1.6g; Cholesterol 0mg; Calcium 146mg; Fibre 5.5g; Sodium 223mg.

STUFFED VINE LEAVES

THIS POPULAR GREEK DISH, DOLMADES, *KEEPS MOIST WHEN COOKED SLOWLY IN A CLAY POT. FRESH VINE LEAVES GIVE THE BEST FLAVOUR, BUT PRESERVED OR TINNED WILL ALSO WORK WELL.*

SERVES FOUR

INGREDIENTS

- 12 fresh vine leaves
- 30ml/2 tbsp olive oil
- 1 small onion, chopped
- 30ml/2 tbsp pine nuts
- 1 garlic clove, crushed
- 115g/4oz/1 cup cooked long grain rice
- 2 tomatoes, skinned, seeded and finely chopped
- 15ml/1 tbsp chopped fresh mint
- 1 lemon, sliced
- 150ml/¼ pint/⅔ cup dry white wine
- 200ml/7fl oz/scant 1 cup vegetable stock
- salt and ground black pepper
- lemon wedges and fresh mint sprigs, to garnish

COOK'S TIPS

- You can use preserved vine leaves; do not rinse, but blanch them before use.
- A lidded clay pot, or "brick", is a useful piece of equipment for sealing in the juices of food while it cooks. It must be thoroughly soaked in water before use.

1 Soak the clay pot in cold water for 20 minutes, then drain. Blanch the vine leaves in a pan of boiling water for about 2 minutes or until they darken and soften. Rinse the leaves under cold running water and leave to drain.

2 Heat the olive oil in a frying pan, add the onion and fry for 5–6 minutes, stirring frequently, until softened. Add the pine nuts and crushed garlic and cook, stirring continuously, until the onions and pine nuts are golden.

3 Stir the onion mixture into the rice, then add and stir in the chopped tomatoes and fresh mint. Season to taste with salt and freshly ground black pepper.

4 Place a spoonful of the rice mixture at the stalk end of each vine leaf. Fold the sides over the filling and roll up tightly.

5 Place the stuffed vine leaves close together, seam side down, in the clay pot. Place the lemon slices on top and in between the stuffed vine leaves. Pour over the white wine and sufficient stock just to cover the stuffed vine leaves and lemon slices.

6 Cover the dish with the lid and place in an unheated oven. Set the oven to 200°C/400°F/Gas 6 and cook for 30 minutes. Reduce to 160°C/325°F/Gas 3 and cook for a further 30 minutes.

7 Serve hot or cold, and drizzle with a fruity extra virgin olive oil. This dish can be a starter or part of a meze table, garnished with lemon wedges and a few sprigs of fresh mint.

VARIATIONS

Stuffed vine leaves form the basis of a number of dishes that simply add extra ingredients and flavourings. Try adding red mullet or sardines. Minced (ground) lamb filling is also popular.

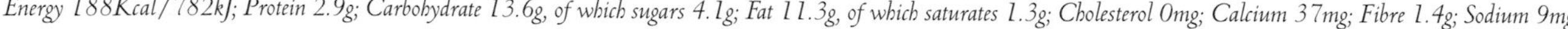

Energy 188Kcal/782kJ; Protein 2.9g; Carbohydrate 13.6g, of which sugars 4.1g; Fat 11.3g, of which saturates 1.3g; Cholesterol 0mg; Calcium 37mg; Fibre 1.4g; Sodium 9mg.

HALF-MOON CHEESE PIES

These delicious small pies, called SKALTSOUNAKIA, *always dazzle people and are a favourite at every meze table. In Crete, where they are very popular, there are several variations, including one with a filling of sautéed wild greens.*

MAKES TWELVE TO FOURTEEN

INGREDIENTS

- 1 large (US extra large) egg, plus 1 egg yolk for glazing
- 150g/5oz feta cheese, chopped and crumbled
- 30ml/2 tbsp milk
- 30ml/2 tbsp chopped fresh mint leaves
- 15ml/1 tbsp raisins
- 15ml/1 tbsp pine nuts, lightly toasted
- a little vegetable oil, for greasing
- a few sprigs of fresh mint, to garnish

For the pastry

- 225g/8oz/2 cups self-raising (self-rising) flour
- 45ml/3 tbsp extra virgin olive oil
- 15g/½oz/1 tbsp butter, melted
- 90g/3½oz/scant ½ cup Greek (US strained plain) yogurt

1 To make the pastry, put the flour in a bowl and mix in the oil, butter and yogurt by hand. Cover and rest in the refrigerator for 15 minutes.

2 Meanwhile, make the filling. Beat the egg lightly in a bowl. Crumble in the cheese, then mix in the milk, mint, raisins and pine nuts.

3 Preheat the oven to 190°C/375°F/Gas 5. Cut the pastry into two pieces and cover one with clear film (plastic wrap) or a dish towel. Thinly roll out the remainder and cut out 7.5cm/3in rounds.

4 Place a heaped teaspoonful of filling on each round and fold the pastry over to make a half-moon shape. Press the edges to seal, then place the pies on a greased baking sheet. Repeat with the remaining pastry. Brush the pies with egg yolk and bake for 20 minutes, or until golden. Serve hot.

Energy 160Kcal/669kJ; Protein 5g; Carbohydrate 16.4g, of which sugars 2.5g; Fat 8.8g, of which saturates 3.4g; Cholesterol 31mg; Calcium 129mg; Fibre 0.7g; Sodium 270mg.

Feta Pastries

Known as börek, these crisp, cheese-filled pastries are a common feature of street food throughout much of the Mediterranean, where they are often taken with aperitifs. They are easy to make at home, but require a little time and patience.

MAKES TEN

INGREDIENTS

- 250g/9oz feta cheese, crumbled
- 2.5ml/½ tsp freshly grated nutmeg
- 30ml/2 tbsp each chopped fresh parsley, dill and mint
- 10 filo pastry sheets, each about 30 x 18cm/12 x 7in, thawed
- 75g/3oz/6 tbsp melted butter or 90ml/6 tbsp olive oil
- ground black pepper

1 Preheat the oven to 190°C/375°F/Gas 5. Mix the feta, nutmeg and herbs in a bowl. Add pepper to taste and mix.

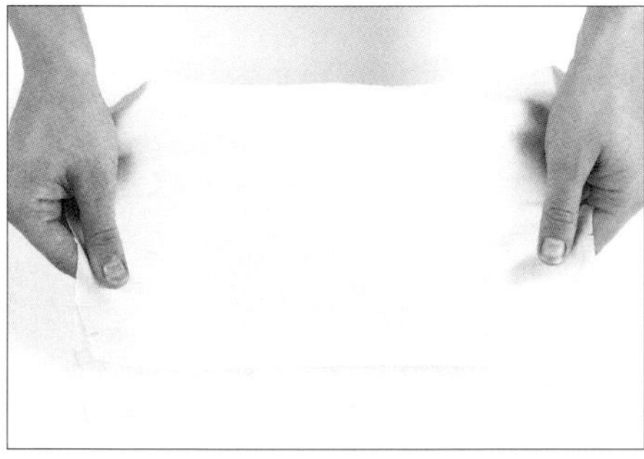

2 Brush a sheet of filo pastry lightly with butter or oil, place another on top of it and brush that too.

3 Cut the buttered sheets in half lengthways to make 10 strips, each 30 x 9cm/12 x 3½in. Place 5ml/1 tsp of the cheese filling at the base of a long strip, fold the corners in diagonally to enclose it, then roll the pastry up into a cigar shape.

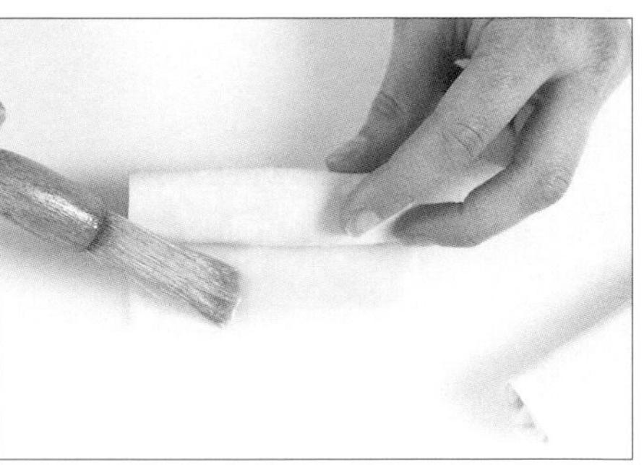

4 Brush the end with a little butter or oil to seal, then place join-side down on a non-stick baking sheet. Repeat with the remaining pastry and filling. Brush the pastries with more butter or oil and bake for 20 minutes, or until crisp and golden. Cool on a wire rack.

COOK'S TIP

When using filo pastry, it is important to keep the unused sheets covered so that they don't dry out. The quantities for filo pastry in this recipe are approximate, as the size of filo sheets varies. Any unused pastry will keep in the refrigerator for a week or so, if it is well wrapped.

Energy 145Kcal/602kJ; Protein 4.7g; Carbohydrate 6.3g, of which sugars 0.6g; Fat 11.4g, of which saturates 7.4g; Cholesterol 33mg; Calcium 108mg; Fibre 0.4g; Sodium 407mg.

LAMB AND POTATO CAKES

AN UNUSUAL DISH, THESE MINCED LAMB TRIANGLES ARE EASY TO SERVE HOT FOR A BUFFET, OR THEY CAN BE EATEN COLD AS A SNACK. THEY ARE ALSO EXCELLENT FOR PICNICS.

MAKES TWELVE TO FIFTEEN

INGREDIENTS

- 450g/1lb new or small, firm potatoes
- 3 eggs
- 1 onion, grated
- 30ml/2 tbsp chopped fresh flat leaf parsley
- 450g/1lb/2 cups finely minced (ground) lean lamb
- 115g/4oz/2 cups fresh breadcrumbs
- vegetable oil, for frying
- salt and ground black pepper
- a few sprigs of fresh mint, to garnish
- toasted pitta bread and herby green salad, to serve

1 Cook the potatoes in a large pan of boiling salted water for 20 minutes, or until tender, then drain and leave to one side to cool.

2 Beat the eggs in a large bowl. Add the grated onion, parsley and seasoning and beat together.

3 When the potatoes are cold, grate them coarsely and stir into the egg mixture. Then add the minced lamb and stir in, using your hands to blend the mixture fully. Knead for 3–4 minutes, or until the ingredients are thoroughly blended.

4 Take a handful of the lamb and potato mixture and roll it into a ball, about the size of a golf ball. Repeat this process until all is used.

5 Roll the balls in the breadcrumbs and then mould them into thin triangular shapes, about 13cm/5in long. Coat them in the breadcrumbs again on both sides.

6 Heat a 1cm/½in layer of oil in a frying pan over a medium heat. When the oil is hot, fry the potato cakes for 8–12 minutes, or until golden brown on both sides, turning occasionally. Drain well on a plate covered with a few layers of kitchen paper, changing the paper when necessary. Serve hot, garnished with a few sprigs of fresh mint and accompanied by freshly toasted pitta bread and a green salad.

Energy 181Kcal/760kJ; Protein 10.8g; Carbohydrate 13.9g, of which sugars 1.1g; Fat 9.6g, of which saturates 2.8g; Cholesterol 76mg; Calcium 31mg; Fibre 0.8g; Sodium 128mg.

Courgette Rissoles from Alonnisos

These tasty kolokythokeftees *are an ingenious way of transforming bland-tasting courgettes into a sharply appetizing dish that captivates everyone who tries it.*

SERVES SIX

INGREDIENTS

- 500g/1¼lb courgettes (zucchini)
- 120ml/4fl oz/½ cup extra virgin olive oil
- 1 large onion, finely chopped
- 2 spring onions (scallions), green and white parts finely chopped
- 1 garlic clove, crushed
- 3 medium slices of bread (not from a pre-sliced loaf)
- 2 eggs, lightly beaten
- 200g/7oz feta cheese, crumbled
- 50g/2oz/½ cup freshly grated Greek Graviera or Italian Parmesan cheese
- 45–60ml/3–4 tbsp finely chopped fresh dill or 5ml/1 tsp dried oregano
- 50g/2oz/½ cup plain (all-purpose) flour
- salt and ground black pepper
- 6 lemon wedges, to serve

1 Bring a pan of lightly salted water to the boil. Slice the courgettes into 4cm/1½in lengths and place them in the boiling water. Cover and cook for about 10 minutes. Drain in a colander and let them cool completely.

2 Heat 45ml/3 tbsp of the olive oil in a frying pan, add the onion and spring onions and sauté until translucent. Add the garlic, then, as soon as it becomes aromatic, take the pan off the heat.

3 Squeeze the courgettes with your hands, to extract as much water as possible, then place them in a large bowl. Add the fried onion and garlic mixture and mix well.

4 Toast the bread, cut off and discard the crusts, then break up the toast and crumb it in a food processor. Add the crumbs to the courgette mixture, with the eggs, feta cheese and grated Graviera or Parmesan.

5 Stir the dill or oregano into the courgette mixture, and add salt and pepper to taste. If the mixture seems too wet, add a little flour.

6 Take a heaped tablespoon of the courgette mixture, roll it into a round ball, using your hands, and press it lightly to make a rissole shape. Make more rissoles in the same way.

7 Coat the rissoles lightly in the flour. Heat the remaining extra virgin olive oil in a large, non-stick frying pan, then fry the rissoles in batches until they are crisp and brown, turning them over once. Drain on kitchen paper and serve with the lemon wedges.

Energy 343Kcal/1,424kJ; Protein 14.7g; Carbohydrate 18.5g, of which sugars 4.9g; Fat 23.9g, of which saturates 8.6g; Cholesterol 95mg; Calcium 301mg; Fibre 2.2g; Sodium 668mg.

Chickpea Rissoles

This is one of the frugal mezedes that are typically found on a Greek table. Although the rissoles are very inexpensive to make, they are very appetizing. If you like, you can serve them accompanied by Cauliflower with Egg and Lemon Sauce, or Wilted Spinach with Rice and Dill to make a complete and unusual vegetarian meal.

SERVES FOUR

INGREDIENTS

- 300g/11oz/scant 1½ cups chickpeas, soaked overnight in water to cover
- 105ml/7 tbsp extra virgin olive oil
- 2 large onions, chopped
- 15ml/1 tbsp ground cumin
- 2 garlic cloves, crushed
- 3–4 fresh sage leaves, chopped
- 45ml/3 tbsp chopped flat leaf parsley
- 1 large (US extra large) egg, lightly beaten
- 45ml/3 tbsp self-raising (self-rising) flour
- 50g/2oz/½ cup plain (all-purpose) flour
- salt and ground black pepper
- radishes, rocket (arugula) and olives, to serve

1 Drain the chickpeas, rinse them under cold water and drain again. Tip them into a large pan, cover with plenty of fresh cold water and bring them to the boil. Skim the froth from the surface of the water with a slotted spoon until the liquid is clear.

2 Cover the pan and cook for 1¼–1½ hours, or until the chickpeas are very soft. Alternatively (and this is the better method) cook them in a pressure cooker under full pressure for 20–25 minutes. Once the chickpeas are soft, set aside a few tablespoons of the cooking liquid, then strain them, discarding the rest of the liquid. Tip the chickpeas into a food processor, add 30–45ml/2–3 tbsp of the reserved liquid and process to a velvety mash.

3 Heat 45ml/3 tbsp of the olive oil in a large frying pan, add the onions, and sauté until they are light golden. Add the cumin and the garlic and stir for a few seconds until their aroma rises. Stir in the chopped sage leaves and the parsley, and set aside.

4 Scrape the chickpea mash into a large bowl and add the egg, the self-raising flour, and the fried onion and herb mixture. Add plenty of salt and pepper and mix well. Take large walnut-size pieces of the mixture and flatten them so that they look like thick, round mini-hamburgers.

5 Coat the rissoles lightly in the plain flour. Heat the remaining olive oil in a large frying pan and fry them in batches until they are crisp and golden on both sides. Drain on kitchen paper and serve hot with the radishes, rocket and olives.

COOK'S TIP

Wet your hands slightly when shaping the rissoles, as this helps to prevent the mixture from sticking to them.

Energy 532Kcal/2231kJ; Protein 19.7g; Carbohydrate 63.6g, of which sugars 8.1g; Fat 23.9g, of which saturates 3.2g; Cholesterol 0mg; Calcium 222mg; Fibre 10.7g; Sodium 77mg.

AUBERGINES WITH TOMATO TOPPING

IMAM BAYILDI IS ONE OF THE MOST FAMOUS GREEK DISHES. THIS LIGHTER, EASIER VERSION USES SLICES OF AUBERGINE TOPPED WITH THE RICH TOMATO, HERB AND OLIVE OIL STUFFING. IT CAN BE SERVED HOT OR LEFT TO COOL SLIGHTLY AND SERVED AT ROOM TEMPERATURE, EITHER ACCOMPANIED BY A SALAD AS A MAIN COURSE OR AS PART OF THE MEZEDES.

SERVES FOUR

INGREDIENTS

- 3 medium aubergines (eggplants), total weight about 800g/1¾lb
- 150ml/¼ pint/⅔ cup extra virgin olive oil
- 2 large onions, finely chopped
- 3 garlic cloves, finely chopped
- 500g/1¼lb fresh, very ripe tomatoes, peeled if you like, and chopped
- 2.5ml/½ tsp each dried oregano and thyme
- 2.5ml/½ tsp sugar
- 45ml/3 tbsp chopped fresh flat leaf parsley
- 15ml/1 tbsp tomato purée (paste) diluted in 150ml/¼ pint/⅔ cup hot water
- salt and ground black pepper

1 Trim the aubergines, then slice them into rounds, about 1cm/½in thick. Heat half the olive oil in a large frying pan and shallow-fry the aubergines in batches, turning them over once, until light golden on both sides. As each batch is cooked, lift the slices out and arrange them side by side in a large roasting dish.

2 Heat the rest of the oil in a pan and sauté the onions until lightly coloured. Add the garlic and, when it is aromatic, add the tomatoes and a little water. Season, stir in the oregano, thyme and sugar, then cover and cook for 15 minutes, stirring occasionally.

3 Preheat the oven to 190°C/375°F/Gas 5. Stir the parsley into the sauce, then pile 15–30ml/1–2 tbsp of the mixture on each slice of aubergine. Pour the diluted tomato purée into the dish, adding it to a corner, to avoid disturbing the aubergines. Bake the aubergines for 20–25 minutes, basting them once.

4 Serve hot or at room temperature, either accompanied by a salad as a main course or as part of the mezedes for a party.

Energy 326Kcal/1,354kJ; Protein 4.6g; Carbohydrate 18.6g, of which sugars 15.8g; Fat 26.6g, of which saturates 3.9g; Cholesterol 0mg; Calcium 81mg; Fibre 7.8g; Sodium 32mg.

Grilled Vegetable Terrine

A colourful, layered terrine, using all the vegetables associated with Greece: bright peppers and courgettes and shiny aubergines, with raisins to give a sweet edge. This dish can be served with hot white crusty bread or pitta bread, and feta cheese or grilled halloumi. It could also make a delicious centrepiece in a meze table.

SERVES SIX

INGREDIENTS

- 2 large red (bell) peppers, quartered, cored and seeded
- 2 large yellow (bell) peppers, quartered, cored and seeded
- 1 large aubergine (eggplant), sliced lengthways
- 2 large courgettes (zucchini), sliced lengthways
- 90ml/6 tbsp olive oil
- 1 large red onion, thinly sliced
- 75g/3oz/½ cup raisins
- 15ml/1 tbsp tomato purée (paste)
- 15ml/1 tbsp red wine vinegar
- 400ml/14fl oz/1⅔ cups tomato juice
- 15g/½½oz/2 tbsp powdered gelatine
- fresh basil leaves, to garnish

For the dressing

- 90ml/6 tbsp extra virgin olive oil
- 30ml/2 tbsp red wine vinegar
- salt and ground black pepper

1 Place the prepared red and yellow peppers skin side up under a hot grill (broiler) and cook until the skins are blackened. Transfer to a bowl and cover with a plate. Leave to cool.

2 Arrange the aubergine and courgette slices on separate baking sheets. Brush them with a little oil and cook under the grill, turning occasionally, until tender and golden.

3 Heat the remaining extra virgin olive oil in a frying pan over a medium heat, and add the sliced onion, raisins, tomato purée and red wine vinegar. Cook gently until soft and syrupy. Take the pan away from the heat and set aside to cool in the frying pan.

4 Lightly oil a 1.75 litre/3 pint/7½ cup terrine with extra virgin olive oil, and then line it with clear film (plastic wrap), leaving a little hanging over the sides. Make sure that you ease the clear film right into the corners of the terrine dish so that the finished dish is the right shape.

5 Pour half the tomato juice into a pan, and sprinkle with the gelatine. Dissolve the mixture gently over a low heat, stirring frequently.

6 Place a layer of red peppers in the bottom of the terrine, and pour in enough of the tomato juice and gelatine mixture to cover. Continue layering the aubergine, courgettes, yellow peppers and onion mixture, finishing with another layer of red peppers. Pour tomato juice over each layer of vegetables.

7 Add the remaining tomato juice to any juices left in the pan, stir it in thoroughly and pour it all into the terrine. Give it a sharp tap to disperse the juice evenly throughout. Cover the terrine and chill until set.

8 To make the dressing, whisk together the extra virgin olive oil and vinegar, and season with salt and ground black pepper. Turn out the terrine and remove the clear film. Serve in thick slices, drizzled with dressing. Garnish with a few fresh and fragrant basil leaves.

Energy 205Kcal/853kJ; Protein 3.8g; Carbohydrate 21.7g, of which sugars 20.9g; Fat 12g, of which saturates 1.8g; Cholesterol 0mg; Calcium 47mg; Fibre 4.1g; Sodium 173mg.

RED MULLET DOLMADES

YOU CAN USE BLANCHED LARGE CABBAGE LEAVES OR LARGE SPINACH LEAVES INSTEAD OF VINE LEAVES FOR THIS TASTY AND MORE SUBSTANTIAL VARIATION OF THE TRADITIONAL GREEK DISH.

SERVES FOUR

INGREDIENTS

- 225g/8oz red mullet fillets, scaled
- 45ml/3 tbsp dry white wine
- 115g/4oz/1 cup cooked long grain rice
- 25g/1oz/¼ cup pine nuts
- 45ml/3 tbsp chopped fresh parsley
- grated rind and juice of ½ lemon
- 8 vine leaves in brine, rinsed and dried
- salt and ground black pepper

For the orange butter sauce

- grated rind and juice of 2 oranges
- 2 shallots, very finely chopped
- 25g/1oz/2 tbsp chilled butter, diced

1 Preheat the oven to 200°C/400°F/Gas 6. Put the fish into a shallow pan and season with salt and pepper. Pour over the wine, bring to the boil, and lower the heat. Poach the fish gently for about 3 minutes, until just cooked. Strain, reserving the liquid.

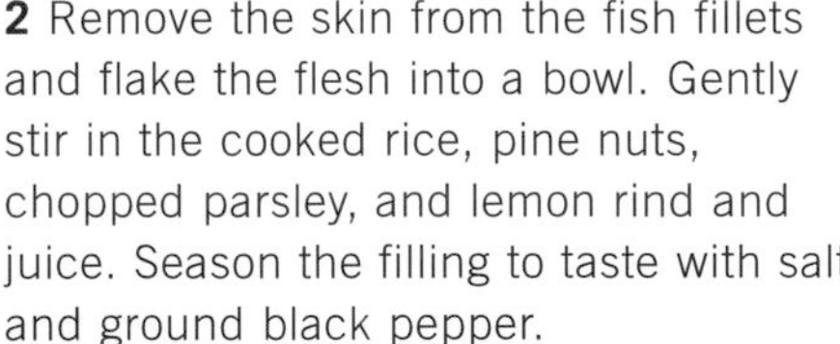

2 Remove the skin from the fish fillets and flake the flesh into a bowl. Gently stir in the cooked rice, pine nuts, chopped parsley, and lemon rind and juice. Season the filling to taste with salt and ground black pepper.

3 Spoon 30–45ml/2–3 tbsp of the filling into the middle of each vine leaf. Roll up each filled leaf, tucking in the ends to make a secure package. Arrange the *dolmades* in an ovenproof dish, with the joins underneath. Pour over the reserved cooking liquid and place the dolmades in the preheated oven for about 5 minutes, until they are heated through thoroughly.

4 Meanwhile, make the sauce. Mix the orange rind and juice and the shallots in a small pan and boil vigorously for a few minutes, until the mixture is reduced and syrupy.

5 Strain the sauce into a clean pan, discarding the shallots. Beat in the butter, one piece at a time. Reheat gently, but do not let the sauce boil. Drizzle the sauce over the hot *dolmades* and serve at once.

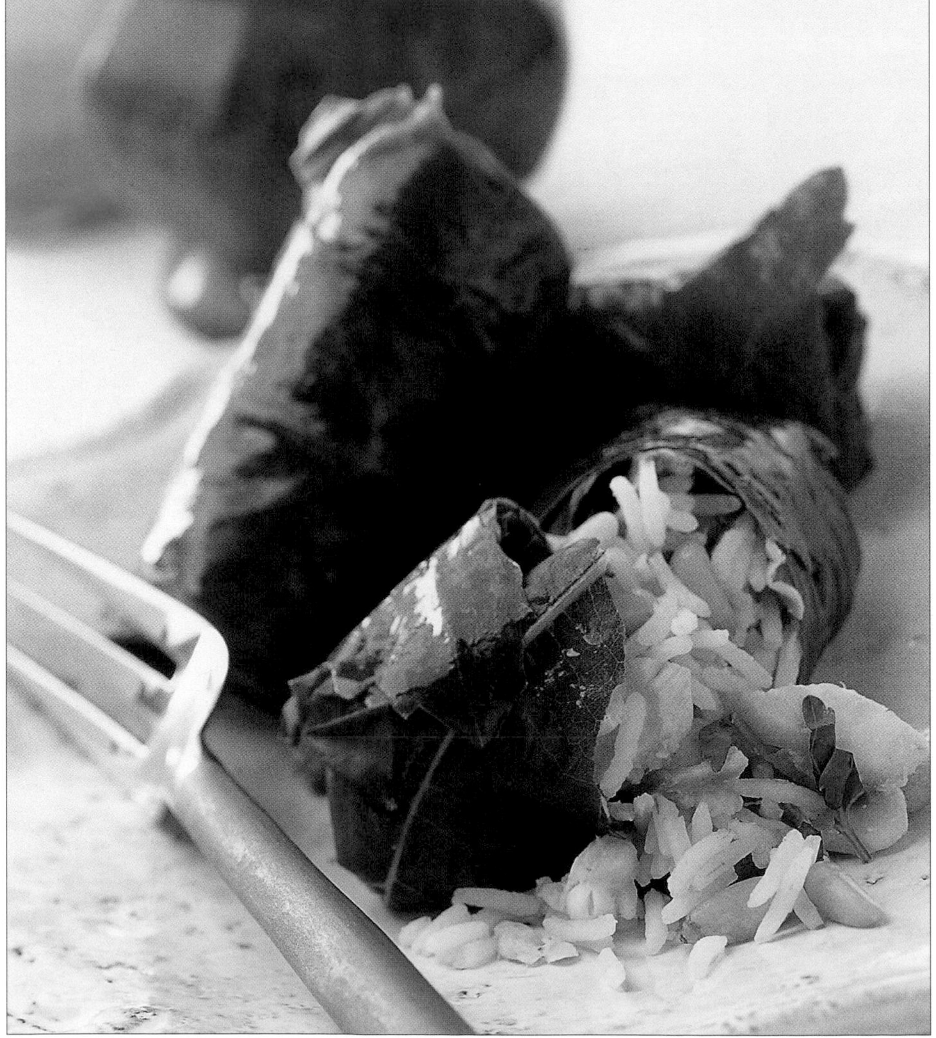

Energy 185Kcal/772kJ; Protein 7.7g; Carbohydrate 12.4g, of which sugars 3.4g; Fat 11.2g, of which saturates 3.6g; Cholesterol 13mg; Calcium 60mg; Fibre 1g; Sodium 74mg.

SALTED AND GRILLED SARDINES

WHOLE GRILLED SARDINES ARE CLASSIC MEDITERRANEAN BEACH FOOD. HERE THEY ARE SERVED WITH A HERB SALSA. THEY CAN ALSO BE COOKED ON SKEWERS OVER A DYING FIRE.

SERVES FOUR TO EIGHT

INGREDIENTS

- 8 sardines, about 800g/1¾lb total weight, scaled and gutted
- 50g/2oz/¼ cup salt
- oil, for brushing
- focaccia, to serve

For the herb salsa

- 5ml/1 tsp sea salt flakes
- 60ml/4 tbsp chopped fresh tarragon leaves
- 40g/1½oz/generous 1 cup chopped flat leaf parsley
- 1 small red onion, very finely chopped
- 105ml/7 tbsp extra virgin olive oil
- 60ml/4 tbsp lemon juice

1 Make the herb salsa by grinding the salt in a mortar and adding the other salsa ingredients one at a time.

2 Wash the sardines thoroughly, both inside and out. Then pat dry with kitchen paper and rub the sardines inside and out with salt. Cover and put in a cool place for 30–45 minutes.

3 Meanwhile, prepare the barbecue. Rinse the salt off the sardines. Pat them dry with kitchen paper, then leave to air-dry for 15 minutes. Once the flames have died down, position a lightly oiled grill rack over the coals to heat.

4 When the coals are cool, or with a thick coating of ash, brush the fish with a little extra virgin olive oil and put them in a small, hinged, wire barbecue fish basket. If you don't have a wire basket, cook the fish directly on the rack in a row, but oil it well first.

5 Cook for about 3 minutes on one side and about 2½ minutes on the other. Serve with the herb salsa and toasted focaccia.

Energy 423Kcal/1,754kJ; Protein 31.5g; Carbohydrate 1.8g, of which sugars 1.4g; Fat 32.1g, of which saturates 6.4g; Cholesterol 0mg; Calcium 187mg; Fibre 1g; Sodium 667mg.

DEEP-FRIED WHITEBAIT

IN GREECE THE SMALLEST FISH OF THE CATCH ARE ALWAYS FRIED. HERE, FISH ARE LIGHTLY FLOURED IN A SPICY MIXTURE AND FRIED INDIVIDUALLY TO MAKE THE FAVOURITE DISH, MARIDES.

SERVES FOUR

INGREDIENTS

- 115g/4oz/1 cup plain (all-purpose) flour
- 2.5ml/½ tsp paprika
- 2.5ml/½ tsp ground cayenne pepper
- 1.1kg/2½lb whitebait
- vegetable oil, for deep frying
- lemon wedges, to serve

1 Put the flour in a large bowl and mix in the paprika, cayenne pepper and salt.

2 Add the whitebait to the bowl in batches and coat evenly with the flour. If you are using frozen whitebait, ensure that it is properly thawed before preparation.

3 Heat the vegetable oil in a large, heavy pan over a medium to high heat until it reaches a temperature of 190°C/375°F. Fry the whitebait in batches of about a dozen in a mesh basket for 2 minutes, or until the fish is golden and crispy.

4 Drain the fried fish well on a plate covered with absorbent kitchen paper and serve hot with lemon wedges. Whitebait are often served with dips, such as Greek yogurt dips, mayonnaise, cocktail or tartar sauce.

COOK'S TIP

Whitebait are not one species of fish, as is often thought, but a mixture of the fry of sprats, herrings and other small fish. There can be as many as 20 different fish in one catch.

Energy 1,444Kcal/5,979kJ; Protein 53.6g; Carbohydrate 14.6g, of which sugars 0.3g; Fat 130.6g, of which saturates 12.1g; Cholesterol 0mg; Calcium 2,365mg; Fibre 0.6g; Sodium 633mg.

Octopus Salad

In the coastal areas of mainland Greece and on the islands, octopus is a particular favourite, and makes a delicious salad.

SERVES FOUR TO SIX

INGREDIENTS

- 900g/2lb baby octopus or squid, skinned
- 175ml/6fl oz/¾ cup olive oil
- 30ml/2 tbsp white wine vinegar
- 30ml/2 tbsp chopped fresh parsley or coriander (cilantro)
- 12 black olives, stoned (pitted)
- 2 shallots, thinly sliced
- 1 red onion, thinly sliced
- salt and ground black pepper
- sprigs of coriander, to garnish
- 8–12 cos or romaine lettuce leaves and lemon wedges, to serve

1 In a large pan, boil the octopus or squid in salted water for 20–25 minutes, or until just soft. Drain and leave to cool completely before covering and chilling for 45 minutes.

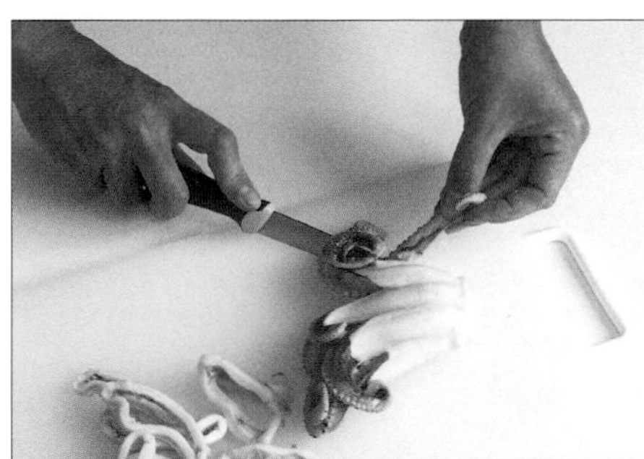

2 Spread out the octopus on a large chopping board. Cut the tentacles from the body and head, then chop all the flesh into even pieces, slicing across the thick part of the tentacles and following the direction of the suckers. If using squid, chop into even rings.

3 In a bowl, combine the olive oil and white wine vinegar.

COOK'S TIP
Take care not to overcook the octopus or squid or it will become tough and rubbery.

4 Add the herbs, olives, shallots, octopus and red onion to the bowl. Season to taste and toss well.

5 Arrange the octopus on a bed of lettuce, garnish with coriander and serve with lemon wedges.

Energy 481Kcal/2,001kJ; Protein 35.2g; Carbohydrate 4.3g, of which sugars 1.2g; Fat 36.1g, of which saturates 5.5g; Cholesterol 506mg; Calcium 56mg; Fibre 0.9g; Sodium 420mg.

FILO FISH PIES

THESE LIGHT, FILO-WRAPPED FISH PIES CAN BE MADE WITH ANY FIRM WHITE FISH FILLETS, SUCH AS ORANGE ROUGHY, COD, HALIBUT OR HOKI. SERVE WITH SALAD LEAVES AND MAYONNAISE ON THE SIDE.

SERVES SIX

INGREDIENTS

- 400g/14oz spinach, trimmed
- 1 egg, lightly beaten
- 2 garlic cloves, crushed
- 450g/1lb orange roughy or other white fish fillet
- juice of 1 lemon
- 50g/2oz/¼ cup butter, melted
- 8–12 filo pastry sheets, thawed if frozen, quartered
- 15ml/1 tbsp finely chopped fresh chives
- 200ml/7fl oz/scant 1 cup half-fat crème fraîche
- 15ml/1 tbsp chopped fresh dill
- salt and ground black pepper

VARIATION

To make one large pie, use a 20cm/8in tin (pan) and cook for 45 minutes.

1 Preheat the oven to 190°C/375°F/Gas 5. Wash the spinach, then cook it in a lidded, heavy pan with just the water that clings to the leaves. As soon as the leaves are tender, drain, squeeze as dry as possible and chop. Put the spinach in a bowl, add the egg and garlic, season with salt and pepper and set aside. Dice the fish and place it in a bowl. Stir in the lemon juice. Season with salt and pepper, and toss lightly.

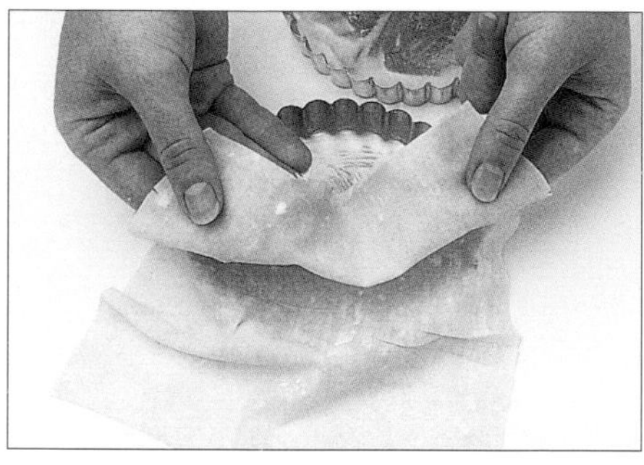

2 Brush the inside of six 13cm/5in tartlet tins (muffin pans) with a little of the melted butter. Fit a piece of filo pastry into one tin, draping it so that it hangs over the sides. Brush with butter, then add another sheet at right angles to the first. Brush with butter. Continue to line the tins with two sheets of filo each.

3 Spread the spinach evenly over the pastry. Add the diced fish and season well. Stir the chives into the crème fraîche and spread the mixture over the top of the fish. Sprinkle the dill over.

4 Draw the overhanging pieces of pastry together and scrunch lightly to make a lid. Brush with butter. Bake for about 15–20 minutes, or until golden brown.

Energy 233Kcal/972kJ; Protein 18.4g; Carbohydrate 9.1g, of which sugars 2.2g; Fat 14g, of which saturates 8.2g; Cholesterol 84mg; Calcium 170mg; Fibre 1.7g; Sodium 213mg.

FRIED SQUID

THERE ARE FEW FOODS MORE APPETIZING THAN FRESHLY CAUGHT FRIED SQUID, ESPECIALLY WHEN IT IS ENJOYED UNDER AN OLIVE TREE ON THE EDGE OF A DAZZLING BEACH.

SERVES FOUR

INGREDIENTS

- 900g/2lb medium to large squid, cleaned
- 50g/2oz/½ cup plain (all-purpose) flour
- 75ml/5 tbsp olive oil or sunflower oil, for frying
- large pinch of dried oregano
- salt and ground black pepper
- 1 lemon, quartered, to serve
- a few sprigs of fresh flat leaf parsley, to garnish

COOK'S TIP

A good fishmonger will prepare the squid for you, especially if you give him or her a little notice. Prepared squid are often available at supermarkets.

1 Do not split the squid bodies. Rinse the bodies thoroughly, inside and out, then drain well. Slice the bodies into 3–4cm/1¼–1½in-wide rings.

2 Season the flour with salt and pepper and put it in a large plastic bag. Add the squid, keeping the rings and tentacles separate, and toss until evenly coated. Shake off any excess flour.

3 Heat the olive or sunflower oil in a large, heavy or non-stick frying pan over a medium to high heat. When it is hot enough to sizzle, but is not smoking, add a batch of squid rings, laying each one in carefully and as round in shape as possible. They should fill the pan but not touch each other.

4 Let the squid rings cook for 2–3 minutes, or until pale golden, then use a fork or tongs to turn the pieces over to ensure that each is evenly cooked. This is a laborious process but worthwhile.

5 Let each ring cook for 1–2 minutes more, then lift out and drain on a platter lined with kitchen paper.

6 Leave the floured tentacles until last. Take care while you fry them, as they spit spitefully. The tentacles will need very little cooking as the oil will have become quite hot. Turn the tentacles over after 1 minute and take them out as soon as they are crisp and golden.

7 Serve the fried squid on a large warmed platter and sprinkle dried oregano on top. Surround with lemon wedges and invite diners to squeeze a little lemon juice over each portion.

Energy 349Kcal/1,464kJ; Protein 35.8g; Carbohydrate 12.4g, of which sugars 0.2g; Fat 17.7g, of which saturates 2.9g; Cholesterol 506mg; Calcium 47mg; Fibre 0.4g; Sodium 248mg.

SOUPS

Greek soups are usually substantial meals in themselves, using pulses and fresh vegetables as well as fish, meat and poultry. A robust, rich flavour is achieved – even when using the simplest of ingredients – by the addition of good-quality extra virgin olive oil.

LENTIL SOUP

PULSES ARE A WINTER STAPLE IN GREECE, LENTILS A PARTICULARLY DELICIOUS VARIETY. AS THEY DO NOT NEED SOAKING, THEY MAKE AN EASY OPTION FOR A QUICK MEAL. THE SECRET OF GOOD LENTIL SOUP IS TO BE GENEROUS WITH THE OLIVE OIL. THE SOUP IS SERVED AS A MAIN MEAL, ACCOMPANIED BY OLIVES, BREAD AND CHEESE OR, FOR A SPECIAL OCCASION, WITH FRIED SQUID OR KEFTEDES.

SERVES FOUR

INGREDIENTS

- 275g/10oz/1¼ cups brown-green lentils, preferably the small variety
- 150ml/¼ pint/⅔ cup extra virgin olive oil
- 1 onion, thinly sliced
- 2 garlic cloves, sliced into thin batons
- 1 carrot, sliced into thin discs
- 400g/14oz can chopped tomatoes
- 15ml/1 tbsp tomato purée (paste)
- 2.5ml/½ tsp dried oregano
- 1 litre/1¾ pints/4 cups hot water
- salt and ground black pepper
- 30ml/2 tbsp roughly chopped fresh herb leaves, to garnish

1 Rinse the brown-green lentils thoroughly, drain them and put them in a large pan with cold water to cover. Bring the water to the boil and boil for 3–4 minutes. Strain, discarding the liquid, and set the lentils aside.

2 Wipe the pan clean and add the extra virgin olive oil. Place it over a medium heat until hot and then add the thinly sliced onion and sauté until translucent. Stir in the sliced garlic, then, as soon as it becomes aromatic, return the lentils to the pan. Add the carrot, tomatoes, tomato purée and oregano. Stir in the hot water and a little ground black pepper to taste.

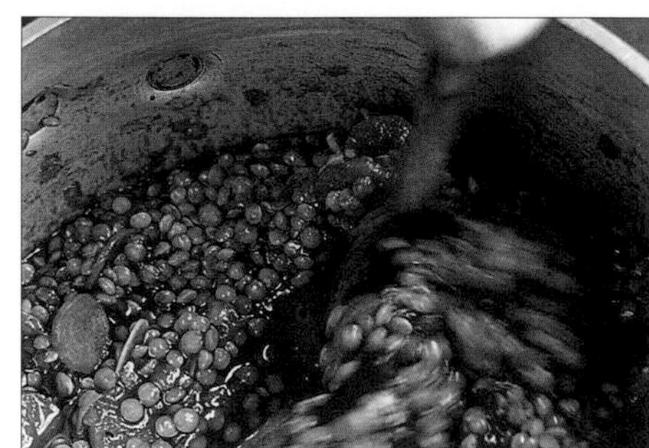

3 Bring the soup to the boil, then lower the heat, cover the pan and cook gently for 20–30 minutes, until the lentils feel soft but have not begun to disintegrate. Add salt and the chopped herbs just before serving.

Energy 462Kcal/1,935kJ; Protein 18.4g; Carbohydrate 40g, of which sugars 6.6g; Fat 26.6g, of which saturates 3.7g; Cholesterol 0mg; Calcium 86mg; Fibre 8g; Sodium 64mg.

Chickpea Soup

This traditional Greek winter staple is enjoyable in any season, even during the hot summer months. Compared to other soups based on pulses, which are often very hearty, this has a unique lightness in terms of both flavour and texture. It can be enjoyed as an appetizer, or can be a delicious healthy main meal with fresh bread and feta cheese.

SERVES FOUR

INGREDIENTS

- 150ml/¼ pint/⅔ cup extra virgin olive oil, plus extra for drizzling and serving
- 1 large onion, chopped
- 350g/12oz/1¾ cups dried chickpeas, soaked in cold water overnight
- 15ml/1 tbsp plain (all-purpose) flour
- juice of 1 lemon, or to taste
- 45ml/3 tbsp chopped fresh flat leaf parsley
- salt and ground black pepper

1 Heat the extra virgin olive oil in a heavy pan, add the onion and sauté until it starts to colour.

2 Meanwhile, drain the chickpeas, rinse them under cold water and drain them again. Shake the colander or sieve to dry the chickpeas as much as possible, then add them to the pan. Turn them with a spatula for a few minutes to coat them well in the oil, then pour in enough hot water to cover them by about 4cm/1½in.

3 Slowly bring to the boil. Skim off any white froth that rises to the surface, using a slotted spoon, and discard. Lower the heat to achieve a simmer, add some freshly ground black pepper, cover and cook for 1–1¼ hours, or until the chickpeas are soft.

4 Put the flour in a cup and stir in the lemon juice with a fork. When the chickpeas are perfectly soft, add this mixture to them. Mix well, then add salt and pepper to taste. Cover the pan and cook gently for 5–10 minutes more, stirring occasionally.

5 To thicken the soup slightly, take out about two cupfuls of the chickpeas and put them in a food processor or blender. Process briefly so that the chickpeas are broken up, but remain slightly rough. Stir into the soup in the pan and mix well.

6 Add the parsley, then taste the soup and add more lemon juice if bland. Serve in heated bowls and offer extra olive oil at the table, for drizzling.

Energy 544Kcal/2,274kJ; Protein 20.1g; Carbohydrate 51.6g, of which sugars 6.1g; Fat 30g, of which saturates 4g; Cholesterol 0mg; Calcium 184mg; Fibre 10.9g; Sodium 40mg.

CANNELLINI BEAN SOUP

IF THERE WERE ONE DISH WITH WHICH THE WHOLE GREEK NATION WOULD IDENTIFY, IT WOULD BE THIS ONE. FROM THE LARGEST CITIES TO THE SMALLEST VILLAGES IT REMAINS THE FAVOURITE. IT IS ALWAYS SERVED WITH BREAD AND OLIVES, AND PERHAPS RAW ONION QUARTERS (OR RAW GARLIC FOR THOSE WITH ROBUST PALATES). PICKLED OR SALTED FISH ARE ALSO TRADITIONAL ACCOMPANIMENTS.

SERVES FOUR

INGREDIENTS

- 275g/10oz/1½ cups dried cannellini beans, soaked overnight in cold water
- 1 large onion, thinly sliced
- 1 celery stick, sliced
- 2 or 3 carrots, sliced
- 400g/14oz can tomatoes
- 15ml/1 tbsp tomato purée (paste)
- 150ml/¼ pint/⅔ cup extra virgin olive oil
- 5ml/1 tsp dried oregano
- 30ml/2 tbsp finely chopped fresh flat leaf parsley
- salt and ground black pepper

1 Drain the beans, rinse them under cold water and drain them again. Tip them into a large pan, pour in enough water to cover and bring to the boil over a medium heat. Cook for about 3 minutes, then drain.

2 Return the beans to the pan, pour in fresh water to cover them by about 3cm/1¼in, then add the sliced onion, celery and carrots, and the tomatoes, and stir in.

3 Add and stir in the tomato purée, extra virgin olive oil and dried oregano. Season to taste with a little freshly ground black pepper, but don't add salt at this stage, as it would toughen the skins of the beans.

4 Bring to the boil, lower the heat and cook for about 1 hour, or until the beans are just tender. Season with salt, stir in the parsley and serve.

COOK'S TIP

For a more substantial meal you could serve this soup with fried squid, marinated anchovies or *keftedes*. Soups are often served in Greece with chunks of crusty bread, feta cheese and olives.

Energy 490Kcal/2,051kJ; Protein 17.9g; Carbohydrate 47.8g, of which sugars 11.3g; Fat 26.6g, of which saturates 4.1g; Cholesterol 0mg; Calcium 89mg; Fibre 8.4g; Sodium 45mg.

Roasted Aubergine and Courgette Soup

A fusion of flavours from the sunny Greek islands creates this fabulous soup, which is served with tzatsiki, the popular combination of cucumber and creamy yogurt. It's worth using a good-quality extra virgin olive oil for this soup as it brings out the richness of the vegetables as they roast.

SERVES FOUR

INGREDIENTS

- 2 large aubergines (eggplant), roughly diced
- 4 large courgettes (zucchini), roughly diced
- 1 onion, roughly chopped
- 4 garlic cloves, roughly chopped
- 45ml/3 tbsp extra virgin olive oil
- 1.2 litres/2 pints/5 cups vegetable stock
- 15ml/1 tbsp chopped fresh oregano
- salt and ground black pepper
- mint sprigs, to garnish

For the tzatsiki

- 1 cucumber, peeled, seeded and diced
- 10ml/2 tsp salt
- 2 garlic cloves, crushed
- 5ml/1 tsp white wine vinegar
- 225g/8oz/1 cup Greek (US strained plain) yogurt
- small bunch of fresh mint leaves, chopped

1 Preheat the oven to 200°C/400°F/ Gas 6. Place the aubergines and courgettes in a roasting pan. Add the onion and garlic, drizzle the oil over and spread out the vegetables in an even layer. Roast for 35 minutes, turning once, until tender and slightly charred.

2 To make the *tzatsiki*, place the cucumber in a colander and sprinkle with the salt. Place on a plate or bowl and leave for 30 minutes.

3 Mix the garlic with the vinegar and stir carefully into the yogurt. Pat the cucumber dry with kitchen paper and fold it gently into the yogurt mixture. Season to taste and then stir in the mint. Chill until required.

4 Place half the roasted vegetables in a food processor or blender. Add the stock and process until almost smooth. (You may have to do this in batches.) Then pour into a large pan and add the remaining vegetables.

5 Bring the soup slowly to the boil and then reduce the heat to let the soup simmer gently for a few minutes. Season well with salt and freshly ground black pepper. Add and then stir in the chopped oregano.

6 Ladle the soup into four bowls. Garnish with mint sprigs and serve immediately. Hand round the bowl of *tzatsiki* so that your guests can add a dollop or two to their soup, swirling it around the top layer.

Energy 222Kcal/920kJ; Protein 9.7g; Carbohydrate 12.7g, of which sugars 11g; Fat 15.7g, of which saturates 4.5g; Cholesterol 0mg; Calcium 192mg; Fibre 6.3g; Sodium 1034mg.

SPICY PUMPKIN SOUP

PUMPKIN IS POPULAR ALL OVER GREECE AND IT'S AN IMPORTANT INGREDIENT IN MIDDLE-EASTERN COOKING, FROM WHICH THIS SOUP IS INSPIRED. GINGER AND CUMIN GIVE THE SOUP ITS WONDERFUL SPICY FLAVOUR, MAKING IT INTO A HEARTY AND FLAVOURSOME MEAL.

SERVES FOUR

INGREDIENTS

- 900g/2lb pumpkin, peeled and seeds removed
- 30ml/2 tbsp extra virgin olive oil
- 2 leeks, trimmed and sliced
- 1 garlic clove, crushed
- 5ml/1 tsp ground ginger
- 5ml/1 tsp ground cumin
- 900ml/1½ pints/3¾ cups chicken stock
- salt and ground black pepper
- coriander (cilantro) leaves, to garnish
- 60ml/4 tbsp Greek (US strained plain) yogurt, to serve

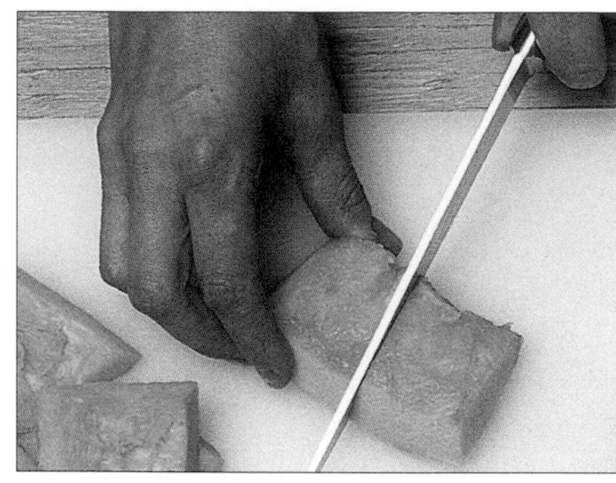

1 Cut the pumpkin flesh into evenly sized chunks. Heat the oil in a large pan and add the leeks and garlic. Cook gently until softened.

2 Add the ground ginger and cumin and cook, stirring, for a further minute. Add the pumpkin chunks and the chicken stock and season with salt and pepper. Bring the mixture to the boil and simmer for 30 minutes, or until the pumpkin is tender. Process the soup, in batches if necessary, in a blender or food processor.

3 Reheat the soup gently, and ladle out into four warmed individual bowls. Add a spoon of Greek yogurt on the top of each and swirl it through the top layer of soup. Garnish with chopped fresh coriander leaves.

Energy 98Kcal/409kJ; Protein 3g; Carbohydrate 7.5g, of which sugars 5.8g; Fat 6.4g, of which saturates 1.1g; Cholesterol 0mg; Calcium 86mg; Fibre 4.2g; Sodium 2mg.

YOGURT AND CUCUMBER SOUP

YOGURT IS FREQUENTLY USED IN GREEK COOKERY, AND IT IS USUALLY MADE AT HOME. SOMETIMES IT IS ADDED AT THE END OF COOKING A DISH, TO PREVENT IT FROM CURDLING, BUT IN THIS COLD SOUP THE YOGURT IS ONE OF THE BASIC INGREDIENTS.

SERVES FOUR

INGREDIENTS

- 1 large cucumber, peeled
- 300ml/½ pint/1¼ cups single (light) cream
- 150ml/¼ pint/⅔ cup natural (plain) yogurt
- 2 garlic cloves, crushed
- 30ml/2 tbsp white wine vinegar
- 15ml/1 tbsp chopped fresh mint
- salt and ground black pepper
- sprigs of fresh mint, to garnish

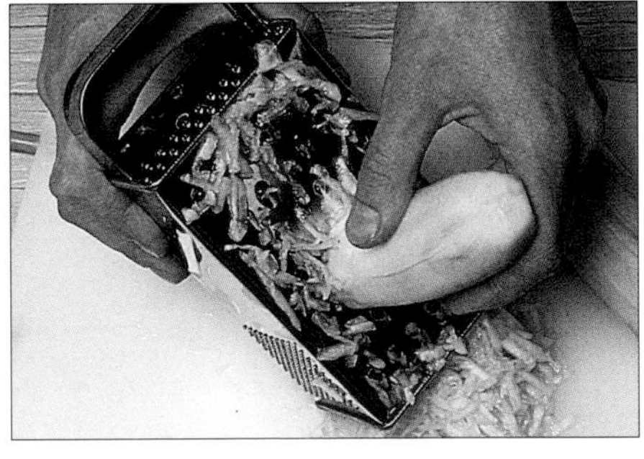

1 Grate the cucumber coarsely. This can be done in a food processor or blender, or you can do it by hand using the coarse side of a grater.

2 Stir it into the cream, yogurt, garlic, vinegar and mint. Season to taste. Chill for at least 2 hours before serving. Stir before serving and garnish with mint.

Energy 170Kcal/704kJ; Protein 4.7g; Carbohydrate 5g, of which sugars 4.8g; Fat 14.8g, of which saturates 9.3g; Cholesterol 42mg; Calcium 151mg; Fibre 0.2g; Sodium 54mg.

AVGOLEMONO

This is a great favourite in Greece and is a fine example of how a few ingredients can make a marvellous dish if carefully chosen and cooked. It is essential to use a well-flavoured stock. Add as little or as much rice as you like.

SERVES 4

INGREDIENTS
- 900ml/1½ pints/3¾ cups chicken stock, preferably home-made
- 50g/2oz/generous ⅓ cup long grain rice
- 3 egg yolks
- 30–60ml/2–4 tbsp lemon juice
- 30ml/2 tbsp finely chopped fresh parsley
- salt and freshly ground black pepper
- lemon slices and parsley sprigs, to garnish

1 Pour the stock into a pan, bring to simmering point, then add the drained rice. Half cover and cook for about 12 minutes until the rice is just tender. Season with salt and pepper.

2 Whisk the egg yolks in a bowl, then add about 30ml/2 tbsp of the lemon juice, whisking constantly until the mixture is smooth and bubbly. Add a ladleful of soup and whisk again.

3 Remove the soup from the heat and slowly add the egg mixture, whisking all the time. The soup will turn a pretty lemon colour and will thicken slightly.

4 Taste and add more lemon juice if necessary. Stir in the parsley. Serve at once, without reheating, garnished with lemon slices and parsley sprigs.

COOK'S TIP

The trick here is to add the egg mixture to the soup without it curdling. Avoid whisking the mixture into boiling liquid. It is safest to remove the soup from the heat entirely and then whisk in the mixture in a slow but steady stream. Do not reheat as curdling would be almost inevitable.

Energy 96Kcal/404kJ; Protein 3.3g; Carbohydrate 10.9g, of which sugars 0.2g; Fat 4.7g, of which saturates 1.2g; Cholesterol 151mg; Calcium 39mg; Fibre 0.4g; Sodium 10mg.

Fish Soup

In Greece fish soup makes a complete meal. The liquid soup is served first, followed by a platter of the fish and vegetables from the pot.

SERVES FOUR

INGREDIENTS
- 1.5 litres/2½ pints/6¼ cups water or fish stock
- 75–90ml/5–6 tbsp extra virgin olive oil
- 2kg/4½lb whole fish (see tip), cleaned and scaled
- 8 small potatoes, peeled and left whole
- 8 small onions, peeled and left whole
- 2 carrots, peeled and cut into 5cm/2in lengths
- 1 or 2 celery sticks, including leaves
- 2 courgettes (zucchini), quartered lengthways
- juice of 1 lemon
- salt and ground black pepper
- extra virgin olive oil, juice of 1 lemon and dried oregano, to serve

1 Mix the water or stock and olive oil in a large pan. Bring to the boil, and boil rapidly for about 4 minutes. Add the fish with salt and pepper and bring slowly back to the boil. Skim the surface until it is clear.

2 Add the potatoes, onions, carrots, celery sticks and leaves, and courgettes to the pan with a little more hot water, if needed, to cover.

3 Put a lid on the pan and cook over a medium heat until the fish is cooked and the flesh flakes when tested with the tip of a sharp knife. Large fish will take up to 35 minutes; smaller ones a little less. Make sure that the fish does not disintegrate.

4 Carefully lift the fish out of the pan and place it on a warm platter. Scoop out the hot vegetables with a draining spoon and arrange them around the fish. Cover and keep hot.

5 Stir the lemon juice into the soup. Serve it first, then bring out the platter of fish and vegetables. Invite guests to help themselves to a piece of fish and a selection of vegetables.

6 Quickly whisk the extra virgin olive oil with the lemon juice and dried oregano. This makes an excellent dressing for the fish and vegetables.

COOK'S TIPS
- In Greece, the favoured fish for this soup would be the bright orange Mediterranean scorpionfish. Its huge, rather ugly head adds a lot of flavour to the broth, and its bones have a glutinous quality, which is indispensable to a good fish soup. Red gurnard is a good alternative. It has a fine, sweet taste.
- It is possible to make this soup from just one type of fish, but if you use two or three different varieties you will achieve better results. In addition to red gurnard, grey mullet, sea bass or snapper are all suitable.

Energy 454Kcal/1,895kJ; Protein 53.8g; Carbohydrate 17g, of which sugars 6.4g; Fat 19.3g, of which saturates 3.1g; Cholesterol 135mg; Calcium 138mg; Fibre 2.5g; Sodium 345mg.

Lamb Meatball Soup with Vegetables

A variety of vegetables makes a tasty base for meatballs in this substantial soup, which will make a hearty meal served with crusty bread.

SERVES FOUR

INGREDIENTS
- 1 litre/1¾ pints/4 cups lamb stock
- 1 onion, finely chopped
- 2 carrots, finely sliced
- ½ celeriac, finely diced
- 75g/3oz/¾ cup frozen peas
- 50g/2oz green beans, cut into 2.5cm/1in pieces
- 3 tomatoes, seeded and chopped
- 1 red (bell) pepper, seeded and diced
- 1 potato, coarsely diced
- 2 lemons, sliced
- salt and ground black pepper
- crusty bread, to serve

For the meatballs
- 225g/8oz/1 cup very lean minced (ground) lamb
- 40g/1½oz/¼ cup short-grain rice
- 30ml/2 tbsp chopped fresh parsley
- plain flour, for coating

1 Put the stock in a large pan over a medium heat. Add the chopped onion, sliced carrot, diced celeriac and peas, and gently stir in.

2 Add the beans, tomatoes, red pepper and potato with the slices of lemon. Add a little salt and freshly ground black pepper and bring the mixture to the boil. Once it is boiling strongly, reduce the heat and simmer for 15–20 minutes.

3 Meanwhile, prepare the meatballs. Mix the minced meat, rice and parsley together in a bowl and season well. It can be useful to use your hands to combine the ingredients, using a kneading action.

4 Take out a rounded teaspoon of the mixture and roll it into a small ball, roughly the size of a walnut. Toss it in the flour and repeat until you have finished the mixture.

5 One by one, drop the meatballs into the soup and simmer gently for 25–30 minutes, stirring occasionally, to prevent the meatballs from sticking. Adjust the seasoning and serve in warmed serving bowls, accompanied by crusty bread.

Energy 226Kcal/948kJ; Protein 15.7g; Carbohydrate 25.1g, of which sugars 11.4g; Fat 7.7g, of which saturates 3.2g; Cholesterol 43mg; Calcium 75mg; Fibre 5.2g; Sodium 102mg.

CHICKEN SOUP WITH EGG AND LEMON SAUCE

THE MUCH-LOVED GREEK CHICKEN AND LEMON SOUP, AVGOLEMONO, *HAS TO BE ONE OF THE MOST DELICIOUS AND NOURISHING SOUPS IN THE WORLD.*

SERVES FOUR TO SIX

INGREDIENTS

- 1 chicken, about 1.6kg/3½lb
- 1.75 litres/3 pints/7½ cups water
- 2 onions, halved
- 2 carrots
- 3 celery sticks, each sliced into 3 or 4 pieces
- a few sprigs of flat leaf parsley
- 3 or 4 black peppercorns
- 50g/2oz/generous ⅓ cup short grain rice
- salt
- lemon wedges, to serve

For the egg and lemon sauce

- 5ml/1 tsp cornflour (cornstarch)
- 2 large (US extra large) eggs, at room temperature
- juice of 1–2 lemons

1 Place the chicken in a large pan with the water. Bring to the boil and skim using a slotted spoon until the surface of the liquid is clear. Add the vegetables, parsley and peppercorns, season with salt and bring to the boil. Lower the heat slightly, then cover the pan and cook for 1 hour (longer if a boiling fowl or stewing chicken is used), until the chicken is very tender.

2 Carefully lift out the chicken and put it on a board. Strain the stock and set it aside, but discard the vegetables. Pull away the chicken breasts, skin them and dice the flesh. Do the same with the legs. Pour the stock back into the pan and add the chicken meat.

3 Shortly before serving, heat the stock and diced chicken. When the stock boils, add the rice.

4 Cover the pan and cook for about 8 minutes, until soft. Take the pan off the heat and let the soup cool a little before adding the sauce.

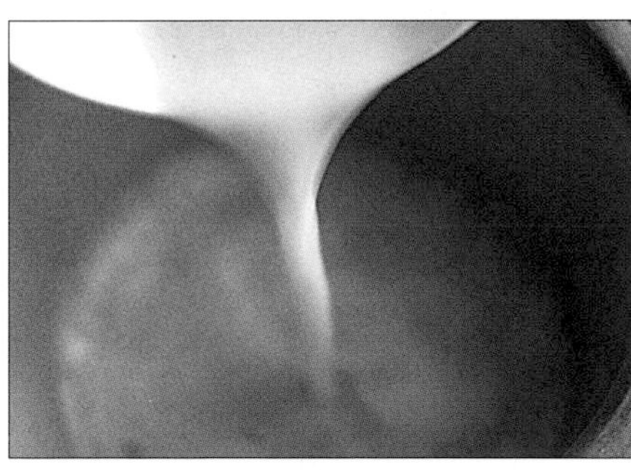

5 To make the sauce, firstly mix the cornflour to a paste with a little water. Beat the eggs in a separate bowl, add the lemon juice and the cornflour mixture and beat together until smooth and well mixed.

6 Gradually beat a ladleful of the chicken stock into the egg mixture, then continue to beat for 1 minute. Add a second ladleful in the same way. By now the sauce will be warm so you can pour it slowly into the soup, and stir vigorously to mix it in.

7 Warm the soup over a gentle heat for no more than 1–2 minutes. Any longer and the eggs may curdle, even though the cornflour should safeguard against that happening. Serve immediately in warmed bowls, with a plate of lemon wedges for those who wish to add extra juice.

COOK'S TIPS

- The soup will have much more character if either a boiling fowl or a large organic chicken is used.
- The chicken soup (without the rice) can be made well in advance up to a day before it is needed. Cool it quickly and keep it in a covered bowl in the refrigerator.

Energy 599Kcal/2,488kJ; Protein 53.5g; Carbohydrate 8.5g, of which sugars 3g; Fat 39.1g, of which saturates 10.9g; Cholesterol 359mg; Calcium 50mg; Fibre 1.2g; Sodium 236mg.

FISH AND SHELLFISH

Because Greece is a peninsula with many islands, fish and shellfish are widely available and enjoyed super-fresh from the sea. Although fish is often simply fried or barbecued, many dishes include rich sauces or are flavoured with combinations of herbs, citrus fruits, spices and vegetables.

FRIED SQUID WITH SPLIT PEA PURÉE

TASTY FRIED SQUID GOES PERFECTLY WITH THIS TRADITIONAL SPLIT PEA PURÉE DISH, KNOWN AS FAVA, THAT HAS LONG BEEN A MAINSTAY OF THE GREEK DIET. FAVA CAN ALSO BE ENJOYED WITH OTHER FISH OR MEATS, OR AS A SIDE DISH WITH CHOPPED ONION AND FLAT LEAF PARSLEY SPRINKLED OVER THE TOP. MEDIUM-SIZED SQUID WORK WELL FOR THIS RECIPE, ALTHOUGH THE TENDER BABY SQUID ARE ALSO POPULAR AND ADD A LOVELY CRISPNESS TO THE TEXTURE.

SERVES FOUR

INGREDIENTS

- 225g/8oz/1 cup Greek fava or yellow split peas
- 1.5 litres/2½ pints/6¼ cups cold water
- 1 onion, finely chopped
- 50g/2oz/½ cup plain (all-purpose) flour
- 4 medium squid, cleaned, total weight about 900g/2lb
- 75ml/5 tbsp olive oil or sunflower oil
- 2 or 3 shallots, finely chopped
- 60–75ml/4–5 tbsp extra virgin olive oil
- juice of ½ lemon
- salt and ground black pepper
- 15ml/1 tbsp finely chopped fresh parsley, to garnish

1 Soak the fava or split peas in cold water to cover for 1 hour. Drain, rinse several times, then drain again and place in a large, heavy pan. Pour in the measured water. Bring to the boil and skim using a slotted spoon.

2 Add the chopped onion and simmer uncovered for 1 hour or more, depending on the age of the peas, stirring occasionally, until soft.

3 Season the flour with salt and freshly ground black pepper and then toss the squid in it until each is evenly coated.

4 Purée the pea mixture in a food processor or blender while it is still hot, as it will solidify if you allow it to cool. The purée should be smooth and have the consistency of thick cream. Add salt to taste.

5 Heat the olive or sunflower oil in a large frying pan. When it is hot enough to sizzle but is not smoking, add the squid bodies, without letting them touch each other. Cook until pale golden underneath, then turn and cook until they are pale golden all over. Add the tentacles and cook until they are crisp and golden all over.

6 Spread the pea mixture on individual plates in a thin layer and let it cool a little. Sprinkle the chopped shallots over the top, then drizzle with the extra virgin olive oil and lemon juice. Place the fried squid on top, with the tentacles arranged at the top. Grind a little black pepper coarsely over the top and add the chopped fresh flat leaf parsley. This dish can be served warm or at room temperature.

COOK'S TIP

Towards the end of the cooking time, watch the pea mixture closely as it may start to stick. Once cooked, the peas should be perfectly soft and moist.

Energy 637Kcal/2,677kJ; Protein 49.6g; Carbohydrate 46.5g, of which sugars 3.3g; Fat 29.5g, of which saturates 4.6g; Cholesterol 506mg; Calcium 83mg; Fibre 3.6g; Sodium 269mg.

GRILLED SQUID STUFFED WITH FETA CHEESE

SQUID IS A POPULAR DISH ON THE GREEK ISLANDS AND IS COOKED IN MANY DIFFERENT WAYS. BARBECUING BRINGS OUT THE SWEETNESS IN THE FLAVOUR, AND IN THIS RECIPE THE SQUID IS STUFFED WITH A RICH AND CREAMY FILLING OF FETA CHEESE THAT HAS BEEN MARINATED IN OLIVE OIL AND MARJORAM. THIS IS A SUMMER SPECIALITY ON THE ISLAND OF ALONNISOS AND IS PERFECT SERVED WITH SALAD AND CRUSTY BREAD.

SERVES FOUR

INGREDIENTS

- 4 medium squid, cleaned, total weight about 900g/2lb
- 4–8 finger-length slices of feta cheese

For the marinade

- 90ml/6 tbsp extra virgin olive oil
- 2 garlic cloves, crushed
- 3 or 4 fresh marjoram sprigs, leaves removed and chopped
- salt and ground black pepper
- lemon wedges, to serve

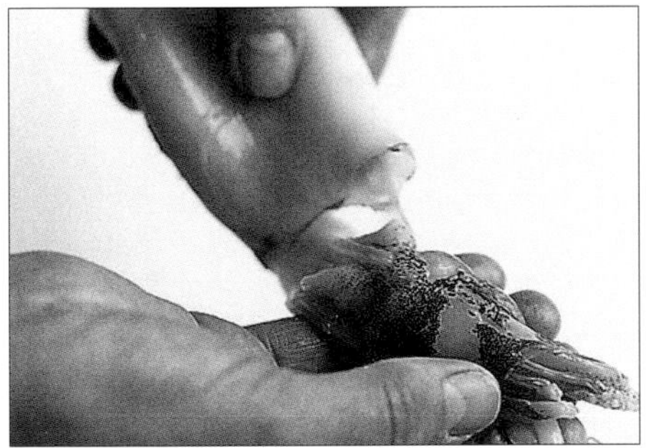

1 Keep the bodies of the cleaned squid intact, with the tentacles attached. Rinse them thoroughly, inside and out, and drain well, using kitchen paper to draw off any residual moisture.

2 Lay the squid bodies and tentacles in a shallow dish that will hold them in a single layer, without squashing them too closely together. Tuck the pieces of feta cheese amongst the squid, and between the squid and the dish.

3 To make the marinade, pour the oil into a jug (pitcher) or bowl and whisk in the crushed garlic and marjoram. Season to taste with salt and pepper. Pour the marinade over the squid and the cheese, then cover and leave in a cool place to marinate for 2–3 hours, turning once.

4 Remove each squid one by one from the marinade and take off the tentacles if they are still attached, keeping them whole. Insert 1 or 2 pieces of cheese and a few bits of marjoram from the marinade into the body of each squid and place them on a lightly oiled grill (broiler) pan or tray. Thread the marinated tentacles on to skewers.

5 Preheat the grill to a fairly low setting or prepare a barbecue. Grill (broil) the stuffed squid gently for about 6 minutes, then turn them over carefully. Grill them for 1–2 minutes more, before adding the skewered tentacles.

6 Grill the tentacles for 2 minutes on each side, until they start to stiffen and scorch slightly. Serve the stuffed squid with the crisp tentacles and lemon wedges.

Energy 393Kcal/1,643kJ; Protein 38.6g; Carbohydrate 3.1g, of which sugars 0.4g; Fat 25.4g, of which saturates 6.7g; Cholesterol 524mg; Calcium 119mg; Fibre 0g; Sodium 608mg.

SQUID WITH SPINACH

This is an unusual dish, which is occasionally made for special feasts on the island of Crete. Squid is a wonderful ingredient, especially when it is used fresh. This dish makes a superb meal with crusty bread and crisp, fresh salad.

SERVES FOUR

INGREDIENTS

- 1kg/2¼lb fresh squid, cleaned
- 120ml/4fl oz/½ cup extra virgin olive oil
- 1 large onion, sliced
- 3 spring onions (scallions), chopped
- 175ml/6fl oz/¾ cup white wine
- 150ml/¼ pint/⅔ cup hot water
- 500g/1¼lb fresh spinach
- juice of ½ lemon
- 45ml/3 tbsp chopped fresh dill
- salt and ground black pepper
- chunks of fresh white bread, to serve

1 Rinse the squid thoroughly inside and out, and drain well. Slice the body in half vertically, then slice into 1cm/½in strips. Cut each tentacle into smaller pieces.

2 Heat the oil in a wide, heavy pan and sauté the onion slices and spring onions gently until the onion slices are translucent.

COOK'S TIP

When buying squid, try to buy the smaller ones as they are generally more tender than larger squid. The wine in this recipe also helps to tenderize the flesh.

3 Increase the heat and add the slices of squid, including the smaller pieces of tentacles. The process will produce some moisture, but keep stirring and this will evaporate. Continue to stir for 10 minutes more, or until the squid starts to turn golden.

4 Pour in the wine and stir in, letting it evaporate slightly. Then add the hot water, with salt and freshly ground black pepper to taste. The flavour will change after further cooking so do not add too much seasoning at this stage. Cover the pan and cook for about 30 minutes, stirring occasionally.

5 Wash the spinach well and drain it carefully, removing any excess moisture with kitchen paper. Remove any stalks and chop it coarsely. Stir into the pan.

6 When the chopped spinach starts to wilt, cover the pan and cook for about 10 minutes. Just before serving, add the lemon juice and dill and mix well. Serve this dish in shallow bowls or on plates with fresh bread. Accompany with a fresh side salad.

Energy 462Kcal/1,931kJ; Protein 42.8g; Carbohydrate 9.5g, of which sugars 5.2g; Fat 25.4g, of which saturates 4g; Cholesterol 563mg; Calcium 264mg; Fibre 3.5g; Sodium 454mg.

Mussel and Rice Pilaff

This is a classic dish and a favourite one in Greece and the Greek islands. Although it is made with very inexpensive ingredients (in Greece, mussels are cheap compared to fish) it always produces spectacular and delicious results.

SERVES FOUR AS A MAIN COURSE, SIX AS A FIRST COURSE

INGREDIENTS

- 1.6kg/3½lb mussels, scrubbed and bearded
- 2 onions, thinly sliced
- 350ml/12fl oz/1½ cups white wine
- 450ml/¾ pint/scant 2 cups hot water
- 150ml/¼ pint/⅔ cup extra virgin olive oil
- 5 or 6 spring onions (scallions), chopped
- 2 garlic cloves, chopped
- large pinch of dried oregano
- 200g/7oz/1 cup long grain rice
- 45ml/3 tbsp finely chopped fresh flat leaf parsley
- 45–60ml/3–4 tbsp chopped fresh dill
- salt and ground black pepper

1 Having prepared the mussels, discard any that are not tightly shut, or which fail to snap shut when tapped. Place the remainder in a large, heavy pan. Add about one-third of the onion slices, then pour in half the wine and 150ml/¼ pint/⅔ cup of the hot water. Cover and cook over a high heat for about 5 minutes, shaking the pan occasionally, until the mussels start to open.

2 Place a colander on top of a large bowl and, using a slotted spoon, transfer the open mussels to the colander so that all their liquid collects in the bowl. Discard any mussels that remain closed or almost closed. Shell most of the mussels, discarding their shells, but keep a dozen or so large or well-presented ones in their shells for decorative purposes.

3 Line a sieve (strainer) with fine muslin (cheesecloth) or kitchen paper and place it over a large bowl. Allow the liquid remaining in the pan to settle, then strain through the lined sieve. Do the same with the liquid from the cooked mussels. Set the strained liquid aside.

4 Heat the olive oil in a deep, heavy pan or sauté pan, add the remaining onion and spring onions, and sauté over a medium heat until golden. Do not allow them to brown. Add the garlic and the oregano and mix in thoroughly. As soon as the garlic becomes aromatic, add the rice and stir to coat the grains well with oil. After a few minutes, add the remaining wine, stirring until it has been absorbed.

5 Stir in the remaining 300ml/½ pint/1¼ cups water, the reserved liquid from cooking the mussels and the chopped flat leaf parsley. Season with salt and ground black pepper, then cover and cook gently over a low to medium heat for about 5 minutes, stirring occasionally.

6 Add the mussels, including the ones in their shells. Sprinkle in half of the chopped fresh dill and mix well, making sure that you keep the mussels in their shells intact. If necessary, add a little more hot water. Cover and cook gently for 5–6 minutes more, or until the rice is cooked but still has a bit of bite at the centre of the grain.

7 Sprinkle the remaining dill on top and serve with a green salad or a cabbage salad with black olives.

Energy 607Kcal/2,529kJ; Protein 23.5g; Carbohydrate 50g, of which sugars 4.9g; Fat 28.5g, of which saturates 4g; Cholesterol 64mg; Calcium 139mg; Fibre 2.2g; Sodium 398mg.

CUTTLEFISH WITH POTATOES

Sautéed cuttlefish is sweeter and more tender than squid, provided you buy small or medium-size specimens. If the only ones available are very large, cook them for a little longer than stated in the recipe. Serve as a sumptuous main course or a tasty meze dish.

SERVES FOUR AS A MAIN COURSE, SIX AS A FIRST COURSE

INGREDIENTS
- 1kg/2¼lb fresh cuttlefish, cleaned
- 150ml/¼ pint/⅔ cup extra virgin olive oil
- 1 large onion, about 225g/8oz, chopped
- 175ml/6fl oz/¾ cup white wine
- 300ml/½ pint/1¼ cups hot water
- 500g/1¼lb potatoes, peeled and cubed
- 4–5 spring onions (scallions), chopped
- juice of 1 lemon
- 60ml/4 tbsp chopped fresh dill
- salt and ground black pepper

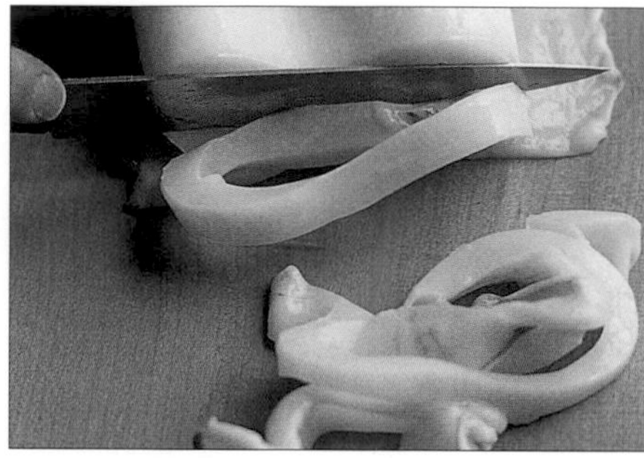

1 Rinse and drain the cleaned cuttlefish well, then slice them into 2cm/¾in wide ribbons.

2 Heat the oil in a heavy pan, add the onion and sauté for about 5 minutes until light golden. Add the cuttlefish and sauté until all the water they exude has evaporated and the flesh starts to change colour. This will take 10–15 minutes.

3 Pour in the wine and, when it has evaporated, add the water. Cover and cook for 10 minutes.

4 Add the potatoes, spring onions, lemon juice, and salt and pepper. There should be enough water almost to cover the ingredients; top up if necessary. Cover and cook gently for 40 minutes, or until the cuttlefish is tender. Add the dill and cook for 5 minutes. Serve hot.

Energy 540Kcal/2,254kJ; Protein 43.3g; Carbohydrate 24.7g, of which sugars 5.1g; Fat 27.3g, of which saturates 4.2g; Cholesterol 275mg; Calcium 176mg; Fibre 2.2g; Sodium 943mg.

OCTOPUS AND PASTA BAKE

A MOUTHWATERING DISH, THIS SLOW-COOKED COMBINATION OF OCTOPUS AND PASTA IN A SPICY TOMATO SAUCE IS QUITE AN EVERYDAY AFFAIR IN GREECE, ESPECIALLY ON THE ISLANDS WHERE OCTOPUS ARE READILY AVAILABLE FROM MARKETS AND AT THE HARBOURS.

SERVES FOUR

INGREDIENTS

- 2 octopuses, total weight about 675–800g/1½–1¾lb, cleaned
- 150ml/¼ pint/⅔ cup extra virgin olive oil
- 2 large onions, sliced
- 3 garlic cloves, chopped
- 1 fresh red or green chilli, seeded and thinly sliced
- 1 or 2 bay leaves
- 5ml/1 tsp dried oregano
- 1 piece of cinnamon stick
- 2 or 3 grains allspice (optional)
- 175ml/6fl oz/¾ cup red wine
- 30ml/2 tbsp tomato purée (paste) diluted in 300ml/½ pint/1¼ cups warm water
- 300ml/½ pint/1¼ cups boiling water
- 225g/8oz/2 cups dried penne or small macaroni-type pasta
- ground black pepper
- 45ml/3 tbsp finely chopped fresh flat leaf parsley, to garnish (optional)

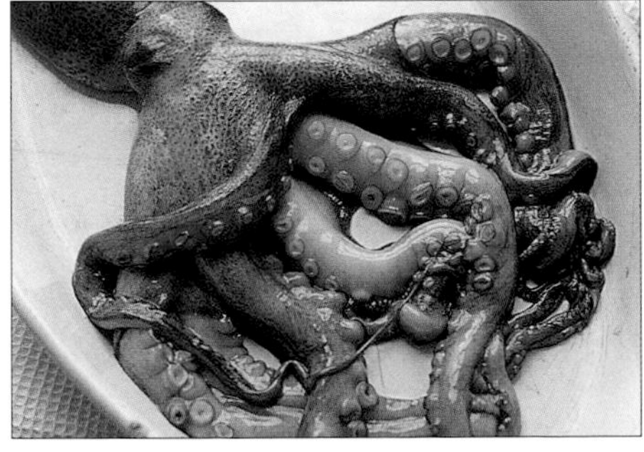

1 Rinse the octopuses well, making sure that there is no sand left in the suckers. Cut the octopuses into large cubes using a sharp knife and place the pieces in a heavy pan over a low heat. Cook gently; they will produce some liquid, the colour of the flesh will change and they will eventually become bright scarlet. Keep turning the pieces of octupus with a wooden spatula until all the liquid has evaporated.

2 Add the olive oil to the pan and sauté the octopus pieces for 4–5 minutes. Add the sliced onions to the pan and cook for a further 4–5 minutes, stirring them constantly until they start to turn golden.

3 Stir in the chopped garlic, chilli, bay leaf or leaves, oregano, cinnamon stick and allspice, if using. As soon as the garlic becomes aromatic, pour in the wine and let it bubble and evaporate for a couple of minutes.

4 Pour in the diluted tomato purée, add some black pepper, cover and cook gently for 1½ hours, or until the octopus is perfectly soft. Stir occasionally and add a little hot water if needed. The dish can be prepared up to this stage well in advance of serving.

5 Preheat the oven to 160°C/325°F/ Gas 3. Bring the octopus mixture to the boil, and then add the boiling water, stirring it into the mixture.

6 Stir in the dried pasta, coating it in the mixture. Tip the mixture into a large roasting dish and level the surface. Transfer to the oven and bake for 30–35 minutes, stirring occasionally and adding a little hot water if the mixture starts to look dry. Sprinkle the parsley on top, if using, and serve.

COOK'S TIPS

- Do not add salt to octopus as it makes it tough and indigestible.
- The octopus mixture can be cooked in a pressure cooker, if you prefer. It will take 20 minutes under full pressure.

Energy 637Kcal/2,669kJ; Protein 38.9g; Carbohydrate 52.9g, of which sugars 10.2g; Fat 28.5g, of which saturates 4.2g; Cholesterol 81mg; Calcium 108mg; Fibre 3.6g; Sodium 25mg.

GRILLED KING PRAWNS WITH PIQUANT SAUCE

THIS WELL-FLAVOURED SAUCE IS SERVED WITH FISH AND SHELLFISH. THE SWEET PEPPER, TOMATOES, GARLIC, CHILLI AND TOASTED ALMONDS GO EXCEEDINGLY WELL WITH ROBUST PRAWNS.

SERVES FOUR

INGREDIENTS

- 24 raw king prawns (jumbo shrimp)
- 30–45ml/2–3 tbsp olive oil
- fresh flat leaf parsley, to garnish
- lemon wedges, to serve

For the sauce

- 2 well-flavoured tomatoes
- 60ml/4 tbsp olive oil
- 1 onion, chopped
- 4 garlic cloves, chopped
- 1 canned pimiento, chopped
- 2.5ml/½ tsp dried chilli flakes
- 75ml/5 tbsp fish stock
- 30ml/2 tbsp white wine
- 10 blanched almonds
- 15ml/1 tbsp red wine vinegar
- salt

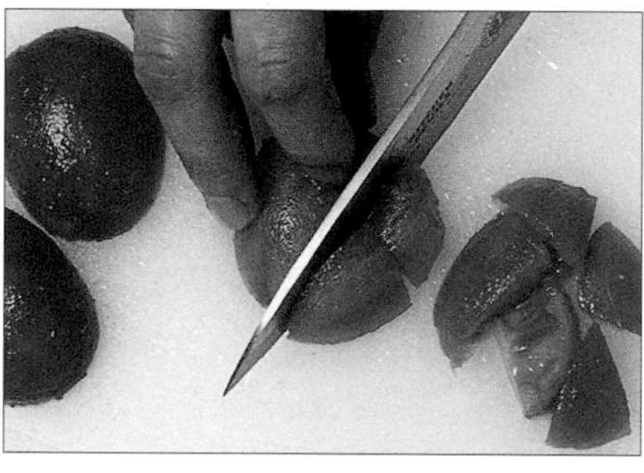

1 For the sauce, immerse the tomatoes in boiling water for 30 seconds. Peel away the skins and chop the flesh.

2 Heat 30ml/2 tbsp of the oil in a pan, add the onion and 3 of the garlic cloves and cook until soft. Add the pimiento, tomatoes, chilli, fish stock and wine, then cover and simmer for 30 minutes.

3 Spread the whole almonds on a baking sheet and toast them under the grill (broiler) until they are golden-brown. Transfer them to a blender or food processor and grind coarsely. Add the remaining 30ml/2 tbsp of olive oil, the vinegar and the last garlic clove and process until evenly combined. Add the tomato and pimiento sauce and process until smooth and well combined. Season with salt.

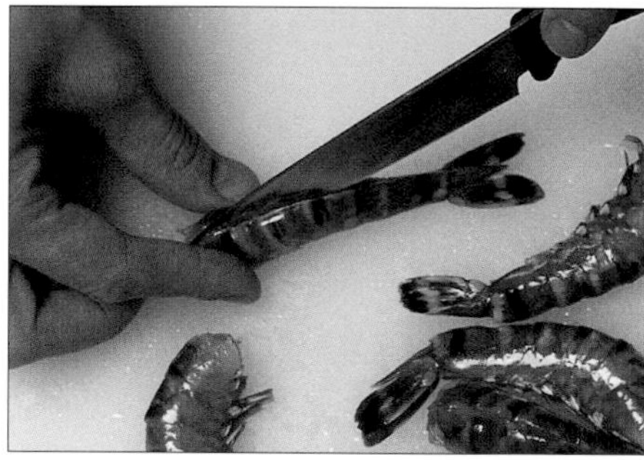

4 Remove the heads from the prawns leaving them otherwise unshelled and, with a sharp knife, slit each one down the back and remove the dark vein. Rinse and pat dry on kitchen paper. Preheat the grill. Toss the prawns in olive oil, then spread out in the grill pan. Grill (broil) for about 2–3 minutes on each side, until pink. Arrange on a platter with lemon wedges and the sauce in a small bowl.

Energy 265Kcal/1,097kJ; Protein 12.9g; Carbohydrate 4.7g, of which sugars 3.6g; Fat 21.2g, of which saturates 2.8g; Cholesterol 117mg; Calcium 78mg; Fibre 1.5g; Sodium 120mg.

PRAWNS WITH TOMATOES AND FETA

THIS LUXURIOUS AND UNUSUAL DISH CALLED YIOUVETSI *TAKES ITS NAME FROM THE ROUND EARTHENWARE BAKING DISH IN WHICH IT IS TRADITIONALLY COOKED.*

SERVES FOUR

INGREDIENTS

- 75ml/5 tbsp extra virgin olive oil
- 1 onion, chopped
- ½ red (bell) pepper, seeded and cubed
- 675g/1½lb ripe tomatoes, peeled and roughly chopped
- generous pinch of sugar
- 2.5ml/½ tsp dried oregano
- 450g/1lb raw tiger prawns (jumbo shrimp), thawed if frozen and peeled (with the tail shells intact)
- 30ml/2 tbsp finely chopped fresh flat leaf parsley
- 75g/3oz feta cheese, cubed
- salt and ground black pepper

1 Heat the oil in a frying pan, add the onion and sauté gently for a few minutes until translucent. Add the cubed red pepper and cook, stirring occasionally, for 2–3 minutes more.

2 Stir in the chopped tomatoes, sugar and oregano, then season with salt and pepper to taste. Cook gently over a low heat for about 15 minutes, stirring occasionally, until the sauce reduces slightly and thickens.

3 Preheat the oven to 180°C/350°F/ Gas 4. Stir the prawns and parsley into the tomato sauce, tip into a baking dish and spread evenly. Sprinkle the cheese cubes on top, then bake for 30 minutes. Serve hot with a fresh green salad.

Energy 308Kcal/1,282kJ; Protein 24.8g; Carbohydrate 10g, of which sugars 9.1g; Fat 19g, of which saturates 4.8g; Cholesterol 233mg; Calcium 194mg; Fibre 2.9g; Sodium 504mg.

FILLETS OF SEA BREAM IN FILO PASTRY

ANY FIRM FISH FILLETS CAN BE USED FOR THIS DISH – BASS, GROUPER AND RED MULLET ARE PARTICULARLY GOOD. EACH LITTLE PARCEL IS A MEAL IN ITSELF AND CAN BE PREPARED SEVERAL HOURS IN ADVANCE, WHICH MAKES THIS AN IDEAL RECIPE FOR ENTERTAINING. IF YOU LIKE, SERVE THE PASTRIES WITH FENNEL BRAISED WITH ORANGE JUICE OR A MIXED LEAF SALAD.

SERVES FOUR

INGREDIENTS

- 8 small waxy salad potatoes, preferably red-skinned
- 200g/7oz sorrel, stalks removed
- 30ml/2 tbsp extra virgin olive oil
- 16 filo pastry sheets, thawed if frozen
- 4 sea bream fillets, about 175g/6oz each, scaled but not skinned
- 50g/2oz/¼ cup butter, melted
- 120ml/4fl oz/½ cup fish stock
- 250ml/8fl oz/1 cup whipping cream
- salt and ground black pepper
- finely diced red (bell) pepper, to garnish

VARIATION

If sorrel isn't available, small spinach leaves or baby chard leaves make a very good substitute.

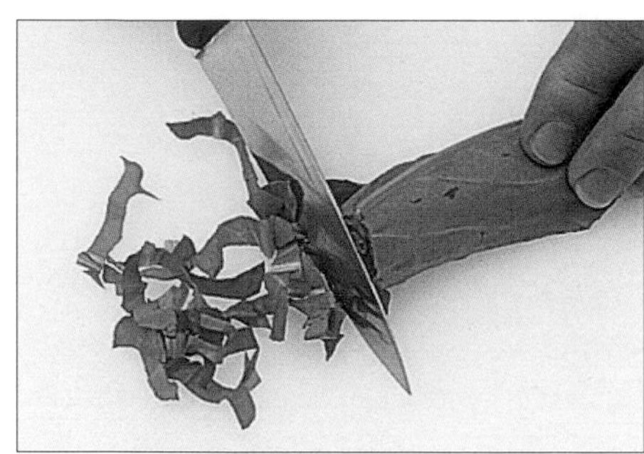

1 Preheat the oven to 200°C/400°F/ Gas 6. Cook the potatoes in a pan of lightly salted boiling water for about 15–20 minutes, or until just tender. Drain and leave to cool. Set about half the sorrel leaves aside. Shred the remaining leaves by piling up 6 or 8 at a time, rolling them up like a fat cigar and slicing them with a sharp knife. Thinly slice the potatoes lengthways.

2 Brush a baking sheet with a little of the oil. Lay a sheet of filo pastry on the sheet, brush it with oil, then lay a second sheet crossways over the first. Repeat with two more sheets. Arrange a quarter of the sliced potatoes in the centre, season and add a quarter of the shredded sorrel. Lay a bream fillet on top, skin-side up. Season with salt and ground black pepper.

3 Loosely fold the filo pastry up and over to make a neat parcel. Make three more parcels; place on the baking sheet. Brush with half the butter. Bake for about 20 minutes, or until the filo is puffed up and golden brown.

4 Meanwhile, make the sorrel sauce. Heat the remaining butter in a pan, add the reserved sorrel and cook gently for 3 minutes, stirring, until it wilts. Stir in the stock and cream. Heat almost to boiling point, stirring so that the sorrel breaks down. Season to taste and keep hot until the fish parcels are ready. Serve garnished with red pepper. Hand round the sauce separately.

Energy 651Kcal/2,710kJ; Protein 35.8g; Carbohydrate 23.2g, of which sugars 3.3g; Fat 46.8g, of which saturates 23.2g; Cholesterol 159mg; Calcium 222mg; Fibre 2g; Sodium 359mg.

FILO-WRAPPED FISH

THE CHOICE OF FISH CAN BE VARIED ACCORDING TO WHAT IS IN SEASON AND WHAT IS FRESHEST ON THE DAY OF PURCHASE. WHEN WORKING WITH FILO PASTRY, KEEP IT COVERED WITH CLEAR FILM (PLASTIC WRAP) OR A DAMP DISH TOWEL AS MUCH AS POSSIBLE. ONCE IT IS EXPOSED TO THE AIR IT DRIES OUT QUICKLY, MAKING IT DIFFICULT TO HANDLE AND COOK PROPERLY.

SERVES THREE TO FOUR

INGREDIENTS

- about 130g/4½oz filo pastry (6–8 large sheets), thawed if frozen
- about 30ml/2 tbsp olive oil, for brushing
- 450g/1lb salmon or cod steaks or fillets
- 550ml/18fl oz/2½ cups fresh tomato sauce (see Cook's Tip)

1 Preheat the oven to 200°C/400°F/Gas 6. Take a sheet of filo pastry, brush with a little olive oil and cover with a second sheet of pastry. Place a piece of fish on top of the pastry, towards the bottom edge, then top with 1–2 spoonfuls of the tomato sauce, spreading it in an even layer.

2 Roll the fish in the pastry, taking care to enclose the filling completely. Brush with a little olive oil. Arrange on a baking sheet and repeat with the remaining fish and pastry. You should have about half the sauce remaining, to serve with the fish.

3 Bake for 10–15 minutes, or until golden. Avoid opening the oven door before 10 minutes as the heat reduction can stop the filo pastry from rising. Meanwhile, reheat the remaining sauce gently in a small pan. Serve the wrapped fish immediately with the remaining heated tomato sauce and a lightly dressed green or mixed salad.

COOK'S TIP

To make the tomato sauce, fry 1 chopped onion and a crushed garlic clove in 15ml/1 tbsp oil until softened. Add a 400g/14oz can chopped tomatoes, 15ml/1 tbsp tomato purée (paste) and 15ml/1 tbsp chopped fresh herbs. Add a pinch of sugar and season to taste. Simmer for 20 minutes.

Energy 458Kcal/1,917kJ; Protein 34.1g; Carbohydrate 26.4g, of which sugars 6.1g; Fat 24.7g, of which saturates 4.1g; Cholesterol 75mg; Calcium 82mg; Fibre 2.7g; Sodium 85mg.

Fish Plaki

The different areas of Greece and the Greek islands have a slightly distinct version of this simple but very delicious dish, which makes the most of the local fresh fish. A whole fish can be used instead of a large fillet, if you prefer. This recipe also works well with sea bass, bream, John Dory, turbot, halibut or brill.

SERVES FOUR

INGREDIENTS

150ml/¼ pint/⅔ cup olive oil
2 large Spanish onions, chopped
2 celery sticks, chopped
4 fat garlic cloves, chopped
4 potatoes, peeled and diced
4 carrots, cut into small dice
15ml/1 tbsp caster (superfine) sugar
2 bay leaves
1 thick middle-cut fillet of grouper or cod, about 1kg/2¼lb
16–20 large black olives (optional)
4 large ripe tomatoes, peeled, seeded and chopped
150ml/¼ pint/⅔ cup dry white wine or vermouth
salt and ground black pepper
herb leaves, to garnish
saffron rice, to serve

1 Preheat the oven to 190°C/375°F/Gas 5. Heat the olive oil in a large frying pan, add the chopped onions and celery and sauté until they are transparent. Add the garlic and cook for 2 minutes more. Stir in the potatoes and carrots and fry for about 5 minutes, stirring occasionally. Sprinkle with the sugar and season to taste with salt and freshly ground black pepper.

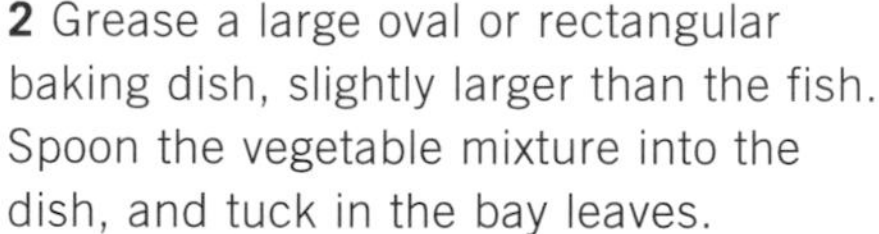

2 Grease a large oval or rectangular baking dish, slightly larger than the fish. Spoon the vegetable mixture into the dish, and tuck in the bay leaves.

3 Season the fish and lay it on the bed of vegetables, skin-side up. Sprinkle the olives evenly around the edge, if you are using them.

4 Spread the chopped tomatoes over the fish, pour over the wine or vermouth and season with salt and freshly ground black pepper.

5 Bake for 30–40 minutes, until the fish is cooked through. The type of fish that you are using and the thickness of the fillet may affect the cooking time, so be sure to test the thickest part of the fish to ensure that it is cooked right through. If you are using a whole fish, the cooking time will probably be longer.

6 Serve straight from the dish, garnished with herb leaves, such as fresh dill, chives and flat leaf parsley. Saffron rice would be the ideal accompaniment for the *plaki*.

COOK'S TIP

If you use a whole fish, be sure to season it inside as well as out. It can also add flavour to place a bay leaf and sprinkle some of the herbs into the fish as well as over the top. The cooking time will probably be longer with a whole fish so be sure to check the thickest part of the fish before taking it out of the oven.

Energy 557Kcal/2,322kJ; Protein 48.8g; Carbohydrate 24.3g, of which sugars 10.2g; Fat 27.3g, of which saturates 3.9g; Cholesterol 115mg; Calcium 74mg; Fibre 3.3g; Sodium 179mg.

SEA BASS IN A SALT CRUST

BAKING FISH IN A CRUST OF SEA SALT KEEPS IN THE FLAVOURS, ENHANCING THE NATURAL TASTE OF THE FISH. IT IS A POPULAR WAY OF COOKING FISH ON THE ISLANDS, WHERE LARGE OUTSIDE OVENS ARE USED TO PREVENT THE INSIDE OF BUILDINGS BECOMING TOO HOT. ANY FIRM FISH CAN BE COOKED WITH A SALT CRUST. BREAK IT OPEN AT THE TABLE TO RELEASE THE GLORIOUS AROMA.

SERVES FOUR

INGREDIENTS

- 1 sea bass, about 1kg/2¼lb, cleaned and scaled
- 1 sprig fresh fennel
- 1 sprig fresh rosemary
- 1 sprig fresh thyme
- 2kg/4½lb coarse sea salt
- mixed peppercorns
- seaweed or samphire, blanched, to garnish
- lemon slices, to serve

1 Preheat the oven to 240°C/475°F/ Gas 9. Make sure that you leave enough time for the oven to heat up properly as a cooler oven will not be able to set the salt crust. Spread half the salt on a shallow baking tray (ideally oval or rectangular).

2 Wash out the sea bass and dry any excess moisture with kitchen paper. Open the fish and lightly season the insides with salt and freshly ground black pepper. Open the fish out and then fill the cavity of the fish with all the herbs. Do not worry if the fish does not close properly as the herbs will become more compact as soon as they have been heated through and cooked.

3 Lay the sea bass on the salt. Cover the fish with a 1cm/½in layer of salt, pressing it down firmly. Moisten the salt lightly by spraying with water from an atomizer. Bake the fish in the hot oven for 30–40 minutes, or until the salt crust is just beginning to colour.

4 Garnish with seaweed or samphire and use a sharp knife to break open the crust. Serve with lemon slices.

Energy 150Kcal/632kJ; Protein 29g; Carbohydrate 0g, of which sugars 0g; Fat 3.8g, of which saturates 0.6g; Cholesterol 120mg; Calcium 195mg; Fibre 0g; Sodium 595mg.

GRILLED SWORDFISH SKEWERS

In Greece, sea-fresh swordfish, often on sale at the local fish market, is perfect for making SOUVLAKI *– skewered and grilled swordfish with garlic and oregano.*

SERVES FOUR

INGREDIENTS

- 2 red onions, quartered
- 2 red or green (bell) peppers, quartered and seeded
- 20–24 thick cubes of swordfish, 675–800g/1½–1¾lb in total
- 75ml/5 tbsp extra virgin olive oil
- 1 garlic clove, crushed
- large pinch of dried oregano
- salt and ground black pepper
- lemon wedges, to garnish

1 Carefully separate the onion quarters in pieces, each composed of two or three layers. Slice each pepper quarter in half widthways, or into thirds if you have very large peppers.

2 Make the *souvlakia* by threading five or six pieces of swordfish on to each of four long metal skewers, alternating with pieces of the pepper and onion. Lay the souvlakia across a grill (broiler) pan or roasting tray and set aside while you make the basting sauce.

3 Whisk the olive oil, crushed garlic and oregano in a bowl. Add salt and pepper, and whisk again. Brush the *souvlakia* generously on all sides with the basting sauce.

4 Preheat the grill to the highest setting, or prepare a barbecue. Slide the grill pan or roasting tray underneath the grill or transfer the skewers to the barbecue, making sure that they are not too close to the heat and that the heat is evenly distributed throughout.

5 Cook for 8–10 minutes, turning the skewers several times, until the fish is cooked and the peppers and onions have begun to scorch around the edges. Every time you turn the skewers, brush them with the basting sauce to increase the flavours.

6 Serve the *souvlakia* immediately, garnished with one or two wedges of lemon. Serve with a salad of cucumber, red onion and fresh olives.

COOK'S TIP

Many fishmongers will prepare the swordfish for you, and cut it into cubes for you too. But if you prefer to do this yourself, or you are buying the swordfish whole, you will need approximately 800g/1¾lb swordfish. The cubes should be fairly big – about 5cm/2in square, as they shrink in size as they are cooking. If you have larger cubes of swordfish, you may need to increase the cooking time slightly to ensure that the fish is completely cooked through. If in doubt, cut a large cube open to check.

Energy 363Kcal/1,511kJ; Protein 32.2g; Carbohydrate 11.5g, of which sugars 9.6g; Fat 21.2g, of which saturates 3.6g; Cholesterol 69mg; Calcium 33mg; Fibre 2.5g; Sodium 225mg.

BAKED SALT COD WITH POTATOES AND OLIVES

SALT COD HAS BEEN A WINTER STAPLE IN GREECE FOR GENERATIONS. IT IS ALSO POPULAR DURING THE PERIOD OF LENT, AND IS OFTEN ON THE MENU AT RESTAURANTS ON FRIDAYS DURING THIS TIME.

SERVES FOUR

INGREDIENTS

- 675g/1½lb salt cod
- 800g/1¾lb potatoes, cut into wedges
- 1 large onion, finely chopped
- 2 or 3 garlic cloves, chopped
- leaves from 1 fresh rosemary sprig
- 30ml/2 tbsp chopped fresh parsley
- 120ml/4fl oz/½ cup olive oil
- 400g/14oz can chopped tomatoes
- 15ml/1 tbsp tomato purée (paste)
- 300ml/½ pint/1¼ cups hot water
- 5ml/1 tsp dried oregano
- 12 black olives
- ground black pepper

1 Soak the cod in cold water overnight, changing the water as often as possible in the course of the evening and during the following morning. The cod does not have to be skinned for this dish, but you may prefer to remove the skin, especially if there is a lot of skin on the fish. You should remove any obvious fins or bones. After soaking, drain the cod and cut it into 7cm/2¾in squares.

2 Preheat the oven to 180°C/350°F/ Gas 4. Mix the potatoes, onion, garlic, rosemary and parsley in a large roasting pan with plenty of black pepper. Add the olive oil and toss until coated.

3 Arrange the pieces of cod between the coated vegetables and spread the tomatoes over the surface. Stir the tomato purée into the hot water until dissolved, then pour the mixture over the contents of the pan. Sprinkle the oregano on top. Bake for 1 hour, basting the fish and potatoes occasionally with the pan juices.

4 Remove the roasting pan from the oven, sprinkle the olives on top, and then cook for 30 minutes more, adding a little more hot water if the mixture seems to be drying out. Garnish with fresh parsley. Serve hot or cold.

COOK'S TIP

Salt cod can often be bought from Italian and Spanish groceries, as well as from Greek food stores. It is often sold in small squares, ready for soaking and draining. If you buy it in one piece, cut it into 7cm/2¾in squares; it will shrink slightly with cooking so it is rarely used in smaller pieces than this. Larger chunks may take longer to cook.

Energy 624Kcal/2,624kJ; Protein 61g; Carbohydrate 45.6g, of which sugars 12.9g; Fat 23.3g, of which saturates 3.5g; Cholesterol 100mg; Calcium 98mg; Fibre 4.8g; Sodium 918mg.

Carp Stuffed with Walnuts

This elaborate dish of carp filled with a spicy walnut stuffing makes a perfect meal to celebrate December 6th, the saint's day of Saint Nicholas, patron saint of fishermen.

SERVES TEN

INGREDIENTS

- about 1.3kg/3lb whole carp, scaled, cleaned and roe reserved
- coarse sea salt

For the stuffing

- 175ml/6fl oz/¾ cup walnut oil
- 675g/1½lb onions, finely sliced
- 5ml/1 tsp paprika
- pinch of cinnamon
- 175g/6oz/1½ cups walnuts, chopped
- 15ml/1 tbsp chopped fresh parsley
- 10ml/2 tsp fresh lemon juice
- 2 tomatoes, sliced
- 250ml/8fl oz/1 cup tomato juice
- salt and ground black pepper
- walnuts and fennel sprigs, to garnish

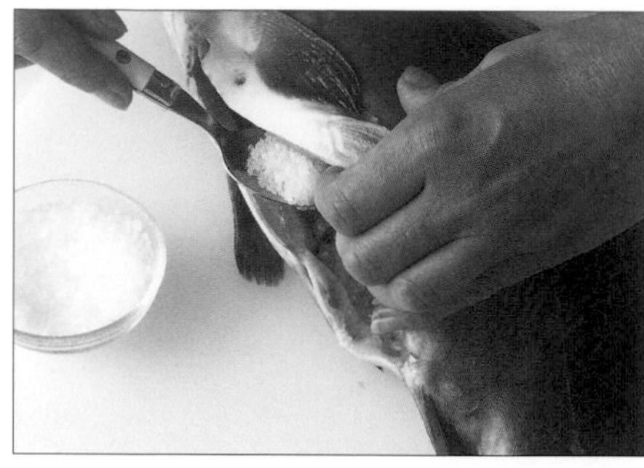

1 Preheat the oven to 180°C/350°F/ Gas 4. Sprinkle the inside of the fish with a little sea salt.

2 To make the stuffing, heat the oil in a large frying pan, then cook the onions, paprika and cinnamon together until soft and the onions are transparent.

3 Clean the roe thoroughly and remove any membrane or skin. Roughly chop it into pieces the same size as the chopped walnuts.

4 Add the roe and walnuts to the frying pan and cook, stirring all the time, for 5–6 minutes. Leave to cool before stirring in the parsley and lemon juice. Season to taste with salt and freshly ground black pepper.

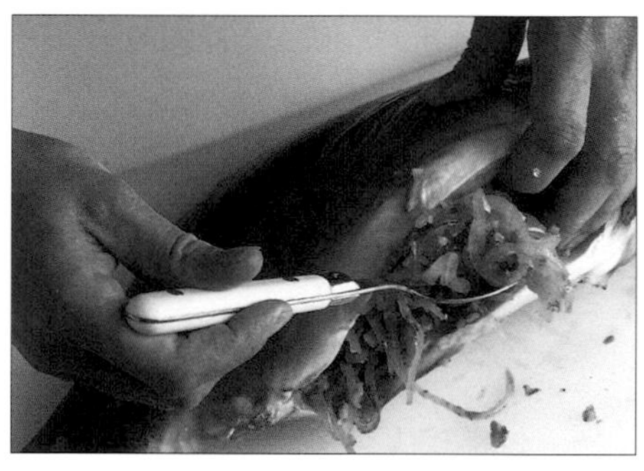

5 Fill the cavity of the fish with half of the filling and secure with cocktail sticks (toothpicks). Spoon the remaining stuffing into the base of a large oval or rectangular ovenproof dish and then place the fish on top.

6 Arrange the sliced tomatoes over the top of the fish and spoon over the tomato juice. Bake in the oven for 30–45 minutes, or until the fish is browned and flakes easily.

7 Carefully transfer the fish to a serving platter or a large dish, and discard the cocktail sticks. Sprinkle the fish with extra walnut pieces and a few sprigs of fennel, and serve.

Energy 380Kcal/1,578kJ; Protein 21.2g; Carbohydrate 7.2g, of which sugars 5.5g; Fat 29.9g, of which saturates 3.1g; Cholesterol 67mg; Calcium 84mg; Fibre 1.9g; Sodium 105mg.

STUFFED RED SNAPPER

THERE ARE A NUMBER OF FLAVOURS COMBINED IN THIS UNUSUAL RECIPE – THE RED SNAPPER FILLED WITH CARP, SHARPENED BY THE SALTY CHEESE AND DILL PICKLE.

SERVES FOUR

INGREDIENTS

- 4 small red snapper, about 900g/2lb in total, filleted
- juice of 1 lemon
- 350g/12oz fish fillets, such as carp, pike or sole, skinned
- 1 egg white
- 2.5ml/½ tsp chopped fresh tarragon
- 1 dill pickle, sliced
- 40g/1½oz/¾ cup fresh breadcrumbs
- 40g/1½oz feta cheese or brinza, roughly crumbled
- 25g/1oz/2 tbsp butter, melted
- salt and ground white pepper
- sprigs of tarragon plus pansies or other edible flowers, to garnish
- lemon wedges, to serve

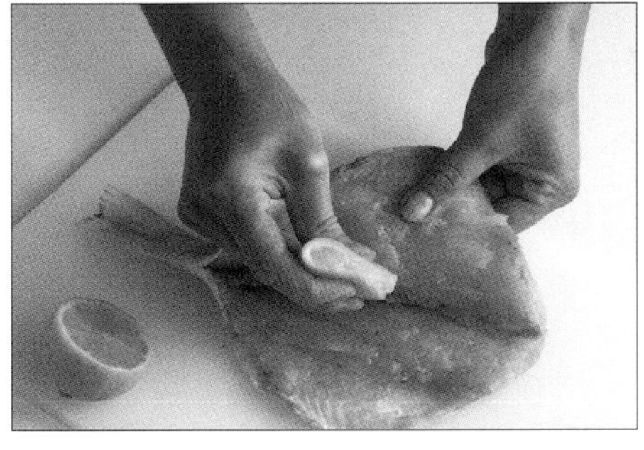

1 Preheat the oven to 180°C/350°F/ Gas 4. Wipe the snapper inside and pat dry. Liberally rub the lemon juice inside the fish.

2 Put the fish fillets in a food processor and process with the egg white, tarragon, dill pickle, breadcrumbs, cheese and a little ground white pepper, until a smooth paste is formed for the stuffing.

3 Using a spoon, fill the fish with the fish fillet mixture. Make sure that you tuck the mixture well inside to prevent it from oozing out during cooking.

COOK'S TIP

Pike has many tiny, soft bones in the flesh, but these will be puréed, so they do not need to be removed.

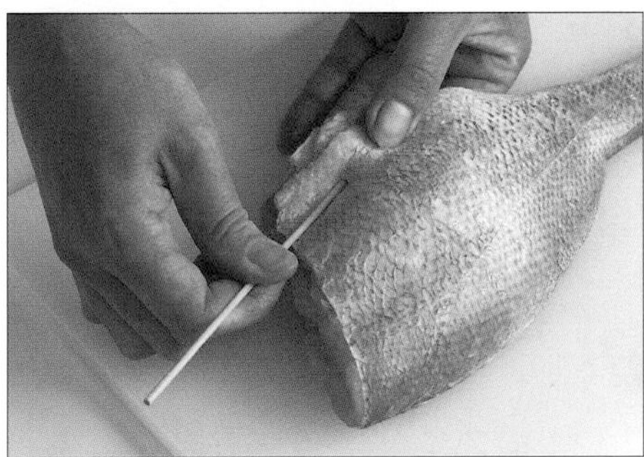

4 Secure the fish with wooden satay sticks and bake for 40–50 minutes. Spoon over the melted butter halfway through cooking.

5 Transfer the fish to a serving plate. Serve with lemon wedges and garnish with fresh sprigs of tarragon and edible flowers, if you like.

Energy 360Kcal/1,515kJ; Protein 58.7g; Carbohydrate 8g, of which sugars 0.5g; Fat 10.6g, of which saturates 5.3g; Cholesterol 135mg; Calcium 139mg; Fibre 0.2g; Sodium 480mg.

PAN-FRIED RED MULLET WITH ANCHOVIES, BASIL AND CITRUS

Oranges and lemons grow all over Greece and are incorporated into many dishes. Here, they make a fine marinade and sauce to accompany red mullet. If you prefer, you can use other fish fillets for this dish, such as lemon sole, haddock, cod or hake. Thicker fish fillets may need to be cooked for longer. Always check the thickest part of a fish to ensure that it is cooked through before you take it out of the oven.

SERVES FOUR

INGREDIENTS

- 4 red mullet, about 225g/8oz each, filleted
- 90ml/6 tbsp olive oil
- 10 peppercorns, crushed
- 2 oranges, one peeled and sliced and one squeezed
- 1 lemon
- 30ml/2 tbsp plain flour
- 15g/½oz/1 tbsp butter
- 2 drained canned anchovies, chopped
- 60ml/4 tbsp shredded fresh basil
- salt and ground black pepper

1 Make sure that the fillets have been cleaned properly and remove any remaining bones or coarse pieces of fin. You can check for bones by inching your thumb and forefinger up each fillet, using gentle pressure and bending the fish slightly to locate any harder or spiny areas that may need to be removed.

2 Place the fish fillets in a shallow dish in a single layer. Pour over the extra virgin olive oil and sprinkle the crushed peppercorns evenly over the top. Lay the orange slices on top of the fish, making sure that each fillet is covered and retaining some orange slices to garnish. Cover the dish, and leave to marinate in the refrigerator for at least 4 hours.

3 Halve the lemon. Remove the skin and pith from one half using a small sharp knife. Slice the lemon flesh thinly, discarding any pips (seeds) and chunks of pith. Cover and set aside.

4 Squeeze the juice from the other lemon half, again discarding any pips. Retain the juice in a small container and set aside.

5 One by one, lift the fillets out of the marinade, and gently shake the excess marinade back into the dish. Pat each fillet dry on kitchen paper. Cover and set aside the marinade and orange slices.

6 Season the fish with salt and freshly ground black pepper. Sprinkle the plain flour on to a large plate or platter and dust each fillet thoroughly yet lightly with flour, turning it over to coat it completely. Shake off any excess flour and set aside.

7 Heat 45ml/3 tbsp of the marinade in a large frying pan until hot. Add the fillets; try not to let them touch each other. Fry for 2 minutes on each side. Remove from the pan, loosely cover and keep warm. Discard the marinade that is left in the pan.

8 Melt the butter in the pan with any of the remaining original marinade. Drain the anchovies and add them to the marinade. Cook them until they are completely softened.

9 Stir in the orange and lemon juice, then check the seasoning, adding salt and freshly ground black pepper as necessary. Simmer until slightly reduced. Stir in the basil.

10 Place the fish on a serving platter and pour over the sauce. Garnish with the reserved orange slices and the lemon slices.

Energy 355Kcal/1,480kJ; Protein 23.4g; Carbohydrate 11g, of which sugars 5.2g; Fat 24.6g, of which saturates 4.4g; Cholesterol 9mg; Calcium 125mg; Fibre 1.3g; Sodium 198mg.

BAKED RED MULLET WITH ORANGES

ORANGES ARE SO PLENTIFUL IN GREECE THAT THEY CAN BE PICKED FROM TREES IN THE STREETS. THE AROMA OF ORANGE ZEST PERVADES MANY OF THE GREEKS' CLASSIC DISHES AND TEMPTS MANY INTO CAFÉS AND RESTAURANTS ON THE MAINLAND AND THROUGHOUT THE ISLANDS.

SERVES FOUR

INGREDIENTS

- a few sprigs of fresh dill
- 4 large red mullet, total weight 1–1.2kg/2¼–2½lb, gutted and cleaned
- 2 large oranges, halved
- ½ lemon
- 60ml/4 tbsp extra virgin olive oil
- 30ml/2 tbsp pine nuts
- salt

1 Place some fresh dill in the cavity of each fish and lay them in a baking dish, preferably one that can be taken straight to the table. Make sure that the fish are not packed too close together. Sprinkle more dill around the fish.

2 Set half an orange aside and squeeze the rest, along with the lemon. Mix the citrus juices with the olive oil, then pour the mixture over the fish. Turn the fish over so that they are evenly coated in the marinade, then cover and leave in a cool place to marinate for 1–2 hours, spooning the marinade over the fish occasionally.

3 Preheat the oven to 180°C/350°F/Gas 4. Slice the reserved half orange into thin rounds, then cut each round into quarters. Cover and set aside.

4 Sprinkle a little salt over each fish. Place two or three of the orange wedges over each fish. Bake for 20 minutes, then remove the dish from the oven, baste the fish with the juices and sprinkle the pine nuts over. Return the dish to the oven and bake for 10–15 minutes more.

5 Test the thickest fish to make sure that it is cooked thoroughly, then remove from the oven. You can transfer the fish to a serving platter, garnished with sprigs of fresh dill, or present them in the baking dish.

Energy 344Kcal/1,434kJ; Protein 30.5g; Carbohydrate 5.4g, of which sugars 5.4g; Fat 22.5g, of which saturates 1.9g; Cholesterol 0mg; Calcium 137mg; Fibre 1.2g; Sodium 153mg.

GRILLED SEA BASS WITH FENNEL

FENNEL GROWS WILD IN THE COUNTRYSIDE IN GREECE AND ADDS ITS DISTINCTIVE ANISEED FLAVOUR TO MANY FISH DISHES. THE ANISEED-FLAVOURED PASTIS ADDS FURTHER WARMTH AND RICHNESS TO THE GRILLED SEA BASS, COMPLEMENTING THE FLAVOUR OF THE FENNEL.

SERVES SIX TO EIGHT

INGREDIENTS

- 1 sea bass, weighing 1.8kg/ 4–4½lb, cleaned
- 60–90ml/4–6 tbsp extra virgin olive oil
- 10–15ml/2–3 tsp fennel seeds
- 2 large fennel bulbs, trimmed and thinly sliced (reserve any fronds)
- 60ml/4 tbsp pastis (such as Pernod or Ricard)
- salt and freshly ground black pepper

VARIATION

If you have access to it, use traditional Greek ouzo instead of pastis. It has a similar aniseed flavour and is frequently used in Greek cooking to enhance the taste of fish and shellfish. You can buy it in Greek stores and it is sometimes also available in Turkish stores.

1 With a sharp knife, make three or four deep cuts in both sides of the fish, more if the fish is large. Brush the fish with extra virgin olive oil and season with salt and freshly ground black pepper, both inside and outside.

2 Sprinkle the fennel seeds into the stomach cavity and push deep down into each of the cuts. Cover loosely and set aside in a cool place while you prepare and cook the fennel.

3 Preheat the grill (broiler) to a medium heat. Put the slices of fennel in a flameproof dish or on the grill rack and brush with extra virgin olive oil. Grill (broil) for 4 minutes on each side until tender. Transfer to a platter and spread evenly to cover the base, loosely cover to keep warm and set aside.

4 Place the fish on the oiled grill rack and position about 10–13cm/4–5in away from a medium heat. Grill for 10–12 minutes on each side, brushing occasionally with extra virgin olive oil.

5 Transfer the fish to the platter, on top of the fennel. Garnish with chopped and whole fennel fronds.

6 Heat the pastis in a small pan, light it and pour it, flaming, over the fish. Serve immediately.

Energy 296Kcal/1,238kJ; Protein 39.2g; Carbohydrate 1.2g, of which sugars 1.1g; Fat 12.5g, of which saturates 1.9g; Cholesterol 160mg; Calcium 276mg; Fibre 1.6g; Sodium 145mg.

Fish Parcels

Sea bass is good for this recipe, but you could also use small whole trout or white fish fillet such as cod or haddock. Serve with chunks of good crusty bread.

SERVES FOUR

INGREDIENTS

- 4 pieces sea bass fillet or 4 whole small sea bass, about 450g/1lb each
- oil, for brushing
- 2 shallots, thinly sliced
- 1 garlic clove, chopped
- 15ml/1 tbsp capers
- 6 sun-dried tomatoes, finely chopped
- 4 black olives, stoned (pitted) and thinly sliced
- grated rind and juice of 1 lemon
- 5ml/1 tsp paprika
- salt and ground black pepper
- a few sprigs of fresh parsley, to garnish
- crusty bread, to serve

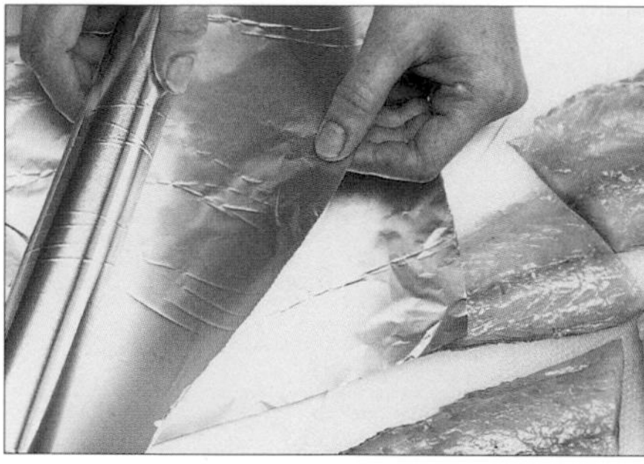

1 Preheat the oven to 200°C/400°F/ Gas 6. Clean the fish, if whole. Cut four large squares of double-thickness foil, large enough to enclose the fish. Brush each square with a little oil.

2 Place a piece of fish in the centre of each piece of foil and season well with salt and freshly ground black pepper.

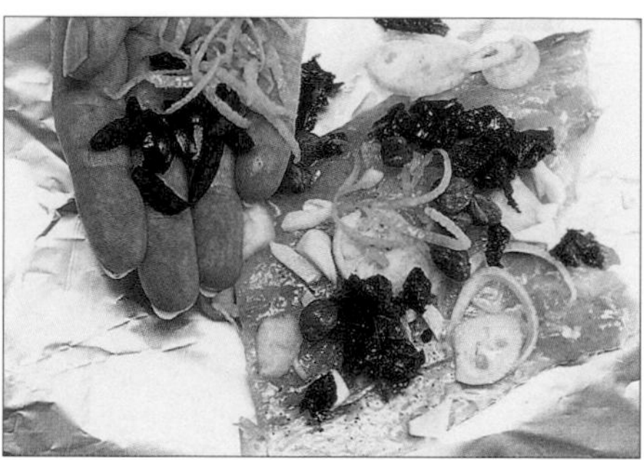

3 Sprinkle over the shallots, garlic, capers, tomatoes, olives and grated lemon rind. Sprinkle with the lemon juice and paprika.

4 Fold the foil over loosely, sealing the edges. Bake in the preheated oven for 15–20 minutes. Remove the foil and serve garnished with parsley.

Energy 343Kcal/1,441kJ; Protein 63.2g; Carbohydrate 2g, of which sugars 1.6g; Fat 9.1g, of which saturates 1.5g; Cholesterol 260mg; Calcium 433mg; Fibre 0.7g; Sodium 396mg.

Baked Fish in the Style of Spetses

All kinds of fish are prepared in this way on the tiny island of Spetses. Serve with a large fresh salad, or with little boiled potatoes and garlicky green beans, for a summer meal.

SERVES FOUR

INGREDIENTS

- 4 cod or hake steaks
- 2 or 3 sprigs of fresh flat leaf parsley
- 4 slices white bread, toasted, then crumbed in a food processor
- salt and ground black pepper

For the sauce

- 75–90ml/5–6 tbsp extra virgin olive oil
- 175ml/6fl oz/¾ cup white wine
- 2 garlic cloves, crushed
- 60ml/4 tbsp finely chopped flat leaf parsley
- 1 fresh red or green chilli, seeded and finely chopped
- 400g/14oz ripe tomatoes, peeled and finely diced

1 Mix all the sauce ingredients in a bowl, and add some salt and pepper. Set the mixture aside.

2 Preheat the oven to 190°C/375°F/ Gas 5. Rinse the fish steaks and pat them dry with kitchen paper. Place the steaks in a single layer in an oiled baking dish and sprinkle over the parsley. Season with salt and pepper.

3 Spoon the sauce over the fish, distributing it evenly over each steak. Then sprinkle over half of the breadcrumbs, again evenly covering each steak. Bake for 10 minutes, then baste with the juices in the dish, trying not to disturb the breadcrumbs. Sprinkle with the remaining breadcrumbs, then bake for a further 10–15 minutes.

VARIATION

If you like, use two whole fish, such as sea bass or grey mullet, total weight about 1kg/2¼lb. Rinse thoroughly inside and out, pat dry, then tuck the parsley sprigs inside. Add the sauce and breadcumbs as above. Bake for 15 minutes, then turn both fish over carefully, and bake for 20–25 minutes more.

Energy 362Kcal/1,510kJ; Protein 31g; Carbohydrate 13.1g, of which sugars 3.7g; Fat 17.9g, of which saturates 2.7g; Cholesterol 36mg; Calcium 49mg; Fibre 1.3g; Sodium 274mg.

BAKED FISH WITH TAHINI SAUCE

THRACE AND THE PELOPONNESE ARE RENOWNED FOR THEIR SESAME SEEDS, WHICH ARE USED TO MAKE THE RICH AND CREAMY PASTE, TAHINI. HERE IT IS USED TO CREATE A FRAGRANT TASTE TO BAKED FISH. HARISSA IS A POPULAR FLAVOURING USED THROUGHOUT MAINLAND GREECE AND THE GREEK ISLANDS, ALTHOUGH IT ORIGINALLY COMES FROM NORTH AFRICA.

SERVES FOUR

INGREDIENTS

- 1 whole fish, about 1.2kg/2½lb, scaled and cleaned
- 10ml/2 tsp coriander seeds
- 4 garlic cloves, sliced
- 10ml/2 tsp harissa sauce
- 90ml/6 tbsp extra virgin olive oil
- 6 plum tomatoes, sliced
- 1 mild onion, sliced
- 3 preserved lemons or 1 fresh lemon
- plenty of fresh herbs, such as bay leaves, thyme and rosemary, plus extra, to garnish
- salt and ground black pepper

For the sauce

- 75ml/3fl oz/⅓ cup light tahini
- juice of 1 lemon
- 1 garlic clove, crushed
- 45ml/3 tbsp finely chopped fresh flat leaf parsley or coriander (cilantro)

1 Preheat the oven to 200°C/400°F/ Gas 6. Grease the base and sides of a large shallow ovenproof dish or roasting pan.

2 Slash the fish diagonally three or four times on both sides with a sharp knife. Cut deeply, right in to the backbone.

3 Finely crush the coriander seeds in a pestle and mortar, add the chopped garlic and crush until it has blended into a fine paste. Mix with the harissa sauce and about 60ml/4 tbsp of the extra virgin olive oil.

4 Spread a little of the harissa, coriander and garlic paste inside the cavity of the fish. Spread the remainder over each side of the fish and set aside.

5 Spread the tomatoes, onion and preserved or fresh lemon in the dish. (Thinly slice the lemon if using fresh.) Sprinkle with the remaining oil and season with salt and pepper. Lay the fish on top and tuck plenty of herbs around it. Bake uncovered for 25 minutes, until the fish has turned opaque. Test by piercing the thickest part with a knife.

6 To make the sauce, put all the ingredients in a small pan with 120ml/ 4fl oz/½ cup water and add a little salt and pepper. Cook gently until smooth and heated through. Transfer the fish, lemons and vegetables to a platter, garnish with herbs and serve with the sauce.

COOK'S TIP

If you can't get a suitable large fish, use small whole fish such as red mullet or even cod or haddock steaks. Remember to reduce the cooking time slightly.

Energy 500Kcal/2,083kJ; Protein 43.8g; Carbohydrate 6.9g, of which sugars 6.4g; Fat 33.2g, of which saturates 4.9g; Cholesterol 160mg; Calcium 426mg; Fibre 4g; Sodium 161mg.

HAKE WITH SPINACH AND LEMON SAUCE

FISH COOKED WITH VARIOUS GREENS HAS ITS ROOTS IN MONASTIC LIFE. RELIGIOUS OBSERVANCE REQUIRED THAT FISH BE EATEN ON CERTAIN DAYS, AND THE COOKS IN THE MONASTERIES INCLUDED WILD GREENS GATHERED FROM THE HILLSIDES TO ADD INTEREST.

SERVES FOUR

INGREDIENTS

- 500g/1¼lb fresh spinach, trimmed of thick stalks
- 4 x 200g/7oz fresh hake steaks or 4 pieces of cod fillet
- 30ml/2 tbsp plain (all-purpose) flour
- 75ml/5 tbsp extra virgin olive oil
- 175ml/6fl oz/¾ cup white wine
- 3–4 strips of pared lemon rind
- salt and ground black pepper

For the egg and lemon sauce

- 2 large (US extra large) eggs, at room temperature
- juice of ½ lemon
- 2.5ml/½ tsp cornflour (cornstarch)

1 Place the spinach leaves in a large pan with just the water that clings to the leaves after washing. Cover the pan tightly and cook over a medium heat for 5–7 minutes, or until they are cooked. Turn the leaves occasionally using a wooden spoon. Drain and set aside.

2 Dust the fish lightly with the flour and shake off any excess. Heat the olive oil in a large frying pan, add the pieces of fish and sauté gently for 2–3 minutes on each side until the flesh starts to turn golden. Pour in the wine, add the lemon rind and some seasoning and carefully shake the pan from side to side to blend the flavourings. Lower the heat and simmer gently for a few minutes until the wine has reduced a little.

3 Add the spinach, distributing it evenly around the fish. Let it simmer for 3–4 minutes more, then pull the pan off the heat and let it stand for a few minutes before adding the sauce.

4 To make the sauce, mix the cornflour to a paste with a little water. Beat the eggs in a bowl, add the lemon juice and the cornflour mixture and beat together until smooth. Gradually beat a ladleful of the liquid from the fish pan into the egg mixture, then beat for 1 minute. Add a second ladleful in the same way, and continue with the rest.

5 Pour the sauce over the fish and spinach, place the pan over a very gentle heat and shake to amalgamate the ingredients. If it appears too dry add a little warm water. Allow to cook gently for 2–3 minutes and serve.

COOK'S TIP

Spinach can be gritty, and the best way to wash it is to swirl the leaves gently in a sink full of cold water, then lift them out by hand into a colander. Repeat the process until the water is clear.

Energy 441Kcal/1,839kJ; Protein 43.6g; Carbohydrate 10.6g, of which sugars 2.3g; Fat 22.1g, of which saturates 3.5g; Cholesterol 141mg; Calcium 273mg; Fibre 2.9g; Sodium 413mg.

BAKED TUNA WITH GOLDEN BROWN POTATOES

SEPTEMBER IS THE MONTH WHEN THE FISHERMEN ON THE ISLANDS LAND THEIR BIGGEST CATCHES OF TUNA, AND IS ALSO THE TIME WHEN THE LOCAL WOMEN ARE HARD AT WORK MAKING THIS DISH. IT IS OFTEN COOKED IN THE OUTSIDE OVENS OF THE LOCAL BAKERS.

SERVES FOUR

INGREDIENTS

- 105ml/7 tbsp extra virgin olive oil
- juice of 1 large lemon
- 3 garlic cloves, crushed
- 4 medium-thick tuna steaks, total weight about 800g/1¾lb
- 45ml/3 tbsp chopped fresh flat leaf parsley
- 15ml/1 tbsp fresh oregano or 5ml/1 tsp dried
- 500g/1¼lb potatoes, peeled and cut into small cubes
- 450g/1lb ripe tomatoes, peeled and chopped
- 150ml/¼ pint/⅔ cup hot water
- salt and ground black pepper
- fresh green salad tossed in olive oil, to serve

1 Mix the olive oil with the lemon juice and garlic, in a shallow dish that will hold all the tuna steaks in a single layer. Stir in salt and pepper, then add the tuna steaks. Sprinkle over the herbs and turn the steaks to coat them in the marinade. Leave to marinate for 1–2 hours. Lift the steaks out and lay them in a roasting pan.

2 Preheat the oven to 180°C/350°F/Gas 4. Drop the cubes of potato into the marinating dish and turn to coat them in the oil mixture. Arrange the potatoes around the tuna steaks, drizzle over any remaining marinade and sprinkle the chopped tomatoes on top. Pour the hot water into the roasting pan.

3 Bake the tuna for 40 minutes, turning it over halfway through and stirring the potatoes and other ingredients.

4 Lift the tuna out of the pan, leaving the other ingredients. Place on a heated platter and cover with foil to keep warm. Increase the oven temperature to 200°C/400°F/Gas 6 and add a little more hot water to the roasting pan.

5 Cook the potatoes for about 15 minutes more to brown them and make them crisp. Serve the tuna and potato mixture with a green salad.

Energy 556Kcal/2,330kJ; Protein 50.7g; Carbohydrate 24g, of which sugars 5.4g; Fat 29.3g, of which saturates 5.4g; Cholesterol 56mg; Calcium 73mg; Fibre 3g; Sodium 122mg.

POULTRY AND GAME

Recipes for poultry and game in Greece always include lots of other flavours: herbs, spices, fruit and nuts, and Mediterranean vegetables. Even the traditional roast will be accompanied by vegetables cooked in a rich and mouthwatering sauce created by the olive oil and juices from the meat.

Spicy Chicken Casserole with Red Wine

This is the traditional chicken dish on the islands. It is usually served with plain rice or orzo, the small tear-shaped pasta, which is called kritharaki *in Greek, but it is even better with thick home-made fried potatoes or homefries.*

SERVES FOUR

INGREDIENTS

- 75ml/5 tbsp extra virgin olive oil
- 1.6kg/3½lb organic or free-range chicken, jointed
- 1 large onion, peeled and roughly chopped
- 250ml/8fl oz/1 cup red wine
- 30ml/2 tbsp tomato purée (paste) diluted in 450ml/¾ pint/ scant 2 cups hot water
- 1 cinnamon stick
- 3 or 4 whole allspice
- 2 bay leaves
- salt and ground black pepper
- boiled rice, orzo or fried potatoes, to serve

1 Heat the olive oil in a large pan or sauté pan and brown the chicken pieces on all sides, ensuring that the skin is cooked and lifts away from the flesh slightly. Lift the chicken pieces out with tongs and set them aside on a plate, cover with another plate or with foil and keep them warm.

2 Add the chopped onion to the hot oil in the same pan and stir it over a medium heat until it becomes translucent.

VARIATION

If you have trouble finding this Greek pasta, you can use Italian pasta. Look for a small pasta shape, Long-grained rice can also be used instead of the pasta, if you prefer.

3 Return the chicken pieces to the pan, pour over the wine and cook for 2–3 minutes, until it has reduced. Add the tomato purée mixture, cinnamon, allspice and bay leaves. Season well with salt and pepper. Cover the pan and cook gently for 1 hour or until the chicken is tender. Serve with rice, orzo or fried potatoes.

Energy 669Kcal/2,775kJ; Protein 48.7g; Carbohydrate 5g, of which sugars 3.8g; Fat 45.9g, of which saturates 11.1g; Cholesterol 250mg; Calcium 37mg; Fibre 0.9g; Sodium 196mg.

CHARGRILLED CHICKEN WITH GARLIC AND PEPPERS

AN IMAGINATIVE MARINADE CAN MAKE ALL THE DIFFERENCE TO THE SOMETIMES BLAND FLAVOUR OF CHICKEN. THIS GARLICKY MARINADE, WITH MUSTARD AND CHILLI, GIVES TENDER CHICKEN A REAL PUNCH. MAKE SURE THE CHICKEN HAS PLENTY OF TIME TO ABSORB THE FLAVOURS BEFORE COOKING.

SERVES FOUR TO SIX

INGREDIENTS

- 1½ chickens, total weight about 2.25kg/5lb, jointed, or 12 chicken pieces
- 2 or 3 red or green (bell) peppers, quartered and seeded
- 4 or 5 ripe tomatoes, halved horizontally
- lemon wedges, to serve

For the marinade

- 90ml/6 tbsp extra virgin olive oil
- juice of 1 large lemon
- 5ml/1 tsp French mustard
- 4 garlic cloves, crushed
- 2 fresh red or green chillies, seeded and chopped
- 5ml/1 tsp dried oregano
- salt and ground black pepper

COOK'S TIP

You can, of course, cook these under the grill (broiler). Have the heat fairly high, but don't place the pieces of chicken too close to the heat. The chicken will probably need less time than when cooked over the coals – allow about 15 minutes each side.

1 If you are jointing the chicken yourself, divide the legs into two. Make a couple of slits in the deepest part of the flesh of each piece of chicken, using a small sharp knife. This will help the marinade to be absorbed more efficiently and will also let the chicken cook thoroughly.

2 Beat together all the marinade ingredients in a large bowl. Add the chicken pieces and turn them over to coat them thoroughly in the marinade. Cover the bowl with clear film (plastic wrap) and place in the refrigerator for 4–8 hours, turning the chicken pieces over in the marinade a couple of times, if possible.

3 Prepare the barbecue. When the coals are ready, lift the chicken pieces out of the marinade and place them on the grill. Add the pepper pieces and the tomatoes to the marinade and set it aside for 15 minutes. Grill the chicken pieces for 20–25 minutes. Watch them closely and move them away from the area where the heat is most fierce if they start to burn.

4 Turn the chicken pieces over and cook them for 20–25 minutes more. Meanwhile, thread the peppers on two long metal skewers. Add them to the barbecue grill, with the tomatoes, for the last 15 minutes of cooking. Remember to keep an eye on them and turn them over at least once. Serve with the lemon wedges.

Energy 760Kcal/3,156kJ; Protein 61.7g; Carbohydrate 11.1g, of which sugars 10.8g; Fat 52.2g, of which saturates 13.3g; Cholesterol 313mg; Calcium 40mg; Fibre 3.1g; Sodium 235mg.

Chicken with Figs and Mint

Grown all over Greece, figs make a rich sauce that complements meat and poultry. They are very popular in savoury dishes, providing a wonderful hearty sweetness which is often balanced out with sharper fruits such as lemon or orange.

SERVES FOUR

INGREDIENTS

- 500g/1¼lb/3¼ cups dried figs
- ½ bottle sweet, fruity white wine
- 4 chicken breast fillets, about 175–225g/6–8oz each, skinned or unskinned as preferred
- 15g/½oz/1 tbsp butter
- 50g/2oz/2 tbsp dark orange marmalade
- 10 fresh mint leaves, finely chopped, plus a few more to garnish
- juice of ½ lemon
- salt and ground black pepper
- a few sprigs of fresh mint, to garnish

1 Place the figs in a pan with the wine and bring to the boil, then simmer very gently for about 1 hour. Allow to cool and refrigerate overnight.

2 Fry the chicken breast fillets in the butter over a medium heat until they are cooked through and golden. Remove and keep warm.

3 Drain any fat from the pan and pour in the juice from the figs. Boil and reduce to about 150ml/¼ pint/⅔ cup.

4 Add the marmalade, mint and lemon juice, and simmer for a few minutes. When the sauce is thick and shiny, pour it over the chicken, garnish with figs and mint leaves, and serve.

Energy 460Kcal/1,941kJ; Protein 50.2g; Carbohydrate 38.4g, of which sugars 38.4g; Fat 6.2g, of which saturates 2.6g; Cholesterol 148mg; Calcium 168mg; Fibre 4.4g; Sodium 190mg.

Chicken Kebabs

These are a great favourite all over Greece, and taste wonderful flavoured with paprika, garlic and saffron. They are ideal for summer barbecues as they can be prepared and marinated in advance and are quick to cook.

SERVES SIX TO EIGHT

INGREDIENTS

- 1 large onion, grated
- 2 garlic cloves, crushed
- 120ml/4fl oz/½ cup extra virgin olive oil
- juice of 1 lemon
- 5ml/1 tsp paprika
- 2 or 3 saffron strands, soaked in 15ml/1 tbsp boiling water
- 2 young chickens
- salt and ground black pepper
- pitta bread and salad leaves, to serve

1 In a bowl, mix the onion, garlic, olive oil, lemon juice, paprika and soaked saffron strands, and season to taste with salt and pepper to make a marinade.

2 Cut the chickens into small pieces, removing the bone and skin if preferred, and place them into a shallow dish. Pour over the marinade, turning the chicken so that all the pieces are covered evenly. If you have boned the chicken, open the cuts and pour a little of the marinade into each one. Cover the bowl loosely with clear film (plastic wrap) and leave in a cool place to marinate for at least 2 hours.

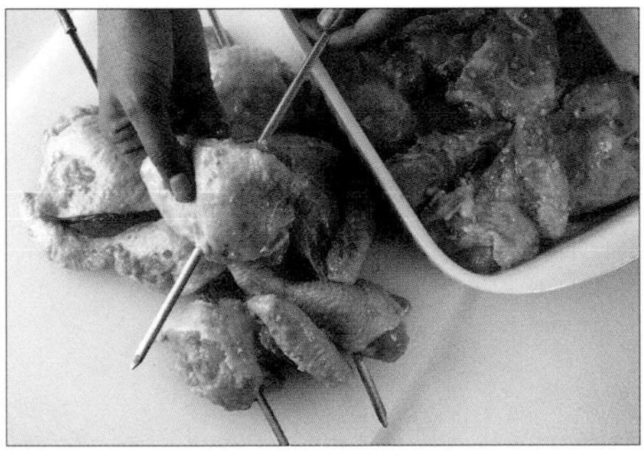

3 Thread the chicken on to long kebab skewers. Thread the wings on to the skewer twice or three times to open them out so they cook more evenly.

4 The kebabs can be barbecued or cooked under a moderately hot grill (broiler) for 10–15 minutes, turning once. If you are using a barbecue, make sure the coals are evenly spread and hot enough to cook the chicken pieces thoroughly without overly scorching the outside. The chicken is cooked when the juices run clear when the meat is pierced with a sharp knife. Serve with pitta bread and salad leaves.

Energy 329Kcal/1,362kJ; Protein 16.3g; Carbohydrate 2.6g, of which sugars 1.9g; Fat 28.2g, of which saturates 5.6g; Cholesterol 83mg; Calcium 14mg; Fibre 0.5g; Sodium 59mg.

Chicken and Apricot Filo Pie

Apricots grow in the fertile areas of Greece, such as along the coastline of Epirus, and are enjoyed in savoury as well as sweet dishes, such as this spicy chicken pie.

SERVES SIX

INGREDIENTS
- 75g/3oz/½ cup bulgur wheat
- 75g/3oz/6 tbsp butter
- 2 small onions, chopped
- 450g/1lb/2 cups minced (ground) chicken
- 50g/2oz/¼ cup ready-to-eat dried apricots, finely chopped
- 25g/1oz/¼ cup blanched almonds, chopped
- 5ml/1 tsp ground cinnamon
- 2.5ml/½ tsp ground allspice
- 50ml/2fl oz/¼ cup Greek (US strained plain) yogurt
- 15ml/1 tbsp chopped fresh chives
- 30ml/2 tbsp chopped fresh flat leaf parsley
- 6 large sheets filo pastry, thawed if frozen
- salt and ground black pepper
- chives, to garnish

1 Preheat the oven to 200°C/400°F/Gas 6. Put the bulgur wheat in a bowl with 120ml/4fl oz/½ cup boiling water. Soak for 5–10 minutes, or until the water is absorbed.

2 Heat 25g/1oz/2 tbsp of the butter in a pan, and gently fry the onions and chicken until pale golden.

3 Stir in the apricots, almonds and bulgur wheat and cook for a further 2 minutes.

4 Remove from the heat and stir in the cinnamon, allspice, yogurt, chives and parsley. Season to taste with salt and ground black pepper.

5 Melt the remaining butter in a pan. Unroll the filo pastry and cut into 25cm/10in rounds. Keep the pastry rounds covered with a clean, damp dish towel to prevent drying.

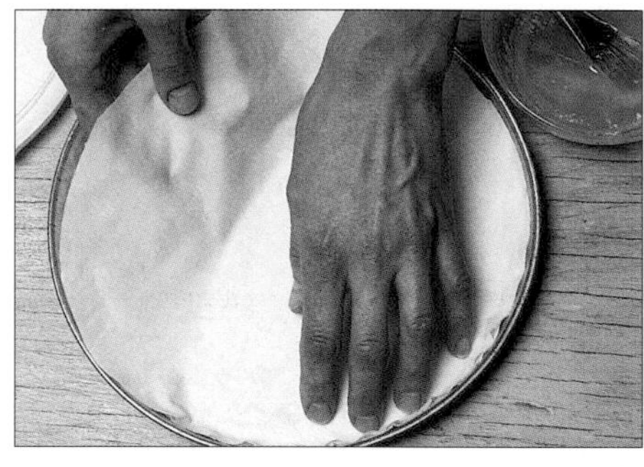

6 Line a 23cm/9in loose-based flan tin (pie pan) with three of the pastry rounds, brushing each one with butter as you layer them. Spoon in the chicken mixture, and cover with three more pastry rounds, brushed with melted butter as before.

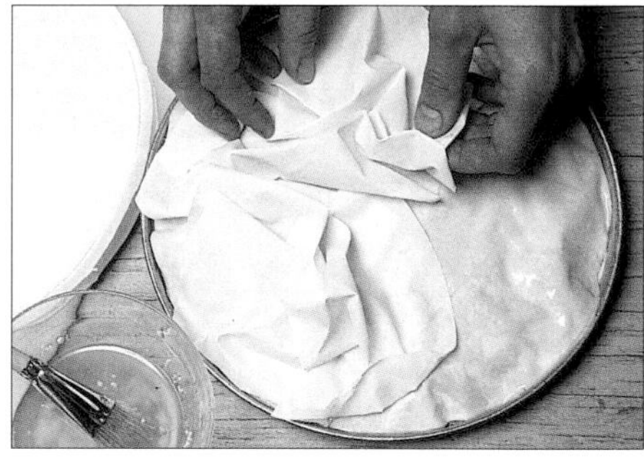

7 Crumple the remaining rounds of filo pastry and place them on top of the pie, then brush over any remaining melted butter. Bake the pie for about 30 minutes, or until the pastry is golden brown and crisp. Try not to open the oven door during the first 20 minutes as a sudden reduction in heat can affect the rising of the pastry. Serve the pie hot or cold, in wedges, and garnished with trimmed chives.

Energy 294Kcal/1230kJ; Protein 21.7g; Carbohydrate 17.6g, of which sugars 2.1g; Fat 15.8g, of which saturates 7.5g; Cholesterol 79mg; Calcium 62mg; Fibre 1.5g; Sodium 131mg.

Chicken Casserole with Olives

This is a very simple dish to prepare and cook, but with its typical Mediterranean undertones it is also full of flavour. It is delicious served with French fries or plain boiled rice, but it goes equally well with boiled new potatoes.

SERVES FOUR

INGREDIENTS

- 75ml/5 tbsp extra virgin olive oil
- 1 organic or free-range chicken, about 1.6kg/3½lb, jointed
- 3 or 4 shallots, finely chopped
- 2 carrots, sliced
- 1 celery stick, roughly chopped
- 2 garlic cloves, chopped
- juice of 1 lemon
- 300ml/½ pint/1¼ cups hot water
- 30ml/2 tbsp chopped flat leaf parsley
- 12 black or green olives
- salt and ground black pepper

1 Preheat the oven to 180°C/350°F/Gas 4. Heat the olive oil in a wide flameproof casserole and brown the chicken pieces on both sides. Lift them out and set them aside.

2 Add the shallots, carrots and celery to the oil remaining in the casserole and sauté them for a few minutes. Stir in the garlic. As soon as it becomes aromatic, return the chicken to the pan and pour the lemon juice over the mixture. Let it bubble for a few minutes, then add the water and season with salt and pepper.

3 Cover the casserole and bake for 1 hour, turning the chicken pieces over occasionally.

4 Remove the casserole from the oven and stir in the parsley and olives. Re-cover the casserole and return it to the oven for about 30 minutes more. Check that it is cooked by piercing with a sharp knife. The juices should run clear. Serve immediately.

Energy 726Kcal/3,008kJ; Protein 54.9g; Carbohydrate 3.8g, of which sugars 3.5g; Fat 54.5g, of which saturates 13.1g; Cholesterol 289mg; Calcium 55mg; Fibre 1.9g; Sodium 435mg.

ROAST CHICKEN WITH POTATOES AND LEMON

THIS IS A LOVELY, EASY DISH FOR A FAMILY MEAL. AS WITH OTHER GREEK ROASTS, EVERYTHING IS BAKED TOGETHER SO THAT THE POTATOES ABSORB ALL THE DIFFERENT FLAVOURS, ESPECIALLY THAT OF THE LEMON AND THE LOVELY JUICES AND FATS FROM THE CHICKEN.

SERVES FOUR

INGREDIENTS

- 1 organic or free-range chicken, about 1.6kg/3½lb
- 2 garlic cloves, peeled but left whole
- 15ml/1 tbsp chopped fresh thyme or oregano, or 5ml/1 tsp dried, plus 2 or 3 fresh sprigs of thyme or oregano
- 800g/1¾lb potatoes
- juice of 1 lemon
- 60ml/4 tbsp extra virgin olive oil
- 300ml/½ pint/1¼ cups hot water
- salt and ground black pepper

1 Preheat the oven to 200°C/400°F/ Gas 6. Place the chicken, breast-side down, in a large roasting pan, then tuck the garlic cloves and the fresh thyme or oregano sprigs inside and around the bird.

2 Peel the potatoes and quarter them lengthways. If they are very large, slice them lengthways into thinner pieces. Arrange the potatoes around the chicken, then pour the lemon juice over the chicken and potatoes.

3 Season the chicken and potatoes with salt and freshly ground black pepper. Drizzle the olive oil over the top and add about three-quarters of the fresh or dried chopped thyme or oregano. Pour the hot water into the roasting pan.

4 Roast the chicken and potatoes for 30 minutes, then remove the roasting pan from the oven and carefully turn the chicken over. Baste, season the bird with a little more salt and pepper, sprinkle over the remaining fresh or dried herbs, and add more hot water, if needed. Reduce the oven temperature to 190°C/375°F/Gas 5.

5 Return the chicken and potatoes to the oven and roast them for another hour, or slightly longer, by which time both the chicken and the potatoes will be a golden colour. Serve with a crisp leafy salad, if you like.

Energy 767Kcal/3,195kJ; Protein 53.3g; Carbohydrate 32.5g, of which sugars 2.9g; Fat 47.7g, of which saturates 11.8g; Cholesterol 264mg; Calcium 51mg; Fibre 2.6g; Sodium 206mg.

ROASTED CHICKEN WITH VEGETABLES

THIS IS A DELICIOUS ALTERNATIVE TO A TRADITIONAL ROAST CHICKEN. THE VEGETABLES BECOME SWEET AND TENDER WITH ROASTING, PROVIDING A WONDERFULLY TASTY AND MOIST ACCOMPANIMENT TO THE ROAST CHICKEN. USE AN ORGANIC, CORN-FED OR FREE-RANGE BIRD, IF AVAILABLE.

SERVES FOUR

INGREDIENTS
- 1.8–2kg/4–4½lb roasting chicken
- 150ml/¼ pint/⅔ cup extra virgin olive oil
- ½ lemon
- 450g/1lb small new potatoes
- 1 aubergine (eggplant), cut into 2.5cm/1in cubes
- 1 red (bell) pepper, seeded and quartered
- 1 fennel bulb, trimmed and quartered
- 8 large garlic cloves, unpeeled
- coarse salt and ground black pepper
- a few sprigs of fresh thyme, to garnish

1 Preheat the oven to 200°C/400°F/ Gas 6. Rub the chicken all over with extra virgin olive oil and season with freshly ground black pepper. Place the lemon wedges inside the bird, with a sprig or two of fresh thyme. Put the chicken, breast-side down, in a large roasting pan, and roast for about 30 minutes.

2 Remove the chicken from the oven and season generously with salt. Turn the chicken right side up, and baste with the juices from the pan. Surround the bird with the potatoes, and roll them in the pan juices, basting where necessary. Return the roasting pan to the oven to cook for a further 30 minutes.

3 Add the aubergine, red pepper, fennel and garlic cloves to the roasting pan. Drizzle with the remaining oil, and season with salt and pepper. Add any remaining thyme sprigs to the vegetables. Return to the oven, and cook for 30–50 minutes more, basting and turning the vegetables occasionally.

4 To check if the chicken is cooked, push the tip of a sharp knife between the thigh and breast. If the juices run clear, it is done. The vegetables should be tender when pierced with a sharp knife, and just beginning to turn a lovely golden brown. Garnish with sprigs of thyme and serve in the roasting dish or transfer to a platter, with the skimmed juices in a gravy boat.

Energy 903Kcal/3,751kJ; Protein 57.5g; Carbohydrate 22.8g, of which sugars 5.9g; Fat 65.2g, of which saturates 14.7g; Cholesterol 289mg; Calcium 44mg; Fibre 3.9g; Sodium 218mg.

BAKED CHICKEN WITH OKRA

OKRA – OR LADY'S FINGERS AS THEY ARE ALSO KNOWN – ARE CONSIDERED TO BE QUITE EXOTIC IN MANY COUNTRIES, BUT IN GREECE THIS VEGETABLE IS A SUMMER STAPLE. IT IS COOKED ON ITS OWN, OR CAN BE COMBINED WITH LAMB OR BEEF, AND TASTES DELICIOUS IN A CHICKEN CASSEROLE.

SERVES FOUR

INGREDIENTS

- 1.6kg/3½lb organic or free-range roasting chicken
- 90ml/6 tbsp extra virgin olive oil
- 5ml/1 tsp dried oregano
- 400g/14oz can plum tomatoes, roughly chopped
- 2 garlic cloves, chopped
- 450ml/¾ pint/scant 2 cups hot water
- 600g/1lb 6oz okra
- 45ml/3 tbsp chopped fresh flat leaf parsley
- salt and ground black pepper
- salad and fresh crusty bread, to serve

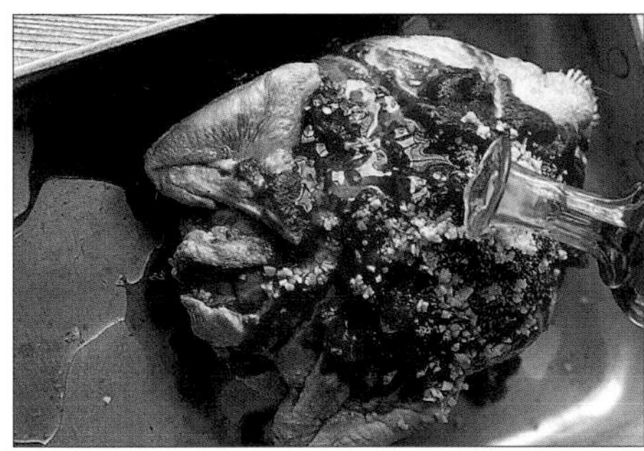

1 Preheat the oven to 200°C/400°F/Gas 6. Place the chicken breast-side down in a large roasting dish. Drizzle half the olive oil over it and sprinkle over half the dried oregano. Add the tomatoes, garlic and 300ml/½ pint/1¼ cups of the hot water to the dish. Transfer to the oven and bake for 30 minutes.

2 Meanwhile, prepare the okra. Leave each okra pod whole and use a small sharp knife to peel the conical end. Be careful not to nick the pod and release the mucilaginous juices. (You will soon get to grips with this task, but it is a good idea to get someone to help you.) Rinse the okra thoroughly in cold water and then drain them well. Repeat until the water appears clear.

3 After 30 minutes, remove the dish from the oven and turn the chicken over. Add the okra, spreading it evenly around the bird. Drizzle the remaining oil over, then sprinkle with the rest of the oregano. Season and add the parsley and the remaining hot water. Turn the okra with a spatula to coat it in the tomato sauce.

4 Reduce the oven temperature to 190°C/375°F/Gas 5 and bake the chicken for 1 hour more, or until it is fully cooked and the okra is tender. Baste the chicken and the okra occasionally during cooking.

5 This dish is best served hot, but will happily wait for 30 minutes. It makes the perfect main course accompanied by a salad and fresh crusty bread.

COOK'S TIP

If you buy a larger chicken, or use large okra pods, you may need to increase the cooking time. The chicken will be cooked when the joints move freely and the juices that flow, when the thickest part of the thigh is pierced with a knife, are clear and no longer pink.

Energy 740Kcal/3,070kJ; Protein 54.9g; Carbohydrate 7.9g, of which sugars 7.1g; Fat 54.4g, of which saturates 12.9g; Cholesterol 264mg; Calcium 286mg; Fibre 7.6g; Sodium 205mg.

Duck Breasts with a Walnut Sauce

Walnuts and pomegranates both grow in Greece and are used here to make an exotic sauce that is perfect with duck. Serve with rice or new potatoes, and a salad.

SERVES SIX

INGREDIENTS

- 60ml/4 tbsp olive oil
- 2 onions, very thinly sliced
- 2.5ml/½ tsp ground turmeric
- 400g/14oz/3½ cups walnuts, roughly chopped
- 1 litre/1¾ pints/4 cups duck or chicken stock
- 6 pomegranates
- 30ml/2 tbsp caster (superfine) sugar
- 60ml/4 tbsp lemon juice
- 4 duck breasts, about 225g/8oz each
- salt and ground black pepper

COOK'S TIP

Pomegranate juice stains, so take care when cutting them. Only the seeds are used in cooking; the pith is discarded.

1 Heat half the olive oil in a frying pan. Add the onions and turmeric, and cook gently until soft. Transfer to a pan, add the roughly chopped walnuts and stock, then season with salt and freshly ground black pepper. Stir well, then bring to the boil and simmer the mixture, uncovered, for 20 minutes, stirring occasionally.

2 Halve the pomegranates and scoop the seeds into a bowl. Reserve the seeds of one pomegranate. Process the remaining seeds in a blender or food processor. Strain through a sieve (strainer), to extract the juice, and stir in the sugar and lemon juice.

3 Score the skin of the duck breasts in a lattice pattern with a sharp knife. Heat the remaining oil in a frying pan or griddle and place the duck breasts in it, skin side down.

4 Cook gently for 10 minutes, pouring off the fat from time to time, until the skin is dark golden and crisp. Turn them over and cook for a further 3–4 minutes. Transfer to a plate and leave to rest.

5 Deglaze the frying pan or griddle with the pomegranate juice mixture, stirring with a wooden spoon, then add the walnut and stock mixture and simmer for 15 minutes, until the sauce has thickened slightly. Serve the duck breasts sliced, drizzled with a little sauce, and garnished with the reserved pomegranate seeds. Pass the remaining sauce around in a serving jug (pitcher) or bowl.

Energy 753Kcal/3,123kJ; Protein 40.2g; Carbohydrate 13.1g, of which sugars 11.5g; Fat 62.9g, of which saturates 6.7g; Cholesterol 165mg; Calcium 105mg; Fibre 3.4g; Sodium 173mg.

RABBIT CASSEROLE WITH BABY ONIONS

THIS TRADITIONAL STIFADO *IS A GOOD WAY TO TRANSFORM MILD-TASTING RABBIT INTO AN EXTREMELY APPETIZING DISH. SERVE WITH A GREEN SALAD TO COUNTERBALANCE ITS RICHNESS.*

SERVES FOUR

INGREDIENTS

- 175ml/6fl oz/¾ cup red wine
- 60ml/4 tbsp red wine vinegar
- 2 bay leaves, crushed
- 1 rabbit, jointed
- 45ml/3 tbsp plain (all-purpose) flour
- 90–105ml/6–7 tbsp extra virgin olive oil
- 2 carrots, cut in thick batons, about 10cm/4in in length
- 2 celery sticks, sliced
- 3 garlic cloves, halved lengthways
- 1 cinnamon stick
- 3–4 whole allspice
- 1–2 fresh rosemary sprigs, plus extra to garnish
- 15ml/1 tbsp tomato purée (paste) diluted in 300ml/½ pint/ 1¼ cups water
- 675g/1½lb small, pickling-size onions, peeled
- 15ml/1 tbsp demerara (raw) sugar
- salt and ground black pepper

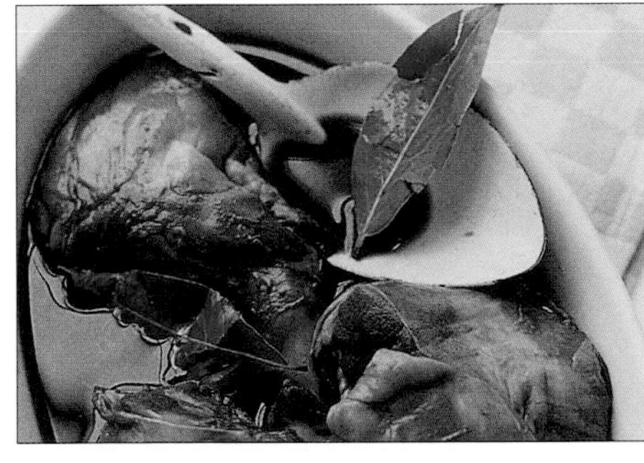

1 Mix together the wine and vinegar in a shallow dish that is large enough to hold the rabbit joints in a single layer. Add the bay leaves and rabbit, turning to coat them in the mixture. Marinate for 4–6 hours, or preferably overnight, turning the pieces over at least once.

2 Lift the rabbit joints out of the marinade and pat them dry with kitchen paper. Reserve the marinade. Coat the pieces of rabbit lightly with the flour.

3 Heat half of the oil in a large, heavy frying pan and add the pieces of rabbit. Fry, turning the pieces occasionally, until they are lightly browned on both sides. They must be in a single layer, so fry them in batches if necessary. Then place them in a flameproof casserole.

4 Preheat the oven to 160°C/325°F/ Gas 3. Add the carrots and celery to the oil remaining in the frying pan. Sauté the vegetables over a gentle heat for about 3 minutes. Add the garlic. As soon as it becomes aromatic, add the contents of the pan to the rabbit joints in the casserole.

5 Place the casserole over a medium heat. Pour in the reserved marinade and let the wine bubble and evaporate. Add the spices, fresh rosemary sprigs and the tomato purée mixture. Stir well, cover and cook in the oven for 1 hour.

6 Heat the remaining oil in the frying pan and sauté the onions in batches until they start to turn light golden. Sprinkle with the demerara sugar, shake the pan, then let them brown and caramelize for 5–6 minutes more.

7 When the rabbit has cooked for an hour, spread the onions on top and add enough hot water almost to cover them. Cover the casserole, return it to the oven and cook for a further 1 hour. Serve with sprigs of rosemary.

Energy 449Kcal/1,874kJ; Protein 30.6g; Carbohydrate 28.7g, of which sugars 16.2g; Fat 21.1g, of which saturates 4.5g; Cholesterol 104mg; Calcium 126mg; Fibre 3.6g; Sodium 95mg.

MEAT DISHES

Tender roasted lamb surrounded with garlic and vegetables, minced meat formed into tasty meatballs or used to fill fresh vegetables, barbecued, grilled or braised cuts of succulent meat – Greek meat dishes are full of flavour.

Fried Meatballs

No Greek celebration or party is complete without keftedes. *They are always a must on the meze table, as they are so appetizing and popular with all the family. Alternatively, they make a luxurious addition to a simple meal such as soup.*

SERVES FOUR

INGREDIENTS
- 2 medium slices of white or wholemeal bread, crusts removed
- 500g/1¼lb/2½ cups minced (ground) lamb or beef
- 1 large onion, peeled and grated
- 5ml/1 tsp each dried thyme and oregano
- 45ml/3 tbsp chopped fresh flat leaf parsley, plus extra sprigs to garnish
- 1 egg, lightly beaten
- salt and ground black pepper
- lemon wedges, to serve (optional)

For frying
- 25g/1oz/¼ cup plain (all-purpose) flour
- 30–45ml/2–3 tbsp pure vegetable oil

1 Soak the slices of bread in a bowl of water for about 10 minutes, then drain. With your hands, squeeze the bread dry before placing it in a large bowl. Add the minced meat, grated onion, dried herbs, fresh parsley, egg, salt and pepper to the bread. Mix it all together, preferably using your hands, until well blended.

2 Shape the meat mixture into walnut-size balls and roll them in the flour to give them a light coating, shaking off any excess.

3 Heat the oil in a large frying pan. Add the meatballs, turning frequently, until they are cooked through. Lift out and drain on kitchen paper. Serve with chopped parsley and lemon wedges.

VARIATION

The meatballs can also be baked for 20 minutes at 190°C/375°F/Gas 5. To finish, cover the meatballs with a mix of 350g/12oz/1½ cups Greek (US strained plain) yogurt with 2 beaten eggs and 15ml/1 tbsp vinegar, and cook for a further 15 minutes.

Energy 375Kcal/1,565kJ; Protein 27.7g; Carbohydrate 13g, of which sugars 1.6g; Fat 24g, of which saturates 8.8g; Cholesterol 144mg; Calcium 78mg; Fibre 1.2g; Sodium 178mg.

MEATBALLS IN RICH TOMATO SAUCE

THIS IS A PRACTICAL ALL-IN-ONE DISH THAT IS VERY EASY TO MAKE. THERE ARE DIFFERENT VERSIONS OF YIOUVARLAKIA, OR MEATBALLS. THIS ONE, WITH ITS RICH TOMATO SAUCE, IS IDEAL IN THE AUTUMN AS IT SEEMS TO BRING BACK ECHOES OF SUMMER WITH ITS SWEETNESS.

SERVES FOUR

INGREDIENTS

- 500g/1¼lb/2½ cups minced (ground) beef or lamb
- 1 onion, grated
- 1 egg, lightly beaten
- 50g/2oz/generous ⅓ cup short grain rice
- 45ml/3 tbsp chopped flat leaf parsley
- finely grated rind of ½ orange, plus extra to garnish (optional)
- extra virgin olive oil, for frying
- salt and freshly ground black pepper
- fresh crusty bread, to serve

For the sauce

- 60ml/4 tbsp extra virgin olive oil
- 1 onion, thinly sliced
- 3–4 fresh sage leaves, finely sliced
- 400g/14oz can tomatoes
- 300ml/½ pint/1¼ cups beef stock or hot water

1 Put the meat in a bowl and add the onion, egg, rice and parsley. Add the grated orange rind to the mixture with salt and pepper. Mix all the ingredients well, then shape the mixture into round balls or small sausage shapes.

2 Heat some olive oil in a large, flat frying pan over a medium heat. When the oil is hot, add the sausages one by one, gently rolling them over to brown the outsides. Take care not to break up the sausages as they can be quite fragile at this stage. Brown around the edges and then remove and set aside.

3 To make the sauce, heat the oil in a wide pan that will take the meatballs in one layer. Sauté the onion slices until they just start to become golden. Add the sage, then the tomatoes, breaking them up with a wooden spoon.

4 Simmer for a few minutes, then add the stock or water, turn up the heat and bring to the boil.

5 Lower the meatballs gently into the sauce. Do not stir but rotate the pan to coat them evenly. Take care not to break them up.

6 Season with salt and freshly ground black pepper, then cover the pan and simmer for about 30 minutes, or until the sauce has thickened. Transfer to a serving platter and sprinkle over a little orange rind to garnish, if you like. Serve with lots of crusty bread to mop up all the juices.

Energy 475Kcal/1,972kJ; Protein 28.5g; Carbohydrate 15.8g, of which sugars 5.1g; Fat 33.2g, of which saturates 10.7g; Cholesterol 123mg; Calcium 58mg; Fibre 2g; Sodium 131mg.

SPRING LAMB CASSEROLE WITH FRESH PEAS

In Greece, milk-fed lamb is at its best in April and May, which is about the time when fresh peas put in an appearance in the markets. Young peas play an important role in many Greek spring recipes. Here, peas and lamb are combined to produce one of the most delicious Greek dishes – a real treat.

SERVES FOUR TO SIX

INGREDIENTS
- 75ml/5 tbsp extra virgin olive oil
- 4–6 thick shoulder of lamb steaks, with the bone in
- 1 large onion, thinly sliced
- 5 or 6 spring onions (scallions), roughly chopped
- 2 carrots, sliced in rounds
- juice of 1 lemon
- 1.2kg/2½lb fresh peas in pods, shelled (this will yield about 500–675g/1¼–1½lb peas)
- 60ml/4 tbsp finely chopped fresh dill
- salt and ground black pepper

1 Heat the olive oil in a wide, heavy pan. Brown the lamb on both sides. Lift the pieces out, and set them to one side.

2 Sauté the onion slices in the oil remaining in the pan until they are translucent. Add the chopped spring onions and, 1 minute later, the sliced carrots. Sauté for 3–4 minutes, until slightly tender.

COOK'S TIP

In Greek cooking, meat is always cooked well so that it is tender and almost falling away from the bone.

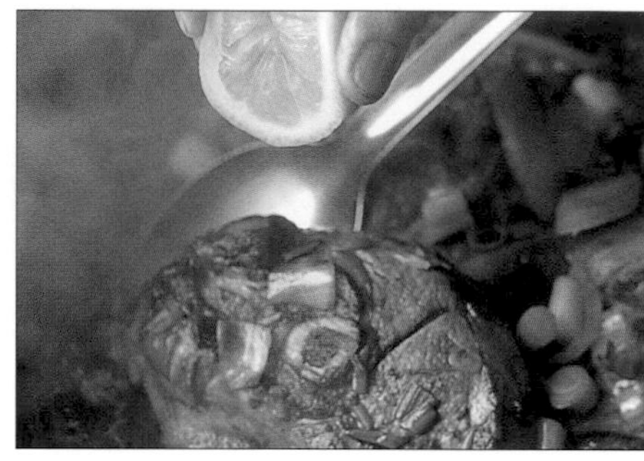

3 Return the lamb steaks to the pan, pour the lemon juice over them and let it evaporate for a few seconds. Pour over enough hot water to cover the meat. Add salt and pepper. Cover and simmer for 45–50 minutes, or until the meat is almost tender, turning the steaks over and stirring the vegetables from time to time.

4 Add the peas and half the dill, with a little more water, if needed. Replace the lid and cook for 20–30 minutes, or until the meat and vegetables are fully cooked. Sprinkle the remaining dill over the casserole just before serving.

Energy 858Kcal/3,551kJ; Protein 40.2g; Carbohydrate 29g, of which sugars 11.8g; Fat 65.6g, of which saturates 26.9g; Cholesterol 119mg; Calcium 79mg; Fibre 10.2g; Sodium 132mg.

LAMB AND COS LETTUCE CASSEROLE

One of the classic Greek dishes, this is found on the islands and the mainland from the Ionian to the Aegean Sea. It is a favourite treat during the period following Easter, when young lambs are at their best and lettuces and fresh dill are to be found in abundance in open-air street markets.

SERVES FOUR TO SIX

INGREDIENTS

- 45ml/3 tbsp olive oil
- 1 onion, chopped
- 1kg/2¼lb boned leg of lamb, sliced into 4–6 medium steaks
- 2 cos or romaine lettuces, coarsely shredded
- 6 spring onions (scallions), sliced
- 60ml/4 tbsp roughly chopped fresh dill, plus extra to garnish (optional)
- 2 eggs
- 15ml/1 tbsp cornflour (cornstarch) mixed to a paste with 120ml/4fl oz/ ½ cup water
- juice of 1 lemon
- salt

1 Heat the olive oil in a large, heavy pan. Add the chopped onion and sauté for 3–5 minutes, until translucent.

2 Increase the heat, add the lamb steaks and cook, turning them over frequently, until all the moisture has been driven off, a process that will take about 15 minutes. Add salt to taste and enough hot water to cover the meat. Cover the pan and simmer for about 1 hour, or until the meat is just tender.

3 Add the lettuces, spring onions and dill. If necessary, pour in a little more hot water so that all the vegetables are almost covered. Replace the pan lid and simmer for 15–20 minutes more. Remove from the heat and leave the dish to stand for 5 minutes.

4 Beat the eggs lightly in a bowl, add the cornflour mixture and beat until smooth. Add the lemon juice and whisk briefly, then continue to whisk while gradually adding 75–90ml/5–6 tbsp of the hot liquid from the pan containing the lamb.

5 Pour the sauce over the meat. Do not stir; instead gently shake and rotate the pan until the sauce is incorporated with the remaining liquid. Return the pan to a gentle heat for 2–3 minutes, just long enough to warm the sauce through. Do not let it boil, or the sauce is likely to curdle. Serve on warmed plates and sprinkle over some extra chopped dill, if you like.

Energy 598Kcal/2,497kJ; Protein 53.8g; Carbohydrate 7.1g, of which sugars 3.2g; Fat 39.8g, of which saturates 15.1g; Cholesterol 285mg; Calcium 95mg; Fibre 1.9g; Sodium 260mg.

GRILLED SKEWERED LAMB

Lamb still makes the best SOUVLAKIA *– kebabs – but in Greece this has now largely been replaced by pork, which is considerably cheaper. Unfortunately, the taste has suffered, as there is nothing to match the succulence and flavour of barbecued lamb.* SOUVLAKIA *are at their best served with* TZATSIKI, *a large tomato salad and barbecued bread.*

SERVES FOUR TO SIX

INGREDIENTS

- 1 small shoulder of lamb, boned and with most of the fat removed
- 2 or 3 onions, preferably red onions, quartered
- 2 red or green (bell) peppers, quartered and seeded
- 75ml/5 tbsp extra virgin olive oil
- juice of 1 lemon
- 2 garlic cloves, crushed
- 5ml/1 tsp dried oregano
- 2.5ml/½ tsp dried thyme or some sprigs of fresh thyme
- salt and ground black pepper

1 Put the olive oil, lemon juice, crushed garlic and herbs in a large bowl. Season with salt and pepper and whisk well to combine. Add the meat cubes, stirring to coat them in the mixture.

2 Cover the bowl tightly and leave to marinate for 4–8 hours in the refrigerator, stirring several times.

3 Separate the onion quarters into pieces, each composed of two or three layers, and slice each pepper quarter in half widthways.

4 Lift out the meat cubes, reserving the marinade, and thread them on to long metal skewers, alternating each piece of meat with a piece of pepper and a piece of onion. Lay them across a grill pan or baking tray and brush them with the reserved marinade.

5 Preheat a grill (broiler) until hot, or prepare a barbecue. Cook the *souvlakia* under a medium to high heat or over the hot coals for 10 minutes, until they start to become scorched. If using the grill, do not place them too close to the heat source. Turn the skewers over, brush again with the marinade (or a little olive oil) and cook for 10–15 minutes more. Serve immediately.

COOK'S TIPS

- Ask your butcher to trim the meat and cut it into 4cm/1½in cubes. A little fat is desirable with *souvlakia*, as it keeps them moist and succulent during cooking. If you prefer, you can use 4–5 best end neck (cross rib) fillets instead of shoulder.
- If you are barbecuing the *souvlakia* you may need to cook them for slightly longer, depending on the intensity of the heat.

Energy 415Kcal/1,724kJ; Protein 31.2g; Carbohydrate 9.6g, of which sugars 8.1g; Fat 28.2g, of which saturates 8.8g; Cholesterol 138mg; Calcium 31mg; Fibre 2.1g; Sodium 86mg.

BAKED LAMB WITH TOMATOES, GARLIC AND PASTA

A lamb YIOUVETSI *is undoubtedly very special in Greece. It is one of the most popular dishes and is often made for the auspicious celebratory family lunch on 15 August, an important date in the Greek Orthodox calendar as it marks the Feast of the Assumption of the Virgin Mary and the end of the long fasting period through the summer months.*

SERVES SIX

INGREDIENTS

1 shoulder of lamb, most of the fat removed, sliced into serving portions
600g/1lb 6oz ripe tomatoes, peeled and chopped, or 400g/14oz can chopped plum tomatoes
4 or 5 garlic cloves, chopped
75ml/5 tbsp extra virgin olive oil
5ml/1 tsp dried oregano
1 litre/1¾ pints/4 cups hot water
400g/14oz/3½ cups orzo pasta, or spaghetti, broken into short lengths
salt and ground black pepper
50g/2oz/½ cup freshly grated Kefalotiri or Parmesan cheese, to serve

VARIATION

The dish can also be made with young goat (kid) or beef, but these have to be boiled first.

1 Preheat the oven to 190°C/375°F/Gas 5. Rinse the meat to remove any obvious bone splinters, and place it in a large roasting pan.

2 Add the fresh or canned tomatoes, and the crushed garlic, extra virgin olive oil and dried oregano. Season with salt and freshly ground black pepper and stir in 300ml/½ pint/1¼ cups of the hot water.

3 Place the lamb in the oven and bake for about 1 hour 10 minutes, basting and turning the meat twice.

4 Remove the lamb from the oven and reduce the oven temperature to 180°C/350°F/Gas 4. Add the remaining 700ml/scant 1¼ pints/2¾ cups hot water to the roasting pan. Stir in the pasta and add more seasoning.

5 Mix well, return the roasting pan to the oven and bake for 30–40 minutes more, stirring occasionally, until the meat is fully cooked and tender, and the pasta feels soft.

6 Serve immediately, with a bowl of grated cheese to be sprinkled over individual portions.

COOK'S TIPS

- As *yiouvetsi* is quite a rich dish, it is a good idea to accompany it with a salad, to refresh the palate.
- If possible, use ripe vine tomatoes, as it is their flavour that really makes the difference.

Energy 528Kcal/2,222kJ; Protein 31.8g; Carbohydrate 52.5g, of which sugars 5.3g; Fat 22.7g, of which saturates 7.8g; Cholesterol 100mg; Calcium 131mg; Fibre 2.9g; Sodium 156mg.

MOUSSAKA

ALTHOUGH FETA IS PERHAPS THEIR BEST-KNOWN CHEESE, THE GREEKS HAVE A NUMBER OF OTHERS THAT CAN BE USED IN COOKING. KEFALOTIRI, A HARD CHEESE MADE WITH SHEEP'S OR GOAT'S MILK, MAKES THE PERFECT TOPPING FOR A CLASSIC MOUSSAKA.

SERVES SIX

INGREDIENTS

- 2 large aubergines (eggplants), thinly sliced
- 45ml/3 tbsp olive oil
- 675g/1½lb/3 cups lean minced (ground) beef
- 1 onion, chopped
- 2 garlic cloves, crushed
- 2 large fresh tomatoes, chopped, or 200g/7oz canned chopped tomatoes
- 120ml/4fl oz/½ cup dry white wine
- 45ml/3 tbsp chopped fresh parsley
- 45ml/3 tbsp fresh breadcrumbs
- 2 egg whites
- salt and ground black pepper

For the topping

- 40g/1½oz/3 tbsp butter
- 40g/1½oz/⅓ cup plain (all-purpose) flour
- 400ml/14fl oz/1⅔ cups milk
- 2.5ml/½ tsp freshly grated nutmeg
- 150g/5oz/1¼ cups grated Kefalotiri cheese
- 2 egg yolks, plus 1 whole egg

1 Layer the aubergines in a colander, sprinkling each layer with salt. Drain over a sink for 20 minutes, then rinse the salt off thoroughly and pat dry with kitchen paper.

VARIATION

Use sliced par-boiled potatoes instead of the aubergines and substitute grated mature Cheddar or Gruyère for the Kefalotiri.

2 Preheat the oven to 190°C/375°F/ Gas 5. Spread out the aubergines in a roasting pan. Brush them with olive oil, then bake for 10 minutes, or until just softened. Remove and cool. Leave the oven on.

3 Make the meat sauce. Heat the olive oil in a large pan and brown the minced beef, stirring frequently. When the meat is.no longer pink and looks crumbly, add the onion and garlic, and cook for 5 minutes.

4 Add the chopped fresh or canned tomatoes to the pan and stir in the wine. Season with plenty of salt and pepper to taste.

5 Bring to the boil, then lower the heat, cover and simmer for 15 minutes. Remove the pan from the heat, leave to cool for about 10 minutes, then stir in the chopped parsley, fresh breadcrumbs and egg whites.

6 Lightly grease a large baking dish, then spread out half the sliced aubergines in an even layer on the base. Spoon over the meat sauce, spread it evenly, then top with the remaining aubergines.

7 To make the topping, put the butter, flour and milk in a pan. Bring to the boil over a low heat, whisking all the time until the mixture thickens to form a smooth, creamy sauce. Lower the heat and simmer for 2 minutes. Remove the pan from the heat, season, then stir in the nutmeg and half the cheese.

8 Cool for 5 minutes, then beat in the egg yolks and the whole egg. Pour the sauce over the aubergine topping and sprinkle with the remaining cheese. Bake for 30–40 minutes, or until golden brown. Allow the dish to stand for 10 minutes before serving.

Energy 588Kcal/2,444kJ; Protein 37.9g; Carbohydrate 14.8g, of which sugars 3.7g; Fat 40.9g, of which saturates 18.2g; Cholesterol 206mg; Calcium 379mg; Fibre 2.4g; Sodium 506mg.

ROAST LAMB WITH FIGS

LAMB FILLET IS AN EXPENSIVE CUT OF MEAT, BUT BECAUSE IT IS VERY LEAN THERE IS VERY LITTLE WASTE. TO MAKE A MORE ECONOMICAL VERSION OF THIS DISH, YOU CAN USE LEG OF LAMB INSTEAD. IT HAS A STRONGER FLAVOUR BUT IS EQUALLY GOOD. SERVE WITH STEAMED GREEN BEANS.

SERVES SIX

INGREDIENTS

- 30ml/2 tbsp extra virgin olive oil
- 1kg/2¼lb lamb fillet, trimmed of excess fat
- 9 fresh figs
- 150ml/¼ pint/⅔ cup ruby port
- salt and ground black pepper
- a few sprigs of fresh parsley, to garnish
- new potatoes and green beans, to serve

1 Preheat the oven to 190°C/375°F/Gas 5. Heat the olive oil in a large roasting pan over a medium heat until the oil is hot and sizzling.

2 Fry the lamb fillet and sear on all sides until evenly browned.

3 Cut the fresh figs in half and arrange them around the lamb. Season the lamb with salt and ground black pepper and roast in the oven for 30 minutes. Pour the port over the figs.

4 Return the lamb to the oven for a further 30–45 minutes. The meat should be slightly pink in the centre.

5 Transfer the lamb to a board and leave to rest for about 5 minutes. Carve into slices, garnish with parsley and serve with new potatoes and green beans.

Energy 517Kcal/2,170kJ; Protein 35.4g; Carbohydrate 41.1g, of which sugars 41.1g; Fat 23.6g, of which saturates 9.2g; Cholesterol 127mg; Calcium 204mg; Fibre 5.7g; Sodium 191mg.

ROAST LAMB WITH POTATOES AND GARLIC

In the old days, Greek homes did not have ovens, so the food was sent to the local baker in the morning and collected at lunchtime. As the meat and vegetables were cooked together with herbs, olives and water, the meal was beautifully moist and flavourful.

SERVES SIX TO EIGHT

INGREDIENTS

- 1 whole leg of lamb, about 2kg/4½lb
- 3 garlic cloves, quartered lengthways, plus 6–8 whole, unpeeled garlic cloves, or 1 or 2 heads of garlic, halved
- 900g/2lb potatoes, peeled and quartered lengthways
- juice of 1 lemon
- 45ml/3 tbsp extra virgin olive oil
- 450ml/¾ pint/scant 2 cups hot water
- 5ml/1 tsp dried Greek oregano
- 2.5ml/½ tsp dried Greek thyme or 5ml/1 tsp chopped fresh thyme
- salt and ground black pepper
- a few sprigs of fresh thyme, to garnish

1 Preheat the oven to 220°C/425°F/ Gas 7. Place the lamb in a large roasting pan. Make several incisions in the meat, pressing the point of a sharp knife deep into the flesh, and insert one or two quartered pieces of peeled garlic into each one.

2 Arrange the quartered potatoes and whole garlic cloves or halved heads of garlic around the meat. Pour over the lemon juice and extra virgin olive oil. Add half the water to the dish, pouring it around the lamb and not on to it. Sprinkle over half the dried Greek oregano and thyme. Season with salt and freshly ground black pepper.

3 Roast the lamb for 15 minutes on the high heat, then reduce the oven temperature to 190°C/375°F/Gas 5. Roast for 1 hour, basting occasionally.

4 After an hour, turn the meat over so that the other side browns as well, sprinkle over the rest of the herbs and seasoning, and turn the potatoes over gently. Add the remaining hot water to the pan and cook for another 25–30 minutes, basting occasionally with the pan juices.

5 Cover the meat with a clean dish towel and rest it for 10 minutes before serving. The cloves of garlic can be popped out of their skins and eaten with the meat; they make a deliciously creamy accompaniment.

Energy 750Kcal/3,132kJ; Protein 73.4g; Carbohydrate 24.3g, of which sugars 2.1g; Fat 40.4g, of which saturates 17.3g; Cholesterol 273mg; Calcium 37mg; Fibre 1.8g; Sodium 175mg.

LAMB SHANKS WITH CANNELLINI BEANS

EARTHY AND SUBSTANTIAL, THIS IS THE IDEAL DISH FOR CHILLY AUTUMN EVENINGS. THE BEANS ACQUIRE LAYERS OF TASTE WHEN SLOW-COOKED IN THE RICH SAUCE PROVIDED BY THE MEAT. A CLEAN-TASTING, LEMON-DRESSED SALAD IS ALL IT NEEDS AS AN ACCOMPANIMENT.

SERVES FOUR TO SIX

INGREDIENTS
- 4 lamb shanks
- 45ml/3 tbsp plain (all-purpose) flour
- 45ml/3 tbsp extra virgin olive oil
- 1 large onion, chopped
- 2 garlic cloves, sliced
- 1 celery stick, sliced
- 1 carrot, sliced
- leaves from 2 fresh rosemary sprigs
- 2 bay leaves
- 175ml/6fl oz/¾ cup white wine
- 30ml/2 tbsp tomato purée (paste)
- 225g/8oz/1¼ cups dried cannellini beans, soaked overnight in water to cover
- 150ml/¼ pint/⅔ cup hot water
- salt and ground black pepper

1 Preheat the oven to 160°C/325°F/Gas 3. Season the lamb shanks and coat them lightly in flour. Heat the oil in a large flameproof casserole over a high heat and brown the meat on all sides. Lift them out and set them aside.

2 Add the onion to the oil remaining in the casserole and sauté gently. As soon as it is light golden, stir in the garlic, celery, carrot, rosemary and bay leaves.

3 Put the meat back in the pan and pour the wine slowly over it. Let it bubble and reduce, then stir in the tomato purée diluted in 450ml/¾ pint/scant 2 cups hot water. Drain the soaked beans and add them to the pan with black pepper to taste. Mix well. Cover the casserole, transfer it to the oven and bake for 1 hour. Stir in salt to taste and add the hot water. Cover and cook for 1 hour more, or until tender.

Energy 588Kcal/2,465kJ; Protein 43.9g; Carbohydrate 39.9g, of which sugars 6.7g; Fat 26.2g, of which saturates 9.1g; Cholesterol 114mg; Calcium 110mg; Fibre 10.5g; Sodium 161mg.

Greek Lamb Sausages with Tomato Sauce

The Greek name for these sausages is souzoukakia. They are more like elongated meatballs than the type of sausage we are accustomed to. They can be served with pasta, rice or fresh, crusty bread, accompanied by a green or mixed salad.

SERVES FOUR

INGREDIENTS

- 50g/2oz/1 cup fresh breadcrumbs
- 150ml/¼ pint/⅔ cup milk
- 675g/1½lb/3 cups minced (ground) lamb
- 30ml/2 tbsp grated onion
- 3 garlic cloves, crushed
- 10ml/2 tsp ground cumin
- 30ml/2 tbsp chopped fresh flat leaf parsley
- flour, for dusting
- olive oil, for frying
- 600ml/1 pint/2½ cups passata (bottled, strained tomatoes)
- 5ml/1 tsp sugar
- 2 bay leaves
- 1 small onion, peeled
- salt and ground black pepper
- a few sprigs of fresh flat leaf parsley, to garnish

1 Mix together the breadcrumbs and milk. Add the minced lamb, onion, garlic, cumin and chopped parsley and season well with salt and freshly ground black pepper.

2 Shape the mixture with your hands into little fat sausages, about 5cm/2in long, and roll them in flour. Heat about 60ml/4 tbsp olive oil in a frying pan.

3 Fry the sausages for about 8 minutes, turning them frequently until they are evenly browned all over. Remove from the pan and drain on a plate covered with a few sheets of kitchen paper.

4 Put the passata, sugar, bay leaves and whole onion in a pan and simmer for 20 minutes. Add the sausages and cook for 10 minutes more. Serve garnished with parsley.

VARIATION

The sausages can also be made with minced (ground) beef.

Energy 477Kcal/1,990kJ; Protein 35.3g; Carbohydrate 13.8g, of which sugars 3.8g; Fat 31.6g, of which saturates 12.1g; Cholesterol 132mg; Calcium 98mg; Fibre 0.7g; Sodium 229mg.

KLEFTIKO

FOR THIS TRADITIONAL GREEK CLASSIC, MARINATED LAMB STEAKS OR CHOPS ARE SLOW-COOKED TO DEVELOP AN UNBEATABLE, MELTINGLY TENDER FLAVOUR. THE DISH IS SEALED, LIKE A PIE, WITH A FLOUR DOUGH LID TO TRAP SUCCULENCE AND FLAVOUR, ALTHOUGH A TIGHT-FITTING FOIL COVER, IF LESS ATTRACTIVE, WILL SERVE EQUALLY WELL.

SERVES FOUR

INGREDIENTS

- juice of 1 lemon
- 15ml/1 tbsp chopped fresh oregano or mint
- 4 lamb leg steaks or chump chops with bones
- 30ml/2 tbsp extra virgin olive oil
- 2 large onions, thinly sliced
- 2 bay leaves
- 150ml/¼ pint/⅔ cup dry white wine
- 225g/8oz/2 cups plain (all-purpose) flour
- salt and freshly ground black pepper

COOK'S TIP

They are not absolutely essential for this dish, but lamb steaks or chops with bones will provide lots of additional flavour. As the bones cook they will slowly add to the taste. Boiled potatoes with extra virgin olive oil make a delicious accompaniment to the dish.

1 Mix the lemon juice, oregano and seasoning, and brush over the lamb.

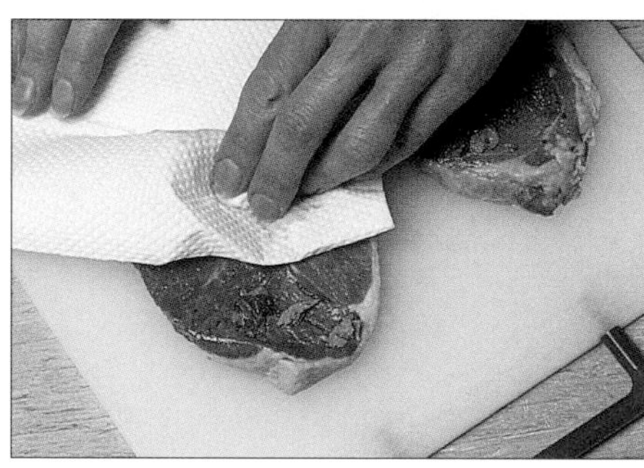

2 Leave to marinate for 4 hours. Then drain the lamb, reserving the marinade, and pat dry with kitchen paper.

3 Preheat the oven to 160°C/325°F/ Gas 3. Heat the olive oil in a large frying pan and fry the lamb over a high heat until browned on both sides.

4 Transfer the lamb to a shallow pie dish, forming an even layer over the base of the dish.

5 Sprinkle the thinly sliced onions and bay leaves around and over the lamb, then pour over the dry white wine and the reserved marinade.

6 Mix the flour with sufficient water to make a firm dough, kneading it to ensure a good consistency.

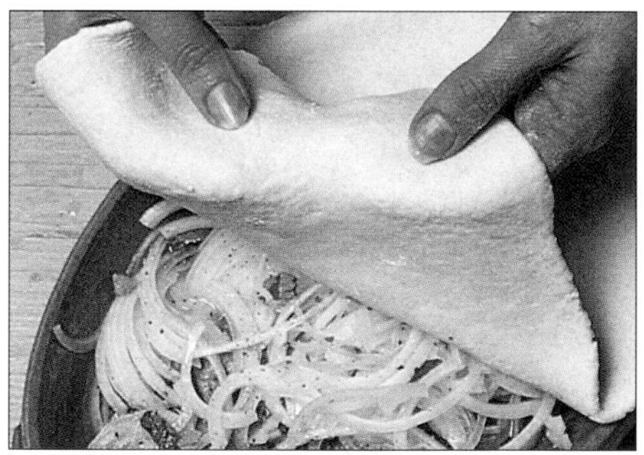

7 Moisten the rim of the pie dish. Roll out the dough on a floured surface so that it is large enough to cover the dish, and roughly cut it into the shape of your dish. Place it over the dish and secure so that it is tightly sealed.

8 Bake for 2 hours, then break away the dough crust and serve the lamb hot, with boiled potatoes.

Energy 658Kcal/2,760kJ; Protein 57.9g; Carbohydrate 53.8g, of which sugars 8.1g; Fat 22.2g, of which saturates 7.2g; Cholesterol 184mg; Calcium 149mg; Fibre 3.5g; Sodium 130mg.

LAMB-STUFFED SQUASH

ACORN SQUASH ARE PERFECT FOR BAKING WITH FILLINGS. HERE, A MELANGE OF LAMB, RICE AND FETA CHEESE IS TOPPED WITH A RICH AND CREAMY TOMATO SAUCE.

SERVES SIX

INGREDIENTS
- 6 acorn squash, halved
- 45ml/3 tbsp lemon juice
- 25g/1oz/2 tbsp butter
- 30ml/2 tbsp plain (all-purpose) flour
- 250ml/8fl oz/1 cup whipping cream
- 175ml/6fl oz/¾ cup passata (bottled strained tomatoes)
- 115g/4oz feta cheese, crumbled, and basil leaves, to garnish, plus extra to serve

For the filling
- 350–450g/12–16oz cooked lean lamb
- 175g/6oz/1½ cups cooked long grain rice
- 25g/1oz/2 tbsp butter, melted
- 25g/1oz/½ cup fresh breadcrumbs
- 50ml/2fl oz/¼ cup milk
- 30ml/2 tbsp finely grated onion
- 30ml/2 tbsp chopped fresh parsley
- 2 eggs, beaten
- salt and ground black pepper

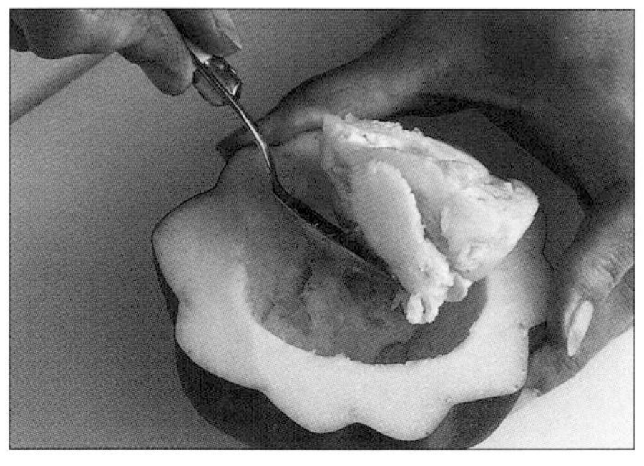

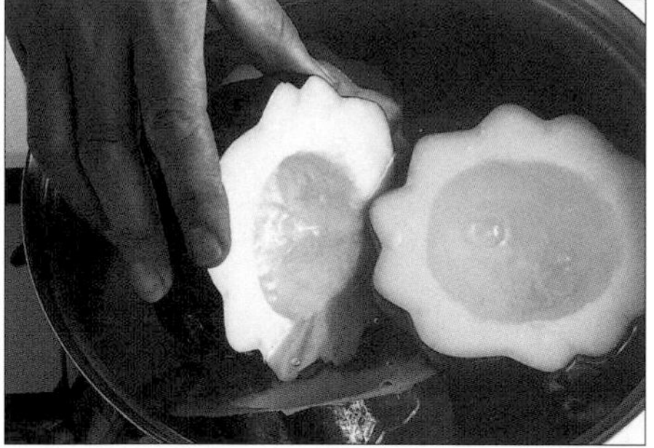

1 Preheat the oven to 180°C/350°F/Gas 4. Trim the bases of the squash, if necessary, so that they will stand up securely. Using a teaspoon, remove the insides of the squash, taking care not to cut the outer skin or the base. Leave about 1cm/½in of flesh at the base.

VARIATION
You could use a thick courgette (zucchini) or a marrow (large zucchini) instead of the squash.

2 Blanch the squash in boiling water with the lemon juice for 2–3 minutes, then plunge them into cold water. Drain well and leave to cool.

3 Meanwhile, make the filling by combining in a bowl the cooked lamb and rice, the butter, fresh breadcrumbs, milk, onion, parsley, beaten eggs and seasoning. Place the squash in a lightly greased ovenproof dish, and fill with the lamb mixture.

4 To make the sauce, put the butter and flour in a pan. Whisk in the cream and bring to the boil, whisking all the time. Cook for 1–2 minutes, or until thickened, then season. Pour the sauce over the squash, then pour over the passata.

5 Bake the squash in the oven for 25–30 minutes. Drizzle with sauce from the pan, and sprinkle with some feta cheese and basil. Serve the remaining sauce, feta and basil separately.

Energy 583Kcal/2,427kJ; Protein 23.3g; Carbohydrate 40g, of which sugars 9.1g; Fat 37g, of which saturates 21.5g; Cholesterol 183mg; Calcium 237mg; Fibre 3.9g; Sodium 513mg.

SPICY ROLLED BEEF

SLICES OF TENDER BEEF ARE DELICIOUS WHEN ROLLED AROUND A FILLING, AND OFTEN APPEAR IN GREEK RECIPES. HERE THE BEEF ENCLOSES HAM AND GREEN PEPPER AND IS SIMMERED IN WINE.

SERVES FOUR

INGREDIENTS

- 4 thick 10–15cm/4–6in beef slices
- 50ml/2fl oz/¼ cup olive or vegetable oil, plus extra for frying
- 30ml/2 tbsp black peppercorns, roughly crushed
- 30ml/2 tbsp whole coriander seeds
- 1 onion, finely sliced
- 300ml/½ pint/1¼ cups dry red wine
- 1 egg, beaten
- 150g/5oz can chopped tomatoes
- flat leaf parsley, to garnish
- polenta and sour cream, to serve

For the filling

- 115g/4oz/½ cup minced (ground) ham
- 40g/1½oz/scant 1 cup fresh breadcrumbs
- 2 spring onions (scallions), finely sliced
- 45ml/3 tbsp chopped fresh parsley
- 1 egg yolk
- 75g/3oz green (bell) pepper, seeded and finely chopped
- 1.5ml/¼ tsp ground allspice
- 15–45ml/1–3 tbsp beef stock, if needed

1 Place the slices of beef between two sheets of dampened clear film (plastic wrap) or baking parchment. Flatten with a meat mallet or rolling pin until the meat is evenly thin. Dip the slices in the oil to wet them lightly.

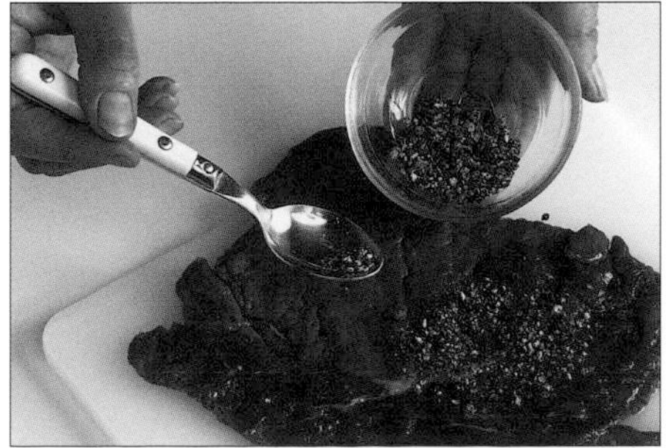

2 Lay the meat out flat and sprinkle over the crushed peppercorns, coriander seeds and onion.

3 Roll up the meat neatly and place in a shallow glass or china dish. Pour over half the wine, cover with clear film and chill for 2 hours.

4 To make the filling, combine the ham, fresh breadcrumbs, spring onions and parsley in a bowl. Add the egg yolk, green pepper, allspice and a little water or beef stock if necessary, to moisten the stuffing.

5 Remove the beef from the bowl and shake off the spices and onion. Spoon 30–45ml/2–3 tbsp of the filling into the middle of each piece of meat.

6 Brush the inner surface with egg and roll up well. Secure with a cocktail stick (toothpick) or tie with string.

7 Heat a little oil in a frying pan and sauté the rolls, turning occasionally, until they are brown on all sides. Reduce the heat and pour over the remaining wine and the canned tomatoes. Simmer for 25–30 minutes, or until tender.

8 Season well and serve the beef with the sauce, the polenta and sour cream and plenty of cracked black pepper. Garnish with a few sprigs of fresh flat leaf parsley.

Energy 508Kcal/2,117kJ; Protein 43.7g; Carbohydrate 12g, of which sugars 4.1g; Fat 26.4g, of which saturates 8.1g; Cholesterol 202mg; Calcium 53mg; Fibre 1.3g; Sodium 547mg.

BEEF CASSEROLE WITH BABY ONIONS

THIS IS THE PERFECT SUNDAY LUNCH FOR A FAMILY, BUT IS ALSO AN EXCELLENT CHOICE FOR A DINNER PARTY. MOSHARI STIFADO IS AN UNUSUAL BUT MOUTHWATERING DISH, WITH THE SMALL PICKLING-SIZE ONIONS MELTING IN THE MOUTH WITH SWEETNESS.

SERVES FOUR

INGREDIENTS

- 75ml/5 tbsp olive oil
- 1kg/2¼lb good stewing or braising steak, cut into large cubes
- 3 garlic cloves, chopped
- 5ml/1 tsp ground cumin
- 5cm/2in piece of cinnamon stick
- 175ml/6fl oz/¾ cup red wine
- 30ml/2 tbsp red wine vinegar
- small sprig of fresh rosemary
- 2 bay leaves, crumbled
- 30ml/2 tbsp tomato purée (paste) diluted in 1 litre/1¾ pints/4 cups hot water
- 675g/1½lb small pickling-size onions, peeled and left whole
- 15ml/1 tbsp demerara (raw) sugar
- salt and freshly ground black pepper

1 Heat the olive oil in a large, heavy pan and brown the meat cubes, in batches if necessary, until pale golden brown all over.

2 Stir in the garlic and cumin. Add the cinnamon stick and cook for a few seconds, then pour the wine and vinegar slowly over the mixture. Let the liquid bubble and evaporate for 3–4 minutes.

3 Add the rosemary and bay leaves, with the diluted tomato purée. Stir well, season with salt and pepper, then cover and simmer gently for about 1½ hours or until the meat is tender.

4 Dot the onions over the meat mixture and shake the pan to distribute them evenly. Sprinkle the demerara sugar over the onions, cover the pan and cook very gently for 30 minutes, until the onions are soft but have not begun to disintegrate. If necessary, add a little hot water at this stage. Do not stir once the onions have been added but gently shake the pan instead to coat them in the sauce. Remove the cinnamon stick and sprig of rosemary and serve.

COOK'S TIP

Stifado can be cooked in the oven, if you prefer. Use a flameproof casserole. Having browned the meat and added the remaining ingredients, with the exception of the onions and sugar, transfer the covered casserole to an oven preheated to 160°C/325°F/Gas 3 and bake for about 2 hours, or until the meat is tender. Add the onions and sugar as above and return the casserole to the oven for 1 hour more.

Energy 672Kcal/2,798kJ; Protein 59.2g; Carbohydrate 18.4g, of which sugars 14.5g; Fat 37.4g, of which saturates 11.5g; Cholesterol 145mg; Calcium 62mg; Fibre 2.6g; Sodium 186mg.

BEEF AND AUBERGINE CASSEROLE

Easy to make but with an exotic taste, this would make an excellent main course for a dinner party. Use good-quality beef and cook it slowly, so that it is meltingly tender and full of flavour. Serve with toasted pitta bread.

SERVES FOUR

INGREDIENTS

- 60ml/4 tbsp extra virgin olive oil
- 1kg/2¼lb good-quality stewing steak or feather steak, sliced in 4 thick pieces
- 1 onion, chopped
- 2.5ml/½ tsp dried oregano
- 2 garlic cloves, chopped
- 175ml/6fl oz/¾ cup white wine
- 400g/14oz can chopped tomatoes
- 2 or 3 aubergines (eggplants), total weight about 675g/1½lb
- 150ml/¼ pint/⅔ cup sunflower oil
- 45ml/3 tbsp finely chopped fresh parsley
- salt and freshly ground black pepper
- toasted pitta bread and green or mixed salad, to serve

1 Heat the olive oil in a large pan and brown the pieces of meat on both sides. As each piece browns, take it out and set it aside on a plate.

2 Add the onion to the oil remaining in the pan and sauté until translucent. Add the oregano and the garlic, then, as soon as the garlic becomes aromatic, return the meat to the pan and pour the wine over. Allow the wine to bubble and evaporate for a few minutes, then add the tomatoes, with enough hot water to just cover the meat. Bring to the boil, lower the heat, cover and cook for about 1 hour, until the meat is tender.

3 Meanwhile, trim the aubergines and slice them into 2cm/¾in thick rounds, then slice each round in half. Heat the sunflower oil and fry the aubergines briefly in batches over a high heat, turning them over as they become light golden. They do not have to cook at this stage and should not be allowed to burn. Lift them out and drain them on kitchen paper. When all the aubergines have been fried, season them.

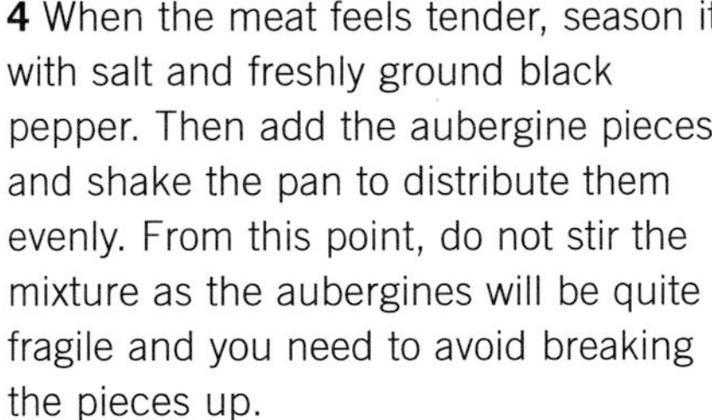

4 When the meat feels tender, season it with salt and freshly ground black pepper. Then add the aubergine pieces and shake the pan to distribute them evenly. From this point, do not stir the mixture as the aubergines will be quite fragile and you need to avoid breaking the pieces up.

5 Add a little more hot water so that the aubergines are submerged in the sauce, cover the pan and simmer for 30 minutes more, or until the meat is very tender and all the flavours have amalgamated.

6 Sprinkle the parsley over the top and simmer gently for a few more minutes before transferring to a serving platter or dish. Serve with hot toasted pitta bread tucked into the folds of a warm, clean dish towel, and accompany with a fresh green or mixed salad.

Energy 838Kcal/3,479kJ; Protein 59.2g; Carbohydrate 8.3g, of which sugars 7.6g; Fat 60.2g, of which saturates 14.4g; Cholesterol 145mg; Calcium 44mg; Fibre 4.6g; Sodium 175mg.

Beef with Quinces

Quinces have a beautiful aroma and complex flavour, but they are sometimes an acquired taste. However, in this sweet and savoury recipe they win everyone over, including the uninitiated. You do not need to serve anything else with this dish.

SERVES FOUR

INGREDIENTS
- juice of ½ lemon
- 2 or 3 large quinces, total weight about 1kg/2¼lb
- 75ml/5 tbsp extra virgin olive oil
- 1kg/2¼lb good-quality feather steak (see tip), cut into large slices
- 175ml/6fl oz/¾ cup white wine
- 300ml/½ pint/1¼ cups hot water
- 1 cinnamon stick
- 45ml/3 tbsp demerara (raw) sugar mixed with 300ml/½ pint/1¼ cups hot water
- 1 whole nutmeg
- salt and freshly ground black pepper

1 Heat the olive oil in a large, heavy pan. When it is almost smoking, brown the meat on both sides, turning the pieces over once. As soon as all the meat has browned, lower the heat, pour the wine over and let it bubble and reduce slightly.

2 Pour the hot water into the pan and add the cinnamon stick. Cover the pan and cook over a gentle heat for about 1 hour or until the meat is tender. Add salt and pepper to taste.

3 Have ready a bowl of water acidulated with the lemon juice. Using a sharp cook's knife, quarter each quince vertically. Core and peel the pieces and drop them into the acidulated water to prevent them from discolouring.

4 Lift the quinces out of the acidulated water, and slice each piece vertically into 2 or 3 elongated pieces. Spread half the quince slices in a single layer in a large frying pan, pour half the sugared water over and cook them gently for 10 minutes, turning occasionally, until all the liquid has been absorbed and they start to brown and caramelize.

5 Spread the caramelized quince slices over the meat in the pan and repeat the caramelizing process with the remaining quince slices.

6 Having added them to the meat, finely grate about one-quarter of a whole nutmeg over the top. If necessary, add more hot water to cover the quince slices completely.

7 Cover the pan and cook for 30 minutes more until both the meat and the quince slices are meltingly soft and sweet. Do not stir the mixture after the quince has been added as it can easily break or disintegrate; instead, shake the pan from side to side occasionally so that the meat is prevented from sticking to the base. Serve hot.

COOK'S TIP

Feather steak is a tender cut of beef, from between the neck and rib, near the chuck. It is particularly good for braising. If you can't find it, use stewing or braising steak instead.

Energy 734Kcal/3,065kJ; Protein 57.6g; Carbohydrate 37g, of which sugars 37g; Fat 37.2g, of which saturates 11.5g; Cholesterol 145mg; Calcium 50mg; Fibre 5.5g; Sodium 170mg.

MEAT RISSOLES WITH GREEN OLIVES

A delicious dish with a Middle Eastern twist that was probably brought back from Asia Minor after the war with Turkey in 1922. It can be cooked in advance and reheated as needed. Serve the soutzoukakia *with plain rice, French fries or pasta.*

SERVES FOUR

INGREDIENTS
- 2 or 3 medium slices of bread, crusts removed
- 675g/1½lb/3 cups minced (ground) lamb or beef
- 2 garlic cloves, crushed
- 15ml/1 tbsp ground cumin
- 1 egg, lightly beaten
- 25g/1oz/¼ cup plain (all-purpose) flour
- 45ml/3 tbsp sunflower oil, for frying
- salt and ground black pepper

For the sauce
- 45ml/3 tbsp olive oil
- 5ml/1 tsp cumin seeds
- 400g/14oz can chopped tomatoes
- 15ml/1 tbsp tomato purée (paste) diluted in 150ml/¼ pint/⅔ cup hot water
- 2.5ml/½ tsp dried oregano
- 12–16 green olives, preferably cracked ones, rinsed and drained

1 Soak the bread in water for 10 minutes, then drain, squeeze dry and place in a large bowl. Add the meat, garlic, cumin and egg. Season with salt and pepper, then mix either with a fork or with your hands, until blended.

2 Take a small handful – the size of a large walnut – and roll it into a short, slim sausage. Set this aside. Continue until all the meat mixture has been used. Roll all the sausage-shaped rissoles lightly in flour, shaking each one to get rid of any excess.

3 Heat the sunflower oil in a large non-stick frying pan and fry the *soutzoukakia*, in batches if necessary, until they are golden on all sides. Lift them out and place them in a bowl. Discard the oil remaining in the pan.

COOK'S TIP

The *soutzoukakia* taste delicious when simmered in the cumin-flavoured tomato sauce, but their aroma is so seductive when they are first fried that you may not be able to wait that long. There's no reason why you shouldn't serve them on their own – just make certain that they are cooked through.

4 To make the sauce, heat the olive oil in a large pan. Add the cumin seeds and swirl them around for a few seconds until aromatic. Add the tomatoes and stir with a wooden spatula to break them up. Pour in the diluted tomato purée, mix well, then add the *soutzoukakia*. Stir in the oregano and olives, with salt and pepper to taste. Spoon the sauce over the *soutzoukakia*, then cover for 30 minutes, shaking the pan occasionally to prevent them from sticking. Tip into a serving dish and serve.

Energy 625Kcal/2,602kJ; Protein 37.3g; Carbohydrate 18.5g, of which sugars 4.3g; Fat 45.2g, of which saturates 13.8g; Cholesterol 178mg; Calcium 98mg; Fibre 2.7g; Sodium 1,101mg.

VEAL ESCALOPES FROM CORFU

THIS DISH COMES FROM THE ISLAND OF CORFU, WHERE THERE IS MORE OF AN ITALIAN INFLUENCE. IT IS CLEARLY DERIVED FROM THE ISLAND'S VENETIAN PAST AS IT WAS NOT KNOWN ELSEWHERE IN GREECE UNTIL RECENTLY AND VEAL IS RARELY EATEN IN GREECE.

SERVES FOUR

INGREDIENTS

- 675g/1½lb thin veal escalopes (scallops)
- 40g/1½oz/⅓ cup plain (all-purpose) flour
- 90ml/6 tbsp extra virgin olive oil
- 1 small onion, thinly sliced
- 3 garlic cloves, finely chopped
- 2 or 3 fresh sage leaves, finely chopped
- 175ml/6fl oz/¾ cup white wine
- juice of ½ lemon
- 450ml/¾ pint/scant 2 cups beef or chicken stock
- 30ml/2 tbsp finely chopped fresh flat leaf parsley
- salt and freshly ground black pepper

1 Sprinkle the veal escalopes with a little salt and pepper, then coat them lightly in the flour.

2 Heat the olive oil in a large frying pan over a medium heat. Add the veal escalopes and brown them lightly on both sides. Transfer them to a wide flameproof casserole.

3 Add the sliced onion to the oil remaining in the frying pan and sauté the slices until translucent, then stir in the chopped garlic and sage. As soon as the garlic becomes aromatic, add the white wine and the lemon juice.

4 Raise the heat to high and cook for 10 minutes, stirring constantly and scraping the base to incorporate any sediment into the pan juices.

5 Pour the pan juices over the meat and add the stock. Sprinkle over salt and freshly ground black pepper to taste, then add the finely chopped flat leaf parsley.

6 Bring to the boil, lower the heat, cover and simmer for 45–50 minutes, or until the meat is tender and the sauce is a velvety consistency.

7 Transfer to a serving platter or dish and serve immediately while it is still piping hot. Garnish with salad leaves, such as rocket (arugula), cos or romaine lettuce, and accompany with new potatoes tossed in extra virgin olive oil, or fresh crusty bread.

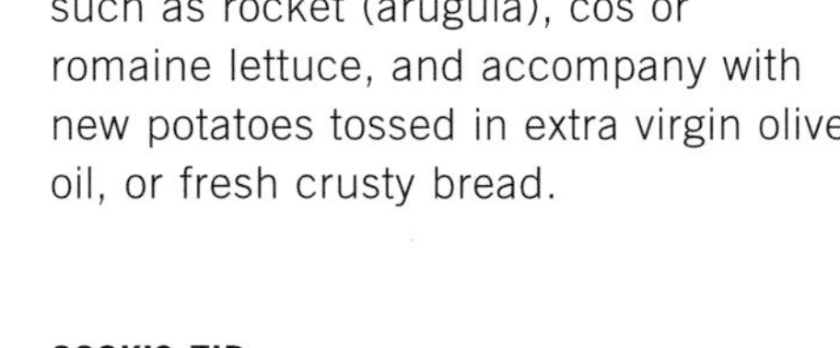

COOK'S TIP

Escalopes (scallops) are thin slices of veal that are cut from the leg. If they are a bit thick, it may be necessary to place them between sheets of clear film (plastic wrap) and beat them with a meat mallet. Thin slices of pork can be cooked in the same way.

Energy 398Kcal/1,666kJ; Protein 39.7g; Carbohydrate 9.4g, of which sugars 1.4g; Fat 19.6g, of which saturates 3.4g; Cholesterol 88mg; Calcium 44mg; Fibre 0.9g; Sodium 105mg.

STUFFED CABBAGE LEAVES

This is the most enticing of Greek winter dishes, and a real favourite with all the family. Dolmades are a traditional classic throughout Greece, with the meat version being especially popular during the winter months.

SERVES FOUR

INGREDIENTS
- 115g/4oz/generous ½ cup long grain rice
- 1 or 2 large green cabbages, total weight about 1.6–2kg/3½–4½lb
- 500g/1¼lb/2½ cups minced (ground) pork, or a mixture of pork and beef
- 1 large onion, roughly grated
- 1 egg, lightly beaten
- 30ml/2 tbsp chopped fresh flat leaf parsley
- 45–60ml/3–4 tbsp chopped fresh dill
- 90ml/6 tbsp extra virgin olive oil
- 25g/1oz/2 tbsp butter
- 15ml/1 tbsp cornflour (cornstarch)
- 2 eggs
- juice of 1½ lemons
- salt and ground black pepper

1 Soak the rice in cold water for 10 minutes, then drain, rinse it under cold water and drain again. Core the cabbage(s) and strip off the outer leaves. Rinse these, drain and pat dry with kitchen paper, and set aside. Peel off the inner leaves, cutting off more of the core as you proceed. When you reach the hard heart, stop peeling. Set the cabbage heart(s) aside.

2 Rinse the leaves and cabbage heart(s) in cold water, then drain them. Bring a large pan of water to the boil and blanch the leaves in batches for 1–2 minutes, or until they become just pliable. Remove with a draining spoon and place them in a colander. Put in the cabbage heart(s) and let them boil for slightly longer. Drain.

3 Combine the minced meat, rice, onion, egg and herbs in a bowl. Mix in half the oil and add seasoning. Cut the larger leaves of the cabbage in half and trim any hard cores and veins.

4 Place 15ml/1 tbsp of the stuffing at one end of a leaf, fold the end over so it looks like a short cigar, then fold in the sides and roll up tightly. Strip as many leaves as possible from the cabbage hearts and stuff them individually. Leave the inner hearts intact, but open the leaves on the top, and add stuffing.

5 Line a large, heavy pan with the uncooked outer leaves. Tightly pack the *dolmades* in the pan, seasoning each layer as you go.

6 Drizzle the remaining oil over the top of the *dolmades* and sprinkle over small knobs (pats) of the butter. Invert a small heatproof plate on top of the *dolmades*. Pour in enough hot water to just cover the top layer. Cover and cook gently for about 50 minutes. Tilt the pan, holding the plate down firmly, and empty most of the liquid into a bowl. Let it cool slightly.

7 Mix the cornflour to a cream with some water. Whisk the eggs in a bowl, then add the lemon juice and the cornflour mixture and whisk again. Whisk, adding tablespoons of the hot cooking liquid from the *dolmades*. Pour the sauce over the *dolmades* and shake the pan gently. Cook over a very gentle heat for 3 minutes to thicken the sauce.

8 Serve with the *dolmades* either hot or cold, as a main course with salad and bread or as a meze.

Energy 589Kcal/2,456kJ; Protein 42g; Carbohydrate 51g, of which sugars 21.9g; Fat 24.7g, of which saturates 7.8g; Cholesterol 235mg; Calcium 293mg; Fibre 11.6g; Sodium 207mg.

Pork with Chickpeas and Orange

This winter speciality is a familiar dish in the Aegean islands, particularly in Crete. In the villages of Mesara it is traditionally offered to family and close friends on the night before a wedding. This version comes from the island of Chios. All you need to serve with this lovely dish is fresh bread and a bowl of black olives.

SERVES FOUR

INGREDIENTS

- 350g/12oz/1¾ cups dried chickpeas, soaked overnight in water to cover
- 75–90ml/5–6 tbsp extra virgin olive oil
- 675g/1½lb boneless leg of pork, cut into large cubes
- 1 large onion, sliced
- 2 garlic cloves, chopped
- 400g/14oz can chopped tomatoes
- grated rind of 1 orange
- 1 small dried red chilli
- salt and ground black pepper

1 Drain the chickpeas, rinse them under cold water and drain them again. Place them in a large, heavy pan. Pour in enough cold water to cover generously, put a lid on the pan and bring to the boil.

2 Skim the surface, replace the lid and cook gently for 1–1½ hours, depending on the age and pedigree of the chickpeas. Alternatively, cook them in a pressure cooker for 20 minutes under full pressure. When the chickpeas are soft, drain them, reserving the cooking liquid, and set them aside.

3 Heat the olive oil in the clean pan and brown the meat cubes in batches. As each cube browns, lift it out with a slotted spoon and put it on a plate. When all the meat cubes have been browned, add the onion to the oil remaining in the pan and sauté the slices until light golden. Stir in the garlic, then as soon as it becomes aromatic, add the tomatoes and orange rind.

4 Crumble in the chilli. Return the chickpeas and meat to the pan, and pour in enough of the reserved cooking liquid to cover. Add the black pepper, but not salt at this stage.

5 Mix well, cover the pan and simmer for about 1 hour, or until the meat is tender. Stir occasionally and add more of the reserved liquid if needed. The result should be a moist casserole; not soupy, but not dry either. Season with salt before serving.

Energy 663Kcal/2,781kJ; Protein 56.7g; Carbohydrate 54.4g, of which sugars 11g; Fat 25.7g, of which saturates 4.9g; Cholesterol 106mg; Calcium 184mg; Fibre 11.8g; Sodium 164mg.

SPICY SAUSAGE AND PEPPER STEW

This dish, SPETZOFAI, *is a speciality of the Pelion on the eastern coast of Greece. The beautiful mountain range towers over the city of Volos on one side and the fresh blue Aegean on the other. You will find* SPETZOFAI *in all its picture-postcard villages, but it is also popular on all the nearby islands of Skiathos, Alonnisos and Skopelos.*

SERVES FOUR

INGREDIENTS

- 675g/1½lb red and green (bell) peppers
- 75ml/5 tbsp extra virgin olive oil
- 500g/1¼lb spicy sausages (Italian garlic sausages, Merguez or Toulouse if you cannot find Greek sausages)
- 400g/14oz tomatoes, skinned and roughly sliced
- 5ml/1 tsp dried oregano or some fresh thyme, chopped
- 150ml/¼ pint/⅔ cup hot water
- 45ml/3 tbsp chopped fresh flat leaf parsley
- salt and ground black pepper
- chopped fresh thyme, to garnish

1 Halve and seed the peppers and cut them into quarters. Heat the olive oil in a large, heavy pan, add the peppers and sauté them over a medium heat for 10–15 minutes until they start to brown.

2 Meanwhile, slice the sausages into bitesize chunks. Then carefully tip the hot olive oil into a frying pan.

3 Add the sausages and fry them briefly, turning them frequently, to get rid of the excess fat but not to cook them. As soon as they are brown, remove from the pan with a slotted spoon and drain on kitchen paper.

4 Add the tomatoes, sausages and herbs to the peppers. Stir in the water and season with salt and pepper, then cover the pan and cook gently for about 30 minutes. Mix in the chopped parsley and serve piping hot.

COOK'S TIP

If you prefer, stir in the parsley, spread the mixture in a medium baking dish and bake in an oven preheated to 180°C/350°F/Gas 4. Cook for about 40 minutes, stirring occasionally.

Energy 573Kcal/2,378kJ; Protein 14.8g; Carbohydrate 28.9g, of which sugars 15.9g; Fat 45g, of which saturates 14.7g; Cholesterol 50mg; Calcium 106mg; Fibre 5g; Sodium 1,033mg.

VEGETARIAN MEALS

Pulses, vegetables, eggs and cheese feature strongly in Greek cuisine, reflecting the abundance of fresh produce that is grown and produced both on the mainland and on the islands. Herbs gathered wild from the countryside are used plentifully, imparting their own distinctive flavours.

Cheese and Leek Pie

This pie, which comes from the Sporades Islands, is unusual by Greek standards because it is not enclosed in pastry. It is called TYROPITTA *and is perfect served with the mezedes, or as a lovely lunch with a fresh green salad.*

SERVES FOUR

INGREDIENTS

- 1 onion, sliced
- 50g/2oz/¼ cup butter
- 60ml/4 tbsp extra virgin olive oil
- 2 large leeks, total weight about 450g/1lb, chopped
- 115g/4oz/1 cup plain (all-purpose) flour
- 2.5ml/½ tsp bicarbonate of soda (baking soda)
- 3 large (US extra large) eggs, lightly beaten
- 200g/7oz/scant 1 cup Greek (US strained plain) yogurt
- 300g/11oz feta cheese, cubed
- 115g/4oz freshly grated Gruyère or Parmesan cheese
- 45–60ml/3–4 tbsp chopped fresh dill
- salt and ground black pepper
- lemon wedges, black olives and radishes, to garnish

1 Sauté the onion in the butter and oil until light golden. Add the leeks and cook over a low heat for 10–12 minutes until soft. Cool a little.

2 Preheat the oven to 180°C/350°F/Gas 4. Lightly grease a 23cm/9in round springform cake tin (pan). Sift the flour and bicarbonate of soda into a bowl. Stir in the eggs, then the yogurt and feta cheese, and finally the leek and onion mixture. Set aside 30ml/2 tbsp of the grated Gruyère or Parmesan cheese and add the rest to the batter, with the dill. Mix well and season.

COOK'S TIP

To remove all the grit from trimmed leeks, cut down through about 10cm/4in of the green part and then turn the leek and cut again, making a cross. Rinse thoroughly in running water.

3 Spoon the mixture into the prepared tin and level the surface. Sprinkle the reserved grated cheese evenly over the top and bake for 40–45 minutes, or until golden brown.

4 Let the pie cool completely before removing it from the tin. Serve in wedges and offer some tasty extra virgin olive oil to be drizzled over the top. Garnish with lemon wedges, black olives and radishes.

Energy 751Kcal/3,124kJ; Protein 35.8g; Carbohydrate 28.9g, of which sugars 5.9g; Fat 56.1g, of which saturates 28.2g; Cholesterol 251mg; Calcium 804mg; Fibre 3.9g; Sodium 1,564mg.

FRIED CHEESE WITH ROCKET SALAD

AT METROPOLITAN PARTIES YOU MAY WELL BE OFFERED THIS AS FINGER FOOD, BUT THERE IS ALSO A MORE ROBUST VERSION, AS SERVED IN TAVERNAS OR PRIVATE HOMES. A SMALL, BLACKENED, CAST-IRON FRYING PAN WILL BE BROUGHT TO THE TABLE, WITH THE SLICES OF CHEESE STILL SIZZLING IN IT.

SERVES FOUR

INGREDIENTS

- 30ml/2 tbsp olive oil, for frying
- 8 slices Greek Kefalotiri or Greek Cypriot halloumi cheese, about 1cm/½in thick
- freshly ground black pepper
- lemon wedges, to serve

For the salad

- 15ml/1 tbsp red wine vinegar
- 60ml/4 tbsp extra virgin olive oil
- a large handful of rocket (arugula) leaves

1 Start by making the salad. Whisk the vinegar and olive oil together in a bowl and dress the rocket leaves. Spread them out on a platter.

2 Heat the olive oil for frying in a large griddle pan or non-stick frying pan until hot. Lay the slices of cheese side by side on the base. Do not allow the slices to touch as they might stick together. Let them sizzle for a couple of minutes, turning each one over using tongs or a metal spatula as it starts to get crisp at the sides.

3 Sprinkle the cheese slices with pepper. As soon as the undersides turn golden, remove them from the pan and arrange them on the dressed rocket. Serve immediately, with the lemon wedges to squeeze over.

Energy 289Kcal/1,195kJ; Protein 10.7g; Carbohydrate 0.8g, of which sugars 0.8g; Fat 27g, of which saturates 9.3g; Cholesterol 29mg; Calcium 266mg; Fibre 1.1g; Sodium 268mg.

Warm Halloumi and Fennel Salad

The firm texture of halloumi cheese makes it perfect for the barbecue, as it keeps its shape very well and doesn't melt in the same way that other cheeses do. It is widely available in most large supermarkets and Greek delicatessens.

SERVES FOUR

INGREDIENTS

- 200g/7oz halloumi cheese, thickly sliced
- 2 fennel bulbs, trimmed and thinly sliced
- 30ml/2 tbsp roughly chopped fresh oregano
- 45ml/3 tbsp lemon-infused extra virgin olive oil
- salt and ground black pepper

COOK'S TIP

If you cannot get lemon-infused extra virgin olive oil, simply use a very fruity extra virgin olive oil and let it soak overnight with some thin slices of lemon. You can also try other flavoured oils, such as garlic or oregano, to produce a different taste.

1 Put the halloumi, fennel and oregano in a bowl and drizzle over the lemon-infused oil. Season with salt and black pepper to taste. (Halloumi is a fairly salty cheese, so be very careful when adding extra salt.)

2 Cover the bowl with clear film (plastic wrap) and chill for about 2 hours to allow the flavours to develop.

3 Remove the halloumi and fennel, reserving the marinade juices. Place on a preheated griddle pan or over the barbecue and cook for about 3 minutes on each side, until lightly charred.

4 Divide the halloumi and fennel among four serving plates and drizzle over the reserved marinade. Serve immediately with crusty bread or toasted pitta bread.

Energy 215Kcal/889kJ; Protein 10.2g; Carbohydrate 1.8g, of which sugars 1.7g; Fat 18.6g, of which saturates 8.1g; Cholesterol 29mg; Calcium 205mg; Fibre 2.4g; Sodium 209mg.

HALLOUMI WITH POTATOES

THIS SALAD CAN BE GRILLED SUCCESSFULLY ON THE STOVETOP, BUT IF YOU ARE PLANNING TO USE THE BARBECUE FOR ANOTHER DISH, USE IT FOR THIS RECIPE, TOO, AND TAKE ADVANTAGE OF THE INITIAL HOT BLAST OF HEAT TO SLIGHTLY CHAR AND SEAL THE CHEESE.

SERVES FOUR

INGREDIENTS

- 20 baby new potatoes, total weight about 300g/11oz
- 200g/7oz extra-fine green beans, trimmed
- 675g/1½lb broad (fava) beans, shelled (about 225g/8oz shelled weight)
- 200g/7oz halloumi cheese, cut into 5mm/¼in slices
- 1 garlic clove, crushed to a paste with a large pinch of salt
- 90ml/6 tbsp olive oil
- 5ml/1 tsp cider vinegar or white wine vinegar
- 15g/½oz/½ cup fresh basil leaves, shredded
- 45ml/3 tbsp chopped fresh savory
- 2 spring onions (scallions), finely sliced
- salt and ground black pepper
- 4 metal or wooden skewers
- a few sprigs of fresh savory, to garnish

1 Divide the potatoes among the 4 skewers, and thread them on. Heat salted water in a pan large enough to take the skewers and, once boiling, add them. Boil for about 7 minutes, or until almost tender.

2 Add the prepared green beans and cook for 3 minutes more. Tip in the broad (fava) beans and cook for just 2 further minutes.

3 Drain all the vegetables in a large colander. Remove the potatoes, still on their skewers, and set to one side.

4 Refresh the cooked broad beans under plenty of cold running water. Pop each broad bean out of its skin to reveal the bright green inner bean. If they do not pop out easily, they may not have been cooked for long enough. Discard the outer shells. Place the beans in a bowl, cover and set aside.

5 Place the halloumi and the potatoes in a wide dish. Whisk the garlic and oil together with a generous grinding of black pepper. Add to the dish and toss with the halloumi and potato skewers.

6 Place the cheese and the potato skewers in a griddle over medium heat and cook for 2 minutes on each side.

7 Add the cider vinegar to the oil and garlic remaining in the dish and whisk to mix. Toss in the beans, herbs and spring onions, with the cooked halloumi. Serve, with the potato skewers laid alongside.

COOK'S TIPS

- To griddle on the barbecue, rake the coals over to one side once the flames have died down. Position a grill rack over the coals to heat. When the coals are hot, or with a light coating of ash, heat the griddle until a few drops of water sprinkled on to the surface evaporate instantly.
- This dish can be cooked directly on the barbecue. When the coals are medium-hot, sear the vegetables and cheese for 2 minutes on each side.

Energy 404Kcal/1,679kJ; Protein 17.5g; Carbohydrate 22.2g, of which sugars 3.5g; Fat 27.8g, of which saturates 9.4g; Cholesterol 29mg; Calcium 280mg; Fibre 7.3g; Sodium 218mg.

Vegetable Moussaka

This is a truly flavoursome main course dish that leaves you feeling wonderfully satisfied. It can be served with warm fresh bread and a salad for a hearty meal.

SERVES SIX

INGREDIENTS

- 450g/1lb aubergines (eggplants), sliced
- 115g/4oz/½ cup whole green lentils
- 600ml/1 pint/2½ cups vegetable stock
- 1 bay leaf
- 45ml/3 tbsp olive oil
- 1 onion, sliced
- 1 garlic clove, crushed
- 225g/8oz/3¼ cups mushrooms, sliced
- 400g/14oz can chickpeas, rinsed and drained
- 400g/14oz can chopped tomatoes
- 30ml/2 tbsp tomato purée (paste)
- 10ml/2 tsp dried herbes de Provence
- 300ml/½ pint/1¼ cups natural (plain) yogurt
- 3 eggs
- 50g/2oz/½ cup grated mature Cheddar cheese
- salt and ground black pepper
- sprigs of fresh flat leaf parsley, to garnish

1 Prepare the aubergines well in advance. Cut into thin to medium slices and arrange them in a colander. You will probably find it necessary to overlap the slices or place one on top of another. Sprinkle each layer liberally with salt. Cover and place a weight or a plate on top. Leave for at least 30 minutes, to allow the bitter juices to be extracted.

2 Meanwhile, place the lentils, stock and bay leaf in a pan, cover, bring to the boil and simmer for about 20 minutes, or until the lentils are just tender but not mushy. Drain thoroughly and keep warm.

3 Heat 15ml/1 tbsp of the oil in a large pan, add the onion and garlic and cook for 5 minutes, stirring. Stir in the lentils, sliced mushrooms, chickpeas, chopped tomatoes, tomato purée, herbs and 45ml/3 tbsp water. Bring to the boil, cover and simmer gently for 10 minutes.

4 Preheat the oven to 180°C/350°F/Gas 4. Rinse the aubergine slices, drain and pat dry. Heat the remaining oil in a frying pan and fry the slices in batches.

5 Season the lentil mixture with salt and freshly ground black pepper. Layer the aubergine slices and lentil mixture alternately in a shallow ovenproof dish or roasting pan, starting with the aubergines. Continue the layers until all the aubergine slices and lentil mixture are used up.

6 Beat the yogurt and eggs together well, and add salt and freshly ground black pepper.

7 Pour the mixture over the aubergines and lentils. Sprinkle generously with the grated Cheddar cheese and bake for about 45 minutes, or until the topping is golden brown and bubbling.

8 Serve immediately, garnished with the sprigs of flat leaf parsley and accompanied by a fresh green or mixed salad, if you like.

VARIATION

Sliced courgettes (zucchini) or potatoes can be used instead of the aubergines in this dish. Simply slice them thinly and sauté them, taking care not to break the slices.

Energy 314Kcal/1,319kJ; Protein 19g; Carbohydrate 29.2g, of which sugars 8.1g; Fat 14.4g, of which saturates 4g; Cholesterol 104mg; Calcium 224mg; Fibre 6.3g; Sodium 300mg.

BRAISED BEANS AND LENTILS

THIS LOVELY CRETAN DISH IS WONDERFULLY EASY TO MAKE, BUT IT IS VITAL THAT YOU START SOAKING THE PULSES AND WHEAT THE DAY BEFORE YOU WANT TO SERVE IT. OFFER SOME TASTY EXTRA VIRGIN OLIVE OIL AT THE TABLE, SO THAT YOUR GUESTS CAN DRIZZLE A LITTLE OVER THEIR FOOD. SERVE WITH WARMED CRUSTY BREAD TO MOP UP THE SAUCE.

SERVES FOUR

INGREDIENTS

- 200g/7oz/generous 1 cup mixed beans and lentils
- 25g/1oz/2 tbsp whole wheat grains
- 150ml/¼ pint/⅔ cup extra virgin olive oil
- 1 large onion, finely chopped
- 2 garlic cloves, crushed
- 5 or 6 fresh sage leaves, chopped
- juice of 1 lemon
- 3 spring onions (scallions), thinly sliced
- 60–75ml/4–5 tbsp chopped fresh dill
- salt and freshly ground black pepper

1 Put the pulses and wheat in a large bowl and cover with cold water. Leave to soak overnight.

2 Next day, drain the pulse mixture, rinse it thoroughly under cold water and drain again. Put the mixture in a large pan. Cover with plenty of cold water, bring to the boil, and cook for about 1½ hours, by which time all the ingredients will be quite soft and tender. Strain, reserving 475ml/16fl oz/2 cups of the cooking liquid. Return the bean mixture to the clean pan.

3 Heat the oil in a frying pan and fry the onion until light golden. Add the garlic and sage. As soon as the garlic becomes aromatic, add the mixture to the beans. Stir in the reserved liquid, add plenty of seasoning and simmer for about 15 minutes, or until the pulses are piping hot. Stir in the lemon juice, then spoon into serving bowls, top with a sprinkling of spring onions and dill, and serve.

Energy 428Kcal/1,788kJ; Protein 13.4g; Carbohydrate 37.7g, of which sugars 4.3g; Fat 26g, of which saturates 3.7g; Cholesterol 0mg; Calcium 62mg; Fibre 3.7g; Sodium 24mg.

GIANT BEANS BAKED WITH TOMATOES

GIGANTES ARE A TYPE OF WHITE BEAN, RESEMBLING BUTTER BEANS BUT LARGER, ROUNDER AND MUCH SWEETER. THEY COME FROM THE NORTH OF GREECE AND THE BEST COME FROM KASTORIA. THEY MAKE A DELICIOUS DISH, WHICH IS OFTEN TO BE FOUND IN TAVERNAS IN GREECE, EVEN IN THE SUMMER. THIS DISH IS USUALLY SERVED AS A MAIN COURSE FOR A FAMILY MEAL.

SERVES FOUR AS A MAIN COURSE
SIX AS A FIRST COURSE

INGREDIENTS

- 400g/14oz/1¾ cups Greek *fasolia gigantes* or similar large dried white beans
- 150ml/¼ pint/⅔ cup extra virgin olive oil
- 2 or 3 onions, total weight about 300g/11oz, chopped
- 1 celery stick, thinly sliced
- 2 carrots, peeled and cubed
- 3 garlic cloves, thinly sliced
- 5ml/1 tsp each dried oregano and thyme
- 400g/14oz can chopped tomatoes
- 30ml/2 tbsp tomato purée (paste) diluted in 300ml/½ pint/1¼ cups hot water
- 2.5ml/½ tsp granulated sugar
- 45ml/3 tbsp finely chopped flat leaf parsley
- salt and ground black pepper

1 Place the beans in a large bowl, cover with plenty of cold water, then leave to soak overnight. The next day, drain the beans, then rinse them under cold water and drain again.

2 Tip the beans into a large pan, pour in plenty of cold water to cover, then bring to the boil. Cover the pan and cook the beans until they are almost tender. *Gigantes* are not like other beans – they cook quickly, so keep testing them after they have been cooking for 30–40 minutes. They should not be allowed to disintegrate through overcooking.

COOK'S TIP

Never add salt to dried beans or pulses of any kind before they are cooked, as it will make their skins leathery and tough. Always taste beans to ensure that you do not overcook them.

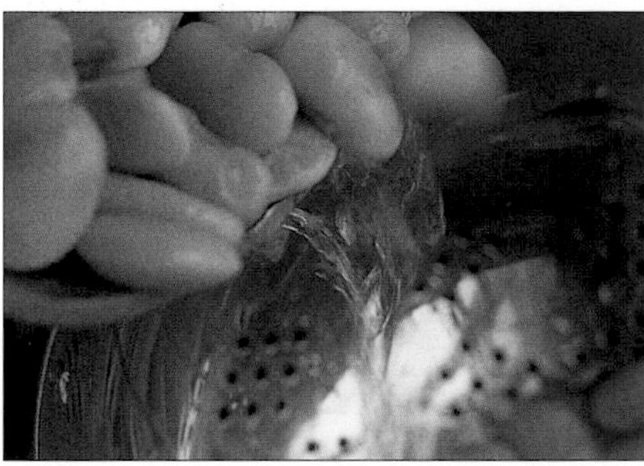

3 When the beans are cooked, tip them into a colander to drain, discarding the cooking liquid, and set them aside. Preheat the oven to 180°C/350°F/Gas 4.

4 Heat the olive oil in the clean pan, add the chopped onions and sauté until light golden. Add the celery, carrots, garlic and dried herbs and stir with a wooden spatula until the garlic becomes aromatic.

5 Stir in the tomatoes, cover and cook for 10 minutes. Pour in the diluted tomato purée, then return the beans to the pan. Stir in the sugar and parsley, with plenty of salt and pepper.

6 Tip the bean mixture into a baking dish and bake for 30 minutes, checking the beans once or twice and adding more hot water if they look dry. The surface should be slightly scorched and sugary.

Energy 562Kcal/2,358kJ; Protein 24.8g; Carbohydrate 58.5g, of which sugars 14.9g; Fat 27.2g, of which saturates 3.9g; Cholesterol 0mg; Calcium 167mg; Fibre 19.8g; Sodium 68mg.

Spicy Chickpea and Aubergine Stew

Spices are especially typical of dishes from the north of Greece, although aubergines and chickpeas are enjoyed all over the country. This stew makes a satisfying meal with rice.

SERVES FOUR

INGREDIENTS

- 3 large aubergines (eggplants), cubed
- 200g/7oz/generous 1 cup chickpeas, soaked overnight in cold water
- 60ml/4 tbsp olive oil
- 3 garlic cloves, finely chopped
- 2 large onions, chopped
- 2.5ml/½ tsp ground cumin
- 2.5ml/½ tsp ground cinnamon
- 2.5ml/½ tsp ground coriander
- 3 x 400g/14oz cans chopped tomatoes
- salt and ground black pepper
- cooked rice, to serve

For the garnish

- 30ml/2 tbsp extra virgin olive oil
- 1 onion, sliced
- 1 garlic clove, sliced
- a few sprigs of fresh coriander (cilantro)

1 Place the diced aubergines in a colander and sprinkle them with plenty of salt. Sit the colander in a bowl and leave for at least 30 minutes, to allow the bitter juices to escape. Rinse thoroughly with cold water and pat dry on kitchen paper.

2 Drain the chickpeas and put them in a large pan with enough water to cover them. Bring to the boil over a medium heat, then reduce the heat and simmer for 30 minutes, or until tender. Drain them thoroughly.

3 Heat the oil in a large pan. Add the garlic and chopped onion and cook gently until soft. Add the spices and cook, stirring, for a few seconds. Add the aubergine cubes and stir to coat with the spices and onion. Cook for 5 minutes. Add the tomatoes and chickpeas. Cover and simmer for 20 minutes.

4 To make the garnish, heat the olive oil in a frying pan and, when very hot, add the sliced onion and garlic. Fry until golden and crisp.

5 Serve the thick stew with rice, topped with the crispy fried onion and garlic, and garnished with sprigs of fresh coriander (cilantro).

Energy 360Kcal/1,512kJ; Protein 15g; Carbohydrate 43.3g, of which sugars 17.8g; Fat 15.4g, of which saturates 2.3g; Cholesterol 0mg; Calcium 135mg; Fibre 12.4g; Sodium 52mg.

SCRAMBLED EGGS WITH TOMATOES

Known in Greece as STRAPATSATHA, *this dish makes a delicious light lunch on a sunny day. All you need add is a salad and slices of crisp toast or fresh bread.*

SERVES FOUR

INGREDIENTS

- 60ml/4 tbsp extra virgin olive oil
- 2 or 3 shallots, finely chopped
- 675g/1½lb sweet tomatoes, roughly chopped
- pinch of dried oregano or 5ml/1 tsp chopped fresh thyme
- 2.5ml/½ tsp sugar
- 6 eggs, lightly beaten
- salt and ground black pepper
- fresh thyme, to garnish

1 Heat the olive oil in a large frying pan and sauté the shallots, stirring occasionally, until they are glistening and translucent.

2 Stir in the chopped tomatoes, dried or fresh herbs and sugar, with salt and freshly ground black pepper to taste. Cook over a low heat for about 15 minutes, stirring occasionally, until most of the liquid has evaporated and the sauce is thick.

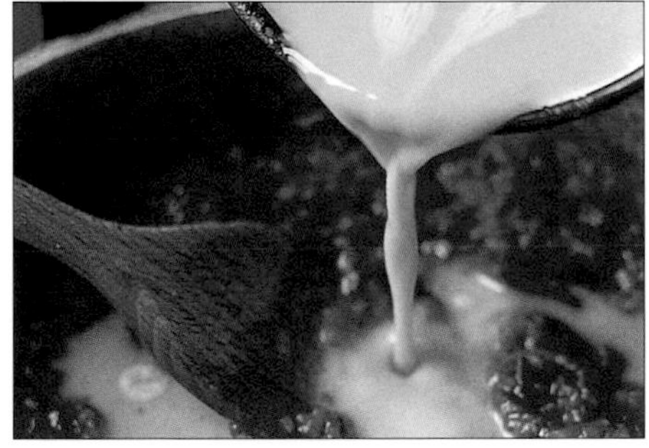

3 Add the beaten eggs to the pan and cook for 2–3 minutes, stirring continuously with a wooden spatula in the same way as when making scrambled eggs. The eggs should be just set, but not overcooked. Serve immediately, garnished with fresh thyme.

Energy 245Kcal/1,020kJ; Protein 10.8g; Carbohydrate 7g, of which sugars 6.6g; Fat 19.9g, of which saturates 4.1g; Cholesterol 285mg; Calcium 59mg; Fibre 1.9g; Sodium 121mg.

ROASTED AUBERGINES WITH FETA CHEESE

AUBERGINES TAKE ON A LOVELY SMOKY FLAVOUR WHEN GRILLED ON A BARBECUE. CHOOSE A GOOD-QUALITY GREEK FETA CHEESE FOR THE BEST FLAVOUR.

SERVES SIX

INGREDIENTS

- 3 medium to large aubergines (eggplant)
- 400g/14oz feta cheese
- a small bunch of fresh coriander (cilantro), roughly chopped, plus extra sprigs to garnish
- 60ml/4 tbsp extra virgin olive oil
- salt and freshly ground black pepper

1 Prepare a barbecue. Cook the aubergines for around 20 minutes on the barbecue, turning occasionally, until they are slightly charred and soft. Remove from the barbecue and cut in half lengthways.

2 Carefully scoop the aubergine flesh into a bowl, reserving the skins. Mash the flesh roughly with a fork.

3 Crumble the feta cheese, and then stir it into the mashed aubergine with the chopped coriander and olive oil. Season with salt and ground black pepper to taste.

4 Spoon the aubergine, feta and chopped coriander mixture back into the skins and return to the barbecue for 5 minutes to warm through.

5 Serve immediately with a fresh green salad coated with fruity extra virgin olive oil, garnished with sprigs of fresh coriander.

Energy 257Kcal/1,066kJ; Protein 12g; Carbohydrate 4.2g, of which sugars 3.9g; Fat 21.5g, of which saturates 10.3g; Cholesterol 47mg; Calcium 286mg; Fibre 3.3g; Sodium 968mg.

AUBERGINES WITH CHEESE SAUCE

THIS WONDERFULLY SIMPLE DISH IS DELICIOUS HOT AND THE PERFECT DISH TO ASSEMBLE AHEAD OF TIME. IT WORKS WELL WITH KASHKAVAL, *A HARD SHEEP'S MILK CHEESE FROM THE BALKANS.*

SERVES FOUR TO SIX

INGREDIENTS

2 large aubergines (eggplants), cut thinly into 5mm/¼in-thick slices
about 60ml/4 tbsp extra virgin olive oil
400g/14oz/3½ cups grated cheese, such as Kashkaval, Gruyère, or a mixture of Parmesan and Cheddar
600ml/1 pint/2½ cups savoury white sauce or béchamel sauce
salt and ground black pepper

1 Layer the aubergine slices in a large bowl or colander, sprinkling each layer with salt, and leave for at least 30 minutes to drain out any bitterness. Rinse each slice well under cold water, then pat dry with kitchen paper.

2 Heat the olive oil in a frying pan, then cook the aubergine slices until golden brown on both sides. Remove from the pan and set aside.

COOK'S TIPS

• To make a white sauce, melt 40g/1½oz/3 tbsp butter in a pan over low heat and add 50g/2oz/½ cup flour. Cook for 3 minutes and then gradually pour in 600ml/1 pint/2½ cups milk, stirring continuously. Simmer for 2–3 minutes. Season.

• Kashkaval cheese is particularly good in this recipe – it is a hard yellow cheese made from sheep's milk and is originally from the Balkans.

3 Preheat the oven to 180°C/350°F/Gas 4. Mix most of the grated cheese into the savoury white or béchamel sauce, reserving a little to sprinkle on top of the finished dish.

4 Arrange a layer of the aubergines in an ovenproof dish, then pour over some sauce. Repeat, ending with sauce. Sprinkle with the reserved cheese. Bake for 35–40 minutes, or until golden.

Energy 729Kcal/3,023kJ; Protein 33.1g; Carbohydrate 18.9g, of which sugars 10.3g; Fat 56.2g, of which saturates 27g; Cholesterol 107mg; Calcium 960mg; Fibre 2.8g; Sodium 1303mg.

STUFFED TOMATOES AND PEPPERS

Colourful peppers and tomatoes make perfect containers for various meat and vegetable stuffings. This rice and herb version uses typically Greek ingredients.

SERVES FOUR

INGREDIENTS

- 2 large ripe tomatoes
- 1 green (bell) pepper
- 1 yellow or orange (bell) pepper
- 60ml/4 tbsp extra virgin olive oil, plus extra for sprinkling
- 2 onions, chopped
- 2 garlic cloves, crushed
- 50g/2oz/½ cup blanched almonds, chopped
- 75g/3oz/scant ½ cup long grain rice, boiled and drained
- 15g/½oz/½ cup fresh mint, roughly chopped
- 15g/½oz/½ cup fresh flat leaf parsley, roughly chopped
- 25g/1oz/2 tbsp sultanas (golden raisins)
- 45ml/3 tbsp ground almonds
- salt and ground black pepper
- chopped fresh mixed herbs, to garnish

1 Cut the tomatoes in half and scoop out the pulp and seeds using a teaspoon. Drain on kitchen paper with cut sides down. Roughly chop the pulp and seeds.

VARIATION

Small aubergines (eggplants) or large courgettes (zucchini) also make good vegetables for stuffing. Halve and scoop out the centres of the vegetables, then oil the vegetable cases and bake for about 15 minutes. Chop the centres, fry for 2–3 minutes and add to the stuffing mixture. Fill the cases with the stuffing and bake as here.

2 Preheat the oven to 190°C/ 375°F/ Gas 5. Halve the peppers, leaving the stalks intact. Scoop out the seeds. Brush the peppers with 15ml/1 tbsp of the oil and bake on a baking tray for 15 minutes. Place the peppers and tomatoes in a shallow ovenproof dish and season with salt and freshly ground black pepper.

3 Fry the onions in the remaining oil for 5 minutes, until they are transparent. Add the garlic and chopped almonds and fry for a further minute or two, until you can smell the garlic aroma.

4 Remove the pan from the heat and stir in the rice, chopped tomatoes, mint, parsley and sultanas. Season well with salt and pepper and spoon the mixture into the tomatoes and peppers.

5 Pour 150ml/¼ pint/⅔ cup boiling water around the tomatoes and peppers and bake, uncovered, for 20 minutes. Sprinkle with the ground almonds and sprinkle with a little extra olive oil. Return to the oven and bake for a further 20 minutes, or until turning golden. Serve garnished with fresh herbs.

Energy 437Kcal/1,816kJ; Protein 9.6g; Carbohydrate 37.3g, of which sugars 20g; Fat 28.2g, of which saturates 3.2g; Cholesterol 0mg; Calcium 122mg; Fibre 6.4g; Sodium 22mg.

AUBERGINES BAKED WITH TOMATOES AND CHEESE

This is a delectable dish, particularly when made in the middle of summer when the aubergines are at their sweetest. In Greece it is usually served as a main course.

SERVES FOUR

INGREDIENTS

- 4 medium to large aubergines (eggplants), total weight about 1.2kg/2½lb
- 150ml/¼ pint/⅔ cup sunflower oil
- 50g/2oz/⅔ cup freshly grated Parmesan or Cheddar cheese

For the sauce

- 45ml/3 tbsp extra virgin olive oil
- 2 garlic cloves, crushed
- 2 x 400g/14oz cans tomatoes
- 5ml/1 tsp tomato purée (paste)
- 2.5ml/½ tsp sugar
- 2.5ml/½ tsp dried Greek oregano
- 30–45ml/2–3 tbsp chopped fresh flat leaf parsley
- salt and ground black pepper

VARIATIONS

- This dish will also work well with sliced courgettes (zucchini).
- You could add thinly sliced red (bell) peppers, quickly fried, to the aubergines, for an enhanced sweet flavour. This can be useful if the aubergines are not properly ripe early in the season.

1 Trim the aubergines and cut them lengthways into 1cm/½in-thick slices. Heat the oil in a large frying pan and fry the slices briefly in batches. Lift out as soon as they are golden on both sides and drain on a plate covered with a few sheets of kitchen paper.

2 Arrange the aubergine slices in two or three layers in a baking dish. Sprinkle liberally with salt and freshly ground black pepper.

3 Make the sauce. Heat the oil gently in a large pan over a medium heat until hot. Add the garlic and sauté for a few seconds, then add the canned tomatoes, tomato purée, sugar and dried Greek oregano and season to taste with salt and ground black pepper. Cover and simmer for 25–30 minutes, or until the sauce is thick and velvety, stirring occasionally. Stir in the chopped parsley and cook for 2–3 minutes.

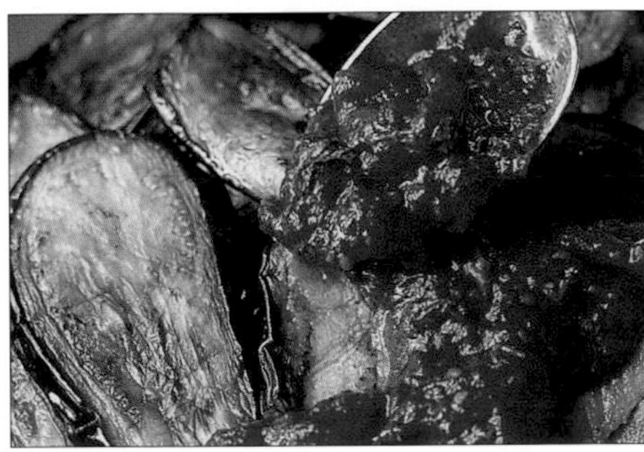

4 Meanwhile, preheat the oven to 180°C/350°F/ Gas 4. Spread the sauce over the aubergines to cover them. Sprinkle the cheese on top and bake for 40 minutes. Serve immediately.

Energy 441Kcal/1,830kJ; Protein 9.6g; Carbohydrate 13.6g, of which sugars 13g; Fat 39.3g, of which saturates 7.3g; Cholesterol 13mg; Calcium 218mg; Fibre 8.7g; Sodium 173mg.

FRIED PEPPERS WITH CHEESE

HERE IS A TRADITIONAL GREEK DISH FOR PEPPERS STUFFED WITH FETA CHEESE AND PARSLEY WITH A HINT OF CHILLI. ANY COLOUR OF PEPPER CAN BE USED, BUT RED OR YELLOW ARE SWEETEST.

SERVES TWO TO FOUR

INGREDIENTS
- 4 long (bell) peppers
- 50g/2oz/½ cup plain (all-purpose) flour, seasoned
- 1 egg, beaten
- olive oil, for shallow frying
- cucumber and tomato salad, to serve

For the filling
- 1 egg, beaten
- 90g/3½oz feta cheese, finely crumbled
- 30ml/2 tbsp chopped fresh flat leaf parsley
- 1 small chilli, seeded and finely chopped
- salt and ground black pepper

1 Make a slit down one side of each pepper lengthways, enabling you to scoop out the seeds and remove the cores, but leaving the peppers in one piece with the stalk intact.

2 Carefully open out the peppers and place under a preheated grill (broiler), skin side uppermost. Cook until the skin is charred and blackened. Place the peppers on a plate, cover with clear film (plastic wrap) and leave for 10 minutes.

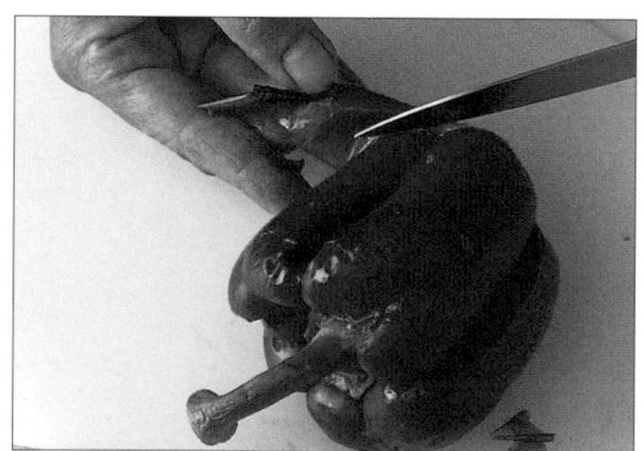

3 Using a sharp knife, carefully peel away the skin from the peppers. If it does not come away easily, you may need to put them back in the oven for another 5 minutes, then cover them with clear film (plastic wrap) again before easing the skin away.

4 In a bowl mix together well all the filling ingredients. Spoon the mixture into each of the peppers.

5 Season the flour with salt and pepper. Reshape the peppers to look whole and dip them into the seasoned flour, then the egg and then the flour again.

6 Fry the peppers gently in a little olive oil for 6–8 minutes, turning once or twice, until they are golden brown all the way around and the filling is set. Drain the peppers on a plate covered with a few layers of kitchen paper. Serve with a cucumber and tomato salad, and a few pieces of toasted pitta.

Energy 587Kcal/2,447kJ; Protein 21.3g; Carbohydrate 52.7g, of which sugars 32.1g; Fat 33.8g, of which saturates 10.6g; Cholesterol 222mg; Calcium 311mg; Fibre 9.9g; Sodium 746mg.

PEPPERS WITH HALLOUMI AND PINE NUTS

HALLOUMI CHEESE IS CREAMY-TASTING AND HAS A FIRM TEXTURE AND SALTY FLAVOUR THAT CONTRASTS WELL WITH THE SUCCULENT SWEET RED, ORANGE AND YELLOW PEPPERS.

SERVES FOUR

INGREDIENTS

- 4 red (bell) peppers
- 2 orange or yellow (bell) peppers
- 60ml/4 tbsp garlic or herb extra virgin olive oil
- 250g/9oz halloumi cheese
- 50g/2oz/½ cup pine nuts

1 Preheat the oven to 220°C/425°F/Gas 7. Halve the 4 red peppers, including their stalks and leaving the stalks attached. Carefully remove the seeds and other unwanted insides with a sharp knife. Halve and seed the 2 orange or yellow peppers. Chop the flesh finely and set to one side.

2 Place the red pepper halves on a baking sheet and fill with the chopped peppers. Drizzle with half the garlic or herb olive oil and bake for 25 minutes, or until the edges of the peppers are beginning to char.

3 With a sharp knife, dice the cheese into pieces about 1cm/½in cubed.

4 Tuck the cheese in the pepper halves among and on top of the chopped peppers. Sprinkle with the pine nuts and drizzle with the remaining garlic or herb extra virgin olive oil. Bake for a further 15 minutes, or until well browned. Serve warm, with a fresh green or mixed salad and toasted pitta or warm crusty bread.

Energy 506Kcal/2,099kJ; Protein 18.4g; Carbohydrate 32.5g, of which sugars 31g; Fat 34.3g, of which saturates 11.3g; Cholesterol 36mg; Calcium 268mg; Fibre 8.3g; Sodium 267mg.

POTATOES WITH FETA CHEESE AND OLIVES

THINLY SLICED POTATOES ARE COOKED WITH GREEK FETA CHEESE AND BLACK AND GREEN OLIVES IN OLIVE OIL FOR THIS FLAVOURSOME DISH. TOASTED PITTA BREAD AND A GREEN SALAD DRESSED WITH A FRUITY EXTRA VIRGIN OLIVE OIL MAKE IDEAL ACCOMPANIMENTS.

SERVES FOUR

INGREDIENTS

- 900g/2lb main-crop potatoes
- 150ml/¼ pint/⅔ cup extra virgin olive oil
- 1 sprig of fresh rosemary
- 275g/10oz feta cheese, sliced and then crumbled
- 115g/4oz/1 cup pitted black and green olives
- 300ml/½ pint/1¼ cups hot vegetable stock
- salt and ground black pepper

COOK'S TIP

A good-quality Greek feta cheese will make all the difference to the warming flavours of this dish.

1 Preheat the oven to 200°C/400°F/Gas 6. Cook the potatoes in plenty of boiling water for 15 minutes. Drain and cool slightly. Peel the potatoes and cut into thin slices.

2 Brush the base and sides of a shallow 1.5 litre/2½ pint/6¼ cup rectangular ovenproof dish with some of the olive oil.

3 Layer the potatoes in the dish with the rosemary, cheese and olives. Drizzle with the remaining olive oil and pour over the stock. Season with salt and plenty of ground black pepper.

4 Cook for 35 minutes, covering with foil to prevent the potatoes from getting too brown. Serve hot, straight from the dish.

Energy 584Kcal/2,429kJ; Protein 14.8g; Carbohydrate 37.3g, of which sugars 4g; Fat 42.7g, of which saturates 13.7g; Cholesterol 48mg; Calcium 279mg; Fibre 3.1g; Sodium 1662mg.

COURGETTE AND POTATO BAKE

COOK THIS DELICIOUS DISH, KNOWN AS BRIAMI *IN GREECE, IN EARLY AUTUMN, AND THE AROMAS SPILLING FROM THE KITCHEN WILL RECALL THE RICH SUMMER TASTES AND COLOURS JUST PAST. IN GREECE, THIS WOULD CONSTITUTE A HEARTY MAIN MEAL, WITH A SALAD, SOME OLIVES AND CHEESE.*

SERVES FOUR AS A MAIN COURSE
SIX AS A FIRST COURSE

INGREDIENTS

- 675g/1½lb courgettes (zucchini)
- 450g/1lb potatoes, peeled and cut into chunks
- 1 onion, finely sliced
- 3 garlic cloves, chopped
- 1 large red (bell) pepper, seeded and cubed
- 400g/14oz can chopped tomatoes
- 150ml/¼ pint/⅔ cup extra virgin olive oil
- 150ml/¼ pint/⅔ cup hot water
- 5ml/1 tsp dried oregano
- 45ml/3 tbsp chopped fresh flat leaf parsley, plus a few extra sprigs, to garnish
- salt and ground black pepper

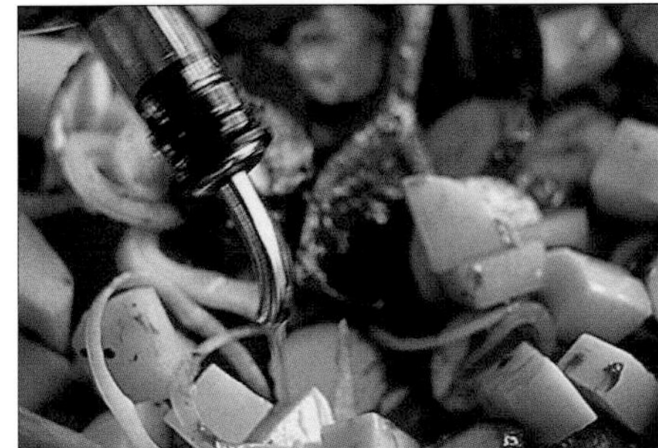

1 Preheat the oven to 190°C/375°F/Gas 5. Scrape the courgettes lightly under running water to dislodge any grit and then slice them into thin rounds. Put them in a large baking dish and add the chopped potatoes, onion, garlic, red pepper and tomatoes. Mix well, then stir in the olive oil, hot water and dried oregano.

2 Spread the mixture evenly, then season with salt and pepper. Bake for 30 minutes, then stir in the parsley and a little more water.

3 Return to the oven and cook for 1 hour, increasing the temperature to 200°C/400°F/Gas 6 for the final 10–15 minutes, so that the potatoes brown.

Energy 374Kcal/1,554kJ; Protein 6.6g; Carbohydrate 28.6g, of which sugars 11.2g; Fat 26.7g, of which saturates 4g; Cholesterol 0mg; Calcium 86mg; Fibre 5.1g; Sodium 29mg.

SPINACH FILO PIE

THIS POPULAR SPINACH AND FILO PASTRY PIE IS SOMETIMES CALLED SPANAKOPITA *IN ITS NATIVE GREECE. THERE ARE SEVERAL WAYS OF MAKING IT, BUT FETA IS INEVITABLY INCLUDED. IT IS OFTEN EATEN AS AN EVERYDAY DISH, OR A SLICE MAY BE TAKEN WITH SALAD FOR A LIGHT LUNCH. OCCASIONALLY IT FORMS PART OF A CELEBRATION MEAL, EITHER AS PART OF A MEZE TABLE OR AS THE MAIN COURSE SERVED WITH SALAD, VEGETABLES AND POTATOES.*

SERVES SIX

INGREDIENTS

- 1kg/2¼lb fresh spinach, thoroughly washed
- 4 spring onions (scallions), chopped
- 300g/11oz feta cheese, crumbled or coarsely grated
- 2 large eggs, beaten
- 30ml/2 tbsp chopped fresh flat leaf parsley
- 15ml/1 tbsp chopped fresh dill, plus a few sprigs to garnish
- 45ml/3 tbsp currants (optional)
- about 8 sheets of filo pastry, each measuring 30 x 18cm/12 x 7in, thawed if frozen
- 150ml/¼ pint/⅔ cup extra virgin olive oil
- ground black pepper

VARIATION

Any crumbly hard cheese will also work well in this pie. Try English Lancashire or Vermont Cheddar for a change.

1 Ensure the spinach is cleaned throughly by rinsing in cold water and draining at least 3 times. Then dry thoroughly with kitchen paper.

2 Break off any thick stalks from the spinach, then blanch the leaves in a very small amount of boiling water for 1–2 minutes, or until just wilted. Drain and refresh under cold water, then drain again, squeeze the spinach dry and chop it roughly.

3 Place the spinach in a bowl with the spring onions and cheese, then add the beaten eggs and stir them in thoroughly. Mix in the fresh herbs and currants, if using. Season with freshly ground black pepper.

4 Preheat the oven to 190°C/375°F/ Gas 5. Brush a sheet of filo pastry with oil and fit it into a 23cm/9in pie dish, allowing it to hang over the edges. Add 3 or 4 more sheets, placing them at different angles and brushing each liberally with olive oil.

5 Spoon the filling into the filo pastry case, then top with all but one of the remaining filo sheets, brushing each filo sheet with olive oil as you go. Fold the overhanging filo pastry over the top sheets to seal. Brush the reserved filo on both sides with olive oil and scrunch it over the top of the pie.

6 Brush the pie with olive oil. Sprinkle with a little water to stop the filo edges from curling, then place on a baking sheet. Bake for about 40 minutes, or until golden and crisp. Allow the pie to cool for 15 minutes before serving. Serve with a crisp salad.

Energy 396Kcal/1,640kJ; Protein 16.8g; Carbohydrate 13.8g, of which sugars 4g; Fat 30.7g, of which saturates 10.1g; Cholesterol 111mg; Calcium 528mg; Fibre 4.8g; Sodium 988mg.

TOMATO, FETA CHEESE AND OLIVE TARTS

THESE UPSIDE-DOWN TARTLETS ARE FILLED WITH VEGETABLES AND CHUNKS OF FETA CHEESE. THEY ARE A PERFECT MEAL AND MAKE A FAVOURITE FOR OUTDOOR EATING AND AT PICNICS.

SERVES FOUR

INGREDIENTS

- 25g/1oz sun-dried aubergine (eggplant) slices
- 300ml/½ pint/1¼ cups boiling water
- 45ml/3 tbsp sunflower oil
- 1 onion, thinly sliced
- 150g/5oz/2 cups button (white) mushrooms, sliced
- 1 garlic clove, crushed
- 12–16 cherry tomatoes, halved
- 8 black or green olives, pitted and chopped
- 115g/4oz feta cheese, sliced and then crumbled
- 350g/12oz ready-made puff pastry, thawed if frozen
- salt and ground black pepper

1 Preheat the oven to 200°C/400°F/Gas 6.

2 Place the aubergine slices in a shallow dish. Pour over the boiling water and leave to soak for 10 minutes. Rinse in cold water, and then drain on kitchen paper. Cut the aubergine slices in half or quarters, depending on size.

3 Heat 30ml/2 tbsp of the oil in a frying pan and fry the onion over a medium heat for 5 minutes. Add the mushrooms and cook for 3–4 minutes, or until the onions are light golden. Set aside.

4 Heat the remaining oil in the frying pan, add the aubergine slices and garlic and lightly fry for 1–2 minutes. Lightly oil four individual dishes.

5 Mix the halved tomatoes with the onions, mushrooms, aubergines, olives and feta cheese and divide among the dishes. Season well.

6 Roll out the pastry thinly into an oblong, then cut out four rounds, each slightly larger than the diameter of the dishes. Place the pastry on top of the vegetable and cheese mixture, tucking the overlap down inside the dish.

7 Bake for 20 minutes, or until the pastry is risen and golden. Cool slightly then invert on to individual warmed serving plates to serve. Garnish with black and green olives and serve with a fruity extra virgin olive oil for drizzling. A fresh mixed salad and new potatoes make wonderful accompaniment for these tarts.

COOK'S TIP

Choose cherry tomatoes on the vine for the very best flavour.

Energy 520Kcal/2,167kJ; Protein 12g; Carbohydrate 38.8g, of which sugars 6.9g; Fat 37.2g, of which saturates 5.3g; Cholesterol 20mg; Calcium 182mg; Fibre 4g; Sodium 865mg.

HERBED GREEK MINI TARTS

IF YOU CAN, USE LARGE TARTLET TINS TO MAKE THESE LITTLE PIES. THEY PROVIDE A DEEP CASE TO HOLD PLENTY OF THE DELICIOUSLY TANGY YOGURT FILLING. THESE ARE IDEAL FOR PICNICS.

MAKES EIGHT

INGREDIENTS
- 45–60ml/3–4 tbsp tapenade or sun-dried tomato paste
- 1 large egg
- 100g/3¾oz/scant ½ cup thick Greek (US strained plain) yogurt
- 90ml/6 tbsp milk
- 1 garlic clove, crushed
- 30ml/2 tbsp chopped mixed herbs, such as thyme, marjoram, basil and parsley
- salt and ground black pepper

For the pastry
- 115g/4oz/1 cup plain (all-purpose) flour
- pinch of salt
- 50g/2oz/¼ cup butter, diced
- 30ml/2 tbsp chilled water

1 To make the pastry, sift the flour and salt into a large bowl. Rub or cut in the butter. Sprinkle over the water and mix to a dough. Knead briefly, then wrap and chill for 20 minutes.

2 Roll out the pastry and cut out eight rounds. Use to line deep tartlet tins (muffin pans).

3 Chill the pastry cases for 30 minutes. Meanwhile, preheat the oven to 190°C/375°F/Gas 5. Line each pastry case with a small piece of foil. Bake for about 15 minutes. Remove the foil and bake for a further 5 minutes, until crisp.

4 Spread a little tapenade or tomato paste in the base of each pastry case.

5 Whisk together the egg, yogurt, milk, garlic, herbs and seasoning.

6 Carefully spoon the egg mixture into the pastry cases and bake for about 30 minutes, or until the filling is just firm to the touch and the pastry golden. Allow the pies to cool slightly before carefully removing them from the tins and serving with a crisp salad tossed in extra virgin olive oil.

VARIATION

A few chopped green or black olives would be a tasty addition to the filling for these pies.

Energy 133Kcal/555kJ; Protein 4g; Carbohydrate 13g, of which sugars 2g; Fat 7.7g, of which saturates 4.3g; Cholesterol 43mg; Calcium 74mg; Fibre 1g; Sodium 78mg.

Greek Picnic Pie

Aubergines layered with spinach, feta cheese and rice make a marvellous filling for a pie that is perfect for picnics. It can be served warm or cold and makes a good vegetarian dish for a buffet lunch in summer or autumn.

SERVES SIX

INGREDIENTS
- 45–60ml/3–4 tbsp olive oil
- 1 large aubergine (eggplant), sliced into rounds
- 1 onion, chopped
- 1 garlic clove, crushed
- 175g/6oz fresh spinach, washed
- 4 eggs
- 75g/3oz feta cheese, crumbled
- 40g/1½oz/½ cup freshly grated Parmesan cheese
- 60ml/4 tbsp natural (plain) yogurt
- 90ml/6 tbsp creamy milk
- 225g/8oz/2 cups cooked white or brown long grain rice
- salt and ground black pepper

For the pastry
- 225g/8oz/2 cups plain (all-purpose) flour
- pinch of salt
- 5ml/1 tsp dried basil
- 115g/4oz/½ cup butter, diced
- 45–60ml/3–4 tbsp chilled water

1 To make the pastry, sift the flour and salt into a mixing bowl. Stir in the basil, then rub or cut in the butter until the mixture resembles fine breadcrumbs. Sprinkle over most of the water and mix to a dough, adding more water if required. Wrap in clear film (plastic wrap) and chill for 30 minutes.

2 Roll out the pastry thinly and use to line a 25cm/10in flan ring or flan tin (quiche pan). Cover with clear film and chill for 30 minutes more. Meanwhile, preheat the oven to 180°C/350°F/Gas 4.

VARIATION
Courgettes (zucchini) make a good alternative to the aubergines (eggplants). Fry the sliced courgettes in a little oil for 3–4 minutes, or until golden. You will need three to four medium-size courgettes. Or, use baby courgettes and thinly slice them horizontally; these would look particularly attractive arranged on top of the pie.

3 Prick around the base of the chilled pastry case all over with a fork and bake blind in the oven for 10–12 minutes, or until the pastry is just turning golden. (If you prefer, you can bake the pastry case lined with baking parchment and weighted with baking beans, dried lentils or chickpeas. Remove the paper and beans for the last few minutes of baking.)

4 To make the filling, heat 45ml/3 tbsp of the oil in a frying pan and gently fry the aubergine slices for 6–8 minutes on each side until golden. You may need to add a little more olive oil at first, but this will be released as the flesh softens. Lift out the aubergine slices and drain on a plate covered with a few layers of kitchen paper.

5 Add the onion and garlic to the oil remaining in the pan and fry over a gentle heat for 4–5 minutes until soft, adding a little extra oil if necessary.

6 Chop the spinach finely, by hand or in a food processor. Beat the eggs in a large mixing bowl.

7 Add the spinach, crumbled feta, Parmesan, yogurt, milk and the onion mixture to the eggs. Season well with salt and pepper and stir thoroughly.

8 Spread the cooked rice in an even layer over the base of the pastry case. Reserve about 8 aubergine slices – save the best ones as these will be placed over the top – and arrange the rest in an even layer over the rice.

9 Spoon the spinach and feta mixture over the aubergines and place the reserved slices of aubergine on top. Bake the pie for 30–40 minutes, or until lightly browned. Serve warm or cold, with a mixed salad.

Energy 554Kcal/2,309kJ; Protein 16.6g; Carbohydrate 53.3g, of which sugars 4.3g; Fat 31.4g, of which saturates 15.5g; Cholesterol 185mg; Calcium 299mg; Fibre 2.7g; Sodium 473mg.

SIDE DISHES AND SALADS

The wealth of vegetables available in Greece provides a range of tasty side dishes and salads to accompany main courses. Many can be added to the meze table or eaten as a light lunch or main course. Vegetables are always used as fresh as possible, either straight from the garden or the market.

Fresh Green Beans with Tomato Sauce

This is one of the standard summer dishes in Greece and is made with different kinds of fresh beans according to what is available. When the beans are tender and the tomatoes sweet, the dish, although frugal, can have an astoundingly good flavour. It is usually accompanied by feta cheese and fresh bread.

SERVES FOUR

INGREDIENTS

- 800g/1¾lb green beans, trimmed
- 150ml/¼ pint/⅔ cup extra virgin olive oil
- 1 large onion, thinly sliced
- 2 garlic cloves, chopped
- 2 small potatoes, peeled and chopped into cubes
- 675g/1½lb tomatoes or a 400g/14oz can plum tomatoes, chopped
- 150ml/¼ pint/⅔ cup hot water
- 45–60ml/3–4 tbsp chopped fresh parsley
- salt and ground black pepper

1 If the green beans are very long, cut them in half. Drop them into a bowl of cold water so that they are completely submerged. Leave them to absorb the water for a few minutes.

2 Heat the olive oil in a large pan, add the onion and sauté until translucent. Add the garlic, then, when it becomes aromatic, stir in the potatoes and sauté the mixture for a few minutes.

3 Add the tomatoes and the hot water and cook for 5 minutes. Drain the beans, rinse them and drain again, then add them to the pan with a little salt and pepper to season. Cover and simmer for 30 minutes. Stir in the chopped parsley, with a little more hot water if the mixture looks dry. Cook for 10 minutes more, until the beans are very tender. Serve hot with slices of feta cheese, if you like.

Energy 350Kcal/1,448kJ; Protein 6.6g; Carbohydrate 21.9g, of which sugars 13.4g; Fat 26.9g, of which saturates 4g; Cholesterol 0mg; Calcium 121mg; Fibre 7.7g; Sodium 25mg.

SLOW-COOKED OKRA WITH TOMATOES

OKRA MAKES A DELICIOUSLY SWEET CASSEROLE AND, AS FAR AS VEGETABLE DISHES GO, THIS IS ONE OF THE BEST. MADE WITH FRESH TOMATOES, AT THE HEIGHT OF THE SUMMER, IT IS CERTAINLY A FAVOURITE LUNCH, ESPECIALLY WHEN SERVED WITH A FRESH-TASTING FETA CHEESE AND CRUSTY BREAD. IT CAN BE SERVED HOT OR AT ROOM TEMPERATURE.

SERVES FOUR AS A MAIN COURSE
SIX AS A FIRST COURSE

INGREDIENTS

- 675g/1½lb fresh okra
- 150ml/¼ pint/⅔ cup extra virgin olive oil
- 1 large onion, sliced
- 675g/1½lb fresh tomatoes, sliced, or 400g/14oz can chopped tomatoes
- 2.5ml/½ tsp sugar
- 30ml/2 tbsp finely chopped flat leaf parsley
- salt and ground black pepper

COOK'S TIP
When cooking okra whole be careful not to cut into the pod itself or the mucilaginous liquid will be released during cooking.

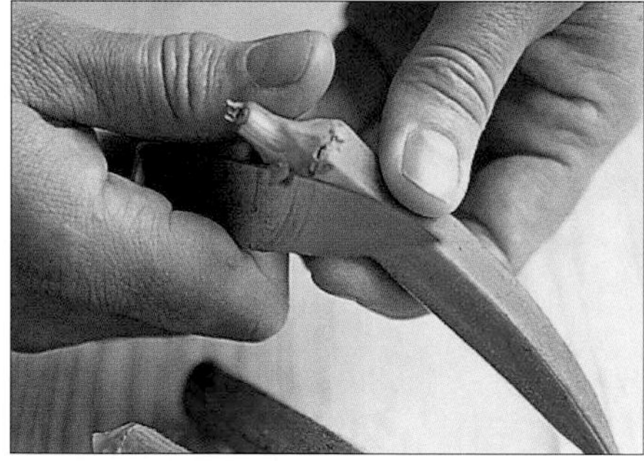

1 Cut off the conical head from each okra pod, without cutting into the body of the okra. Remove the black tip at the other end and rinse the pod.

2 Heat the oil in a large, deep pan or sauté pan and fry the onion slices until light golden. Stir in the fresh or canned tomatoes, with the sugar, and salt and pepper to taste. Cook for 5 minutes.

3 Add the okra and shake the pan to distribute them evenly and coat them in the sauce. The okra should be immersed in the sauce, so add a little hot water if necessary.

4 Cook gently for 30–40 minutes, depending on the size of the okra. Shake the pan occasionally, but do not stir. Add the parsley just before serving.

Energy 326Kcal/1,350kJ; Protein 6.5g; Carbohydrate 14.8g, of which sugars 12.8g; Fat 27.3g, of which saturates 4.3g; Cholesterol 0mg; Calcium 295mg; Fibre 9.1g; Sodium 30mg.

ARTICHOKES WITH NEW POTATOES

AMONG THE FIRST SPRING VEGETABLES, ARTICHOKES APPEAR IN GREECE IN THE MIDDLE OF MARCH, TOGETHER WITH FRESH BROAD BEANS AND AROMATIC BUNCHES OF DILL. THEY ARE COOKED IN VARIOUS COMBINATIONS WITH MANY SPRING VEGETABLES.

SERVES FOUR AS A FIRST COURSE

INGREDIENTS

- 4 globe artichokes
- juice of 1½ lemons
- 150ml/¼ pint/⅔ cup extra virgin olive oil
- 1 large onion, thinly sliced
- 3 carrots, peeled and sliced into long batons
- 300ml/½ pint/1¼ cups hot water
- 400g/14oz small new potatoes, scrubbed or peeled
- 4 or 5 spring onions (scallions), chopped
- 60–75ml/4–5 tbsp chopped fresh dill
- salt and ground black pepper

1 Remove and discard the outer leaves of the artichoke until you reach the tender ones. Cut off the top, halfway down. Scoop out the hairy choke. Cut off the stalk, leaving 4cm/1½in, and peel away its outer surface. Drop them into a bowl of cold water acidulated with about one-third of the lemon juice, which is about half a lemon. Add enough hot water to just about cover the artichokes.

2 Heat the extra virgin olive oil in a pan and sauté the onion slices gently over a low to medium heat until they become translucent. Next add the baton carrots and sauté for 2–3 minutes. Add the remaining lemon juice and the hot water, stir, and bring to the boil.

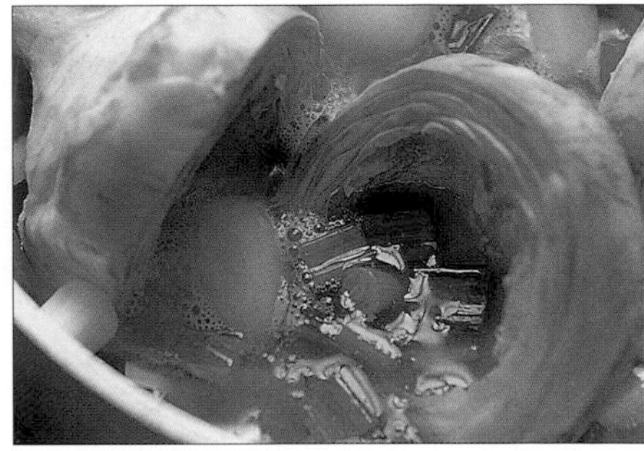

3 Drain the artichokes and add them to the pan with the potatoes, spring onions and seasoning. The vegetables should be almost covered with the sauce, so add a little more hot water if needed. Cover and cook gently for 40–45 minutes. Sprinkle the dill over the top and cook for 2–3 minutes more.

Energy 373Kcal/1,552kJ; Protein 5.6g; Carbohydrate 30.2g, of which sugars 13.7g; Fat 26.5g, of which saturates 3.9g; Cholesterol 0mg; Calcium 142mg; Fibre 6.7g; Sodium 103mg.

BRAISED ARTICHOKES WITH FRESH PEAS

This artichoke dish is uniquely delicate. Shelling fresh peas is rather time-consuming but their matchless flavour makes the task very worthwhile. Sit on a step outside in the sunshine, and what at first seems a chore will become positively sybaritic.

SERVES FOUR

INGREDIENTS
- 4 medium to large globe artichokes
- juice of 1½ lemons
- 150ml/¼ pint/⅔ cup extra virgin olive oil
- 1 onion, thinly sliced
- 4 or 5 spring onions (scallions), roughly chopped
- 2 carrots, peeled and sliced in rounds
- 1.2kg/2½lb fresh peas in pods, shelled (this will give you about 500–675g/1¼–1½lb peas)
- 450ml/¾ pint/scant 2 cups hot water
- 60ml/4 tbsp finely chopped fresh dill
- salt and ground black pepper
- a few sprigs of fresh dill, to garnish

1 Remove and discard the outer leaves of the artichokes. Cut off the top, and cut the artichoke in half lengthways. Scoop out the hairy choke and cut the stalk to 4cm/1½in. Drop the halves into a bowl of water acidulated with about one-third of the lemon juice.

2 Heat the oil in a pan and add the onion and spring onions, and then a minute later, add the carrots. Sauté the mixture for a few seconds, then add the peas and stir for 1–2 minutes.

3 Pour in the remaining lemon juice. Let it bubble and evaporate for a few seconds, then add the hot water and bring to the boil. Drain the artichokes and add them to the pan, with salt and pepper to taste. Cover and cook gently for about 40–45 minutes, stirring occasionally. Add the dill and cook for 5 minutes more, or until the vegetables are beautifully tender. Serve hot or at room temperature.

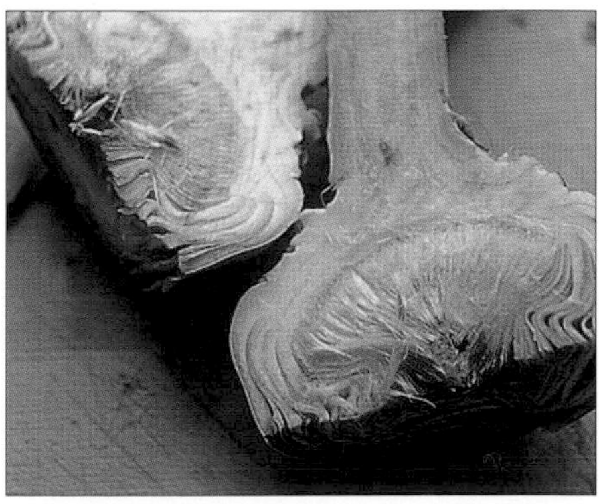

Energy 384Kcal/1,584kJ; Protein 10.5g; Carbohydrate 25.2g, of which sugars 12.4g; Fat 27.5g, of which saturates 4g; Cholesterol 0mg; Calcium 121mg; Fibre 10g; Sodium 85mg.

GLOBE ARTICHOKES WITH GREEN BEANS

PIQUANT GARLIC DRESSING GOES PERFECTLY WITH THESE LIGHTLY COOKED VEGETABLES. SERVE LEMON WEDGES WITH THE ARTICHOKES SO THAT THEIR JUICE MAY BE SQUEEZED OVER TO TASTE. THE VEGETABLES CAN ALSO BE GARNISHED WITH FINELY SHREDDED LEMON RIND.

SERVES FOUR TO SIX

INGREDIENTS

- 225g/8oz green beans
- 3 small globe artichokes
- 15ml/1 tbsp lemon-flavoured extra virgin olive oil
- 250ml/8fl oz/1 cup garlic dressing
- salt and ground black pepper

COOK'S TIP

Artichokes should feel heavy – make sure that the inner leaves are wrapped tightly round the choke and the heart inside.To eat the artichokes, pull the leaves from the base one at a time and use to scoop the dressing. It is only the fleshy end of each leaf that is eaten as well as the base, heart or "fond".

1 Wash the beans thoroughly and cook in boiling water for 1–2 minutes, or until slightly softened. Drain well.

2 Trim the artichoke stalks close to the base. Cook them in a large pan of salted water for about 30 minutes, or until you can easily pull away a leaf from the base. Drain well.

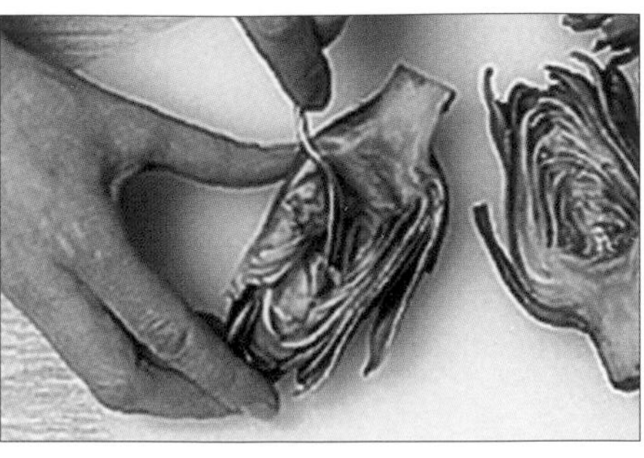

3 Using a sharp knife, halve them lengthways and ease out their chokes using a teaspoon.

4 Arrange the artichokes and beans on serving plates and drizzle with the oil. Season with coarse salt and a little pepper. Spoon the garlic dressing into the hearts and serve warm.

Energy 449Kcal/1,848kJ; Protein 1.6g; Carbohydrate 2.6g, of which sugars 2g; Fat 34.1g, of which saturates 6.7g; Cholesterol 0mg; Calcium 59mg; Fibre 2.1g; Sodium 626mg.

STUFFED MUSHROOMS WITH SPINACH

USE FRESH CEPS, IF YOU CAN FIND THEM, TO ACHIEVE THE TRADITIONAL DISH POPULAR THROUGHOUT THE MAINLAND, ALTHOUGH THE LARGE, FLAT WILD OR CULTIVATED MUSHROOMS WORK VERY WELL TOO. THEY MAKE A PERFECT ACCOMPANIMENT TO BARBECUED MEAT OR CHICKEN.

SERVES SIX

INGREDIENTS

- 12 large flat mushrooms
- 450g/1lb small young spinach leaves
- 3 rindless bacon rashers (strips), cut into 5mm/¼in dice
- 1 onion, finely chopped
- 2 egg yolks, beaten
- 40g/1½ oz/¾ cup fresh breadcrumbs
- 5ml/1 tsp chopped fresh marjoram
- 45ml/3 tbsp olive or vegetable oil
- 115g/4oz feta cheese, crumbled
- salt and ground black pepper

1 Peel the mushrooms only if necessary, otherwise just wipe them. Remove the stalks and chop them finely.

2 Blanch the spinach by dropping it into boiling water for 1–2 minutes, then plunge into cold water. Squeeze dry in kitchen paper, then chop.

3 Dry fry the bacon and onion until golden brown, then add the mushroom stalks. Remove from the heat. Stir in the spinach, egg yolks, breadcrumbs and marjoram, and season to taste.

4 Place the mushrooms underside up on a baking sheet and brush with a little extra virgin olive oil. Do not add too much olive oil as the mushrooms will produce moisture while they are cooking.

5 Place heaped tablespoons of the spinach mixture on to the mushroom caps. Sprinkle over the cheese and cook the mushrooms under a preheated grill (broiler) for about 10 minutes, or until golden brown.

Energy 212Kcal/882kJ; Protein 12g; Carbohydrate 8.1g, of which sugars 2.5g; Fat 14.8g, of which saturates 4.8g; Cholesterol 87mg; Calcium 226mg; Fibre 3.7g; Sodium 636mg.

GREEK TOMATO AND POTATO BAKE

AN ADAPTATION OF A CLASSIC GREEK DISH, WHICH IS USUALLY COOKED ON THE HOB. THIS RECIPE HAS A RICHER FLAVOUR AS IT IS STOVE-COOKED FIRST AND THEN BAKED IN THE OVEN.

SERVES FOUR

INGREDIENTS

- 120ml/4fl oz/½ cup extra virgin olive oil
- 1 large onion, finely chopped
- 3 garlic cloves, crushed
- 4 large ripe tomatoes, peeled, seeded and chopped
- 1kg/2¼lb even-size main-crop waxy potatoes
- salt and freshly ground black pepper
- a few sprigs of fresh flat leaf parsley, to garnish

COOK'S TIP

Make sure that the potatoes are evenly sized and completely coated in the olive oil otherwise they will not cook evenly.

1 Preheat the oven to 180°C/350°F/ Gas 4.

2 Heat the oil in a flameproof casserole. Fry the chopped onion and garlic for 5 minutes, or until softened and just starting to brown.

3 Add the tomatoes to the pan, season and cook for 1 minute.

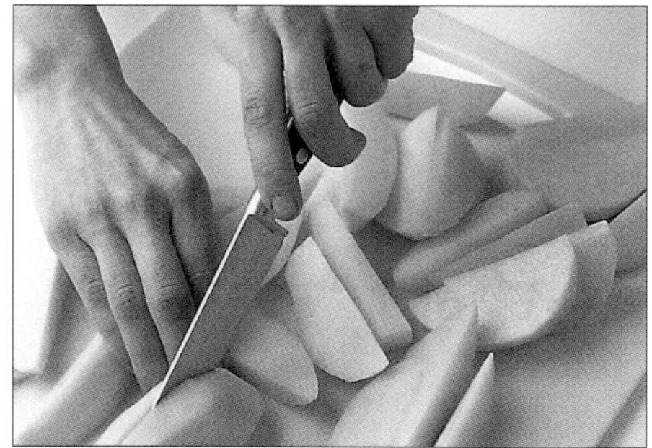

4 Cut the potatoes into wedges. Add to the pan, stirring well. Cook for 10 minutes. Season again with salt and freshly ground black pepper, and cover with a tight-fitting lid.

5 Place the covered casserole on the middle shelf of the oven and cook for 45 minutes–1 hour. Garnish with a few sprigs of fresh flat leaf parsley.

Energy 399Kcal/1,670kJ; Protein 5.9g; Carbohydrate 49.3g, of which sugars 10.6g; Fat 21.2g, of which saturates 3.2g; Cholesterol 0mg; Calcium 41mg; Fibre 4.6g; Sodium 39mg.

CAULIFLOWER WITH EGG AND LEMON

In Greece cauliflower is very popular and is used in many different ways. Here it is teamed with a lemon sauce, a perfect accompaniment for KEFTEDES *(fried meatballs).*

SERVES SIX

INGREDIENTS

- 75–90ml/5–6 tbsp extra virgin olive oil
- 1 medium cauliflower, divided into large florets
- 2 eggs
- juice of 1 lemon
- 5ml/1 tsp cornflour (cornstarch), mixed to a cream with a little cold water
- 30ml/2 tbsp chopped fresh flat leaf parsley
- salt

1 Heat the olive oil in a large, heavy pan, add the cauliflower florets and sauté over a medium heat until they start to brown.

2 Pour in enough hot water to almost cover the cauliflower florets, add salt to taste, bring to the boil, then cover the pan and cook for 7–8 minutes until the florets are just soft.

3 Remove the pan from the heat and leave to stand, retaining the hot water and covering the pan tightly to keep in the heat. Meanwhile, make the sauce.

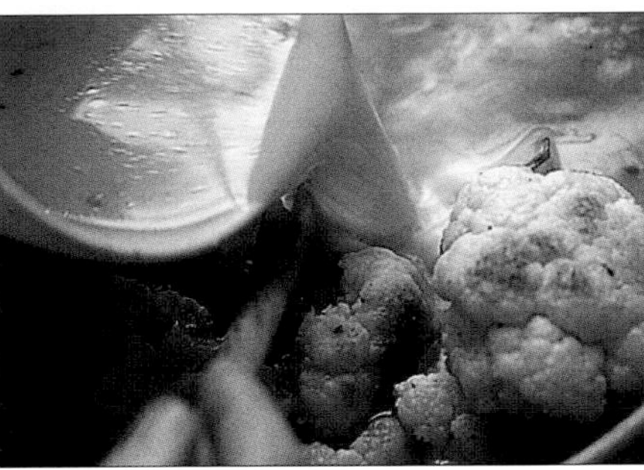

4 Beat the eggs in a bowl, add the lemon juice and cornflour and beat until well mixed. While beating, add a few tablespoons of the hot liquid from the cauliflower. Pour the egg mixture slowly over the cauliflower, then stir gently. Place the pan over a very gentle heat for 2 minutes to thicken the sauce. Spoon into a warmed serving bowl, sprinkle the chopped parsley over the top and serve.

Energy 211Kcal/874kJ; Protein 8g; Carbohydrate 5.2g, of which sugars 3.4g; Fat 17.8g, of which saturates 3g; Cholesterol 95mg; Calcium 63mg; Fibre 2.8g; Sodium 51mg.

ROASTED BEETROOT WITH GARLIC SAUCE

In Greece, beetroot is a favourite winter vegetable, either served solo as a salad or with a layer of the flavourful garlic sauce, known as skordalia, on top.

SERVES FOUR

INGREDIENTS

- 675g/1½lb medium or small beetroot (beets)
- 75–90ml/5–6 tbsp extra virgin olive oil
- salt

For the garlic sauce

- 4 medium slices of bread, crusts removed, soaked in water for 10 minutes
- 2 or 3 garlic cloves, chopped
- 15ml/1 tbsp white wine vinegar
- 60ml/4 tbsp extra virgin olive oil

1 Preheat the oven to 180°C/350°F/ Gas 4. Rinse the beetroot under cold running water and rub off any grit, but be careful not to pierce the skin or the colour will run.

2 Line a roasting pan with a large sheet of foil and place the beetroot on top. Drizzle a little of the olive oil over them, sprinkle lightly with salt and fold over both edges of the foil to enclose the beetroot completely. Bake for about 1½ hours until perfectly soft.

3 Meanwhile, make the garlic sauce. Squeeze most of the water out of the soaked bread, but leave it quite moist.

4 Place the soaked bread in a blender or food processor. Add the garlic and vinegar, with salt to taste, and blend until smooth.

5 While the blender or food processor is running, drizzle in the extra virgin olive oil through the lid or feeder tube. The sauce should be runny. Spoon it into a bowl and set it aside.

6 Remove the beetroot from the foil package. When they are cool enough to handle, carefully peel them. Cut them into thin, round slices and arrange on a flat platter.

7 Drizzle with the remaining oil. Either spread a thin layer of garlic sauce on top, or hand it around separately. Serve with fresh bread, if you like.

Energy 342Kcal/1,425kJ; Protein 5g; Carbohydrate 25.2g, of which sugars 12.5g; Fat 25.4g, of which saturates 3.6g; Cholesterol 0mg; Calcium 61mg; Fibre 3.6g; Sodium 242mg.

Aromatic Braised Leeks in Red Wine

Coriander seeds and oregano give a delicate flavour to this dish of braised leeks. Serve it as part of a mixed meze or as a partner for baked white fish.

SERVES SIX

INGREDIENTS
- 12 baby leeks or 6 thick leeks
- 15ml/1 tbsp coriander seeds, lightly crushed
- 5cm/2in piece of cinnamon stick
- 120ml/4fl oz/½ cup olive oil
- 3 fresh bay leaves
- 2 strips pared orange rind
- 5 or 6 fresh or dried oregano sprigs
- 5ml/1 tsp sugar
- 150ml/¼ pint/⅔ cup fruity red wine
- 10ml/2 tsp balsamic or sherry vinegar
- 30ml/2 tbsp coarsely chopped fresh oregano or marjoram
- salt and ground black pepper

1 If using baby leeks, simply trim the ends, but leave them whole. Cut thick leeks into 5–7.5cm/2–3in lengths.

2 Place the coriander seeds and cinnamon in a pan wide enough to take all the leeks in a single layer. Cook over a medium heat for 2–3 minutes, or until the spices give off a fragrant aroma, then stir in the olive oil, bay leaves, orange rind, fresh or dried oregano, sugar, wine and balsamic or sherry vinegar. Bring to the boil and simmer for 5 minutes.

3 Add the leeks to the pan. Bring back to the boil, reduce the heat and cover the pan. Cook the leeks gently for 5 minutes. Uncover and simmer gently for another 5–8 minutes, or until the leeks are just tender when tested with the tip of a sharp knife.

4 Use a slotted spoon to transfer the leeks to a serving dish. Boil the pan juices rapidly until reduced to about 75–90ml/5–6 tbsp. Add salt and pepper to taste and pour the liquid over the leeks. Leave to cool.

5 The leeks can be left to stand for several hours. If you chill them, bring them back to room temperature again before serving. Sprinkle the chopped herbs over the leeks just before serving.

COOK'S TIP

Balsamic vinegar is ideal for this dish. It has a high sugar content and wonderfully strong bouquet. It is a very dark brown colour and has a deep, rich flavour with hints of herbs and port. Nowadays you can find quite good balsamic vinegar in supermarkets. It is expensive, but the flavour is so rich that you only need to use a little.

Energy 151Kcal/621kJ; Protein 1.1g; Carbohydrate 1.7g, of which sugars 1.3g; Fat 13.7g, of which saturates 2g; Cholesterol 0mg; Calcium 29mg; Fibre 1.5g; Sodium 5mg.

SPINACH WITH RAISINS AND PINE NUTS

RAISINS AND PINE NUTS MAKE DELICIOUS PARTNERS IN DISHES, SPRUCING UP GREEN VEGETABLES TO MAKE THEM INTO FLAVOURSOME SIDE DISHES. HERE, TOSSED WITH WILTED SPINACH AND CROÛTONS, THEY MAKE A TASTY SNACK OR MAIN MEAL ACCOMPANIMENT.

SERVES FOUR

INGREDIENTS

- 50g/2oz/⅓ cup raisins
- 1 large thick slice white bread
- 45ml/3 tbsp olive oil
- 25g/1oz/¼ cup pine nuts
- 500g/1¼lb young spinach, stalks removed
- 2 garlic cloves, crushed
- salt and ground black pepper

VARIATION

You can also use Swiss chard or spinach beet instead of the spinach. They will give a more earthy, rich taste that goes well with red meats. You will need to cook them for a few minutes longer.

1 Put the raisins in a small bowl, cover them with boiling water and leave to soak for 10 minutes. Drain and pat dry with kitchen paper.

2 Cut the bread into small cubes and discard the crusts. Heat 30ml/2 tbsp of the olive oil and fry the bread until golden. Drain.

3 Heat the remaining oil in the pan. Fry the pine nuts until they begin to turn golden brown. Add the spinach and garlic and cook quickly, turning the spinach until it has just wilted.

4 Toss in the raisins and season lightly. Transfer to a warmed serving dish. Sprinkle with croûtons and serve hot.

Energy 198Kcal/824kJ; Protein 5.2g; Carbohydrate 14.3g, of which sugars 11g; Fat 13.7g, of which saturates 1.6g; Cholesterol 0mg; Calcium 226mg; Fibre 3.1g; Sodium 218mg.

RICE WITH LENTILS

LENTILS ARE A FAVOURITE STAPLE IN GREECE, ESPECIALLY DURING PERIODS OF FASTING, WHEN MEAT IS NOT EATEN. HERE THEY ARE COMBINED WITH RICE AND SPICES, MAKING A SATISFYING SIDE DISH TO ACCOMPANY SIMPLY FRIED FISH OR GRILLED MEAT OR AS A MAIN COURSE WITH SALAD.

SERVES SIX

INGREDIENTS

- 350g/12oz/1½ cups large brown lentils, soaked overnight in water
- 2 large onions
- 45ml/3 tbsp olive oil
- 15ml/1 tbsp ground cumin
- 2.5ml/½ tsp ground cinnamon
- 225g/8oz/generous 1 cup long grain rice
- salt and freshly ground black pepper
- a few sprigs of fresh flat leaf parsley, to garnish

1 Drain the lentils and put them in a large pan. Add enough water to cover by 5cm/2in. Bring to the boil, cover and simmer for 40 minutes to 1½ hours, or until tender. Drain thoroughly.

2 Finely chop one of the large onions, and finely slice the other. Heat 15ml/1 tbsp olive oil in a pan, add the finely chopped onion and fry until soft. Do not allow to brown.

3 Add the lentils and gently stir them in. Then add the cumin and coriander and stir in. Season to taste with salt and freshly ground black pepper.

4 Measure the volume of rice and add it, with the same volume of water, to the lentil mixture. Cover and simmer for about 20 minutes, until the rice is tender. Heat the remaining oil in a frying pan, and cook the sliced onion until it is very dark brown. Tip the rice mixture into a serving bowl, sprinkle with the onion and serve hot or cold, garnished with flat leaf parsley.

Energy 394Kcal/1,656kJ; Protein 17.5g; Carbohydrate 68g, of which sugars 5.1g; Fat 6.6g, of which saturates 0.9g; Cholesterol 0mg; Calcium 54mg; Fibre 3.8g; Sodium 23mg.

WILTED SPINACH WITH RICE AND DILL

THIS IS A DELICIOUS DISH THAT CAN BE MADE IN VERY LITTLE TIME. IN GREECE IT IS PARTICULARLY POPULAR DURING PERIODS OF FASTING, WHEN MEAT IS AVOIDED FOR RELIGIOUS REASONS.

SERVES SIX

INGREDIENTS

- 675g/1½lb fresh spinach, trimmed of any hard stalks
- 105ml/7 tbsp extra virgin olive oil
- 1 large onion, chopped
- juice of ½ lemon
- 150ml/¼ pint/⅔ cup water
- 115g/4oz/generous ½ cup long grain rice
- 45ml/3 tbsp chopped fresh dill, plus extra sprigs to garnish
- salt and ground black pepper

1 Thoroughly wash the spinach in cold water and drain. Repeat four or five times until the spinach is completely clean and free of grit, then drain it completely in a colander. Brush off the excess water with kitchen paper and coarsely shred the spinach.

2 Heat the olive oil in a large pan and sauté the onion until translucent. Add the spinach and stir for a few minutes to coat it with the oil.

3 As soon as the spinach looks wilted, add the lemon juice and the measured water and bring to the boil. Add the rice and half of the dill, then cover and cook gently for about 10 minutes or until the rice is cooked to your taste. If it looks too dry, add a little hot water.

4 Spoon into a serving dish and sprinkle the sprigs of dill over the top. Serve hot or at room temperature.

COOK'S TIP

This dish is ideal to accompany fried or barbecued fish or chickpea rissoles. It can also be eaten as a first course.

Energy 325Kcal/1,343kJ; Protein 7.8g; Carbohydrate 29.9g, of which sugars 5.6g; Fat 19.2g, of which saturates 2.7g; Cholesterol 0mg; Calcium 327mg; Fibre 4.8g; Sodium 242mg.

Lentil, Tomato and Cheese Salad

Cheese and lentils are a natural combination, and the small blue-green Puy lentils are perfect in this salad with chunks of crumbly feta cheese.

SERVES SIX

INGREDIENTS

- 200g/7oz/scant 1 cup lentils (preferably Puy lentils), soaked for about 3 hours in cold water to cover
- 1 red onion, chopped
- 1 bay leaf
- 60ml/4 tbsp extra virgin olive oil
- 45ml/3 tbsp chopped fresh flat leaf parsley
- 30ml/2 tbsp chopped fresh oregano or marjoram
- 250g/9oz cherry tomatoes, halved
- 250g/9oz feta, goat's milk cheese or Caerphilly cheese, crumbled
- salt and ground black pepper
- chicory (Belgian endive) or frisée lettuce leaves and fresh herbs, to garnish
- 30–45ml/2–3 tbsp lightly toasted pine nuts, to serve

1 Drain the lentils and place them in a large pan. Pour in plenty of cold water and add the onion and bay leaf. Bring to the boil, boil hard for 10 minutes, then lower the heat and simmer for 20 minutes or according to the instructions on the packet.

VARIATION

Continental, or green, lentils will also work well. Cook for about 30 minutes.

2 Drain the lentils, discard the bay leaf and tip them into a bowl. Add salt and pepper to taste. Toss with the olive oil. Set aside to cool, then mix with the fresh parsley, oregano or marjoram and cherry tomatoes.

3 Add the cheese. Line a serving dish with chicory or frisée leaves and pile the salad in the centre. Sprinkle over the pine nuts and garnish with fresh herbs.

Energy 324Kcal/1,352kJ; Protein 15.8g; Carbohydrate 21.9g, of which sugars 3.7g; Fat 19.9g, of which saturates 7.1g; Cholesterol 29mg; Calcium 188mg; Fibre 2.7g; Sodium 619mg.

Watermelon and Feta Salad with Mixed Seeds and Olives

The combination of sweet watermelon with salty feta cheese is refreshing and flavoursome. The salad may be served plain and light, on a leafy base, or with a herbed dressing drizzled over. It is perfect served as an appetizer or a side salad, or taken as part of a meze table on a summer picnic.

SERVES FOUR

INGREDIENTS

- 4 slices watermelon, chilled
- 130g/4½oz feta cheese, preferably sheep's milk feta, cut into bitesize pieces
- handful of mixed seeds, such as pumpkin seeds and sunflower seeds, lightly toasted
- 10–15 black olives

COOK'S TIP

The best choice of olives for this recipe are plump black ones, such as *kalamata*, other shiny, brined varieties or dry-cured black olives.

1 Cut the rind off the watermelon and remove as many seeds as possible. The sweetest and juiciest part is right in the core, and you may want to cut off any whiter flesh just under the skin.

2 Cut the flesh into triangular chunks. Mix the watermelon, feta cheese, mixed seeds and black olives. Cover and chill the salad for 30 minutes in the refrigerator before serving.

Energy 203Kcal/849kJ; Protein 7.8g; Carbohydrate 16.2g, of which sugars 14.8g; Fat 12.4g, of which saturates 5.2g; Cholesterol 23mg; Calcium 148mg; Fibre 1.1g; Sodium 754mg.

SUN-RIPENED TOMATO AND FETA SALAD WITH PURSLANE

THIS TASTY SALAD IS A VERSION OF A TRADITIONAL GREEK SALAD, WITH PLENTY OF PURSLANE ADDED TO THE TRADITIONAL COMBINATION OF TOMATO, PEPPER, ONION, CUCUMBER, FETA AND OLIVES. THIS RECIPE IS POPULAR IN THE RURAL COMMUNITIES AS FRESH PURSLANE GROWS WILD IN GARDENS AND UNCULTIVATED FIELDS.

SERVES FOUR

INGREDIENTS

- 225g/8oz tomatoes
- 1 red onion, thinly sliced
- 1 green (bell) pepper, cored and sliced in thin ribbons
- 1 piece of cucumber, about 15cm/6in in length, peeled and sliced in rounds
- 150g/5oz feta cheese, cubed
- a large handful of fresh purslane, trimmed of thick stalks
- 8–10 black olives
- 90–105ml/6–7 tbsp extra virgin olive oil
- 15ml/1 tbsp lemon juice
- 1.5ml/¼ tsp dried oregano
- salt and ground black pepper

1 Cut the tomatoes in quarters and place them in a salad bowl. Add the onion, green pepper, cucumber, feta, purslane and olives.

COOK'S TP

If purslane is not available, you can use rocket (arugula) instead.

2 Sprinkle the extra virgin olive oil, lemon juice and oregano on top. Add salt and ground black pepper to taste, then toss to coat everything in the olive oil and lemon, and to amalgamate the flavours. If possible, let the salad stand for 10–15 minutes at room temperature before serving.

Energy 283Kcal/1,168kJ; Protein 7.2g; Carbohydrate 6.8g, of which sugars 6.3g; Fat 25.4g, of which saturates 7.7g; Cholesterol 26mg; Calcium 158mg; Fibre 1.9g; Sodium 717mg.

GREEK SALAD

GREEK TOMATOES ARE RIPENED IN THE SUN AND ARE ABSOLUTELY BURSTING WITH FLAVOUR. THEY MAKE THE PERFECT BASE FOR A REFRESHING SALAD WITH CUCUMBER AND THE BEST-QUALITY FETA CHEESE. USE A GOOD FRUITY EXTRA VIRGIN OLIVE OIL FOR A SUCCESSFUL SALAD.

SERVES SIX

INGREDIENTS

- 1 cos or romaine lettuce, sliced
- 450g/1lb well-flavoured tomatoes, cut into eighths
- 1 cucumber, seeded and chopped
- 200g/7oz feta cheese, crumbled
- 4 spring onions, sliced
- 50g/2oz/½ cup black olives, stoned (pitted) and halved

For the dressing

- 90ml/6 tbsp extra virgin olive oil
- 25ml/1½ tbsp lemon juice
- salt and ground black pepper

1 Put the sliced lettuce, tomatoes and chopped cucumber into a large serving bowl and add the feta cheese, spring onions and black olives. Mix the ingredients together.

2 To make the dressing, mix together the extra virgin olive oil and lemon juice and season with salt and freshly ground black pepper to taste.

3 Pour the dressing over the salad. Toss the dressing into the salad well, and serve immediately with crusty bread or hot toasted pitta.

VARIATION

For a more substantial meze-style variation add red (bell) peppers, cored and chopped into bitesize pieces, and sprinkle with pine nuts if you like, and include mixed salad leaves with the lettuce.

Energy 212Kcal/879kJ; Protein 6.4g; Carbohydrate 4g, of which sugars 4g; Fat 19.1g, of which saturates 6.4g; Cholesterol 23mg; Calcium 147mg; Fibre 1.6g; Sodium 677mg.

POTATO AND FETA SALAD

A potato salad may sound mundane but this one is not, as it is redolent with the aromas of the herbs and has layer upon layer of flavours. It is an easy dish to assemble, so makes a perfect lunch or dinner for a busy day.

SERVES FOUR

INGREDIENTS

- 500g/1¼lb small new potatoes
- 5 spring onions (scallions), green and white parts finely chopped
- 15ml/1 tbsp rinsed bottled capers
- 8–10 black olives
- 115g/4oz feta cheese
- 45ml/3 tbsp finely chopped fresh flat leaf parsley
- 30ml/2 tbsp finely chopped fresh mint
- salt and freshly ground black pepper

For the dressing

- 90–120ml/6–8 tbsp extra virgin olive oil
- juice of 1 lemon, or to taste
- 2 salted or preserved anchovies, rinsed and finely chopped
- 45ml/3 tbsp Greek (US strained plain) yogurt
- 45ml/3 tbsp finely chopped fresh dill, plus a few sprigs, to garnish
- 5ml/1 tsp French mustard

1 Chop the feta cheese into small, evenly sized cubes and crumble slightly.

2 Bring a pan of lightly salted water to the boil and cook the potatoes in their skins for 25–30 minutes, or until tender. Take care not to let them become soggy and disintegrate. Drain them thoroughly and let them cool a little.

3 When the potatoes are cool enough to handle, peel them with your fingers and place them in a large bowl. If they are very small, keep them whole; otherwise cut them into large cubes. Add the chopped spring onions, capers, olives, feta cheese and fresh herbs, and toss gently to mix.

4 To make the dressing, place the extra virgin olive oil in a bowl with the lemon juice and anchovies.

5 Whisk thoroughly for a few minutes until the dressing emulsifies and thickens; you may need to add a little more olive oil if it does not thicken. Whisk in the yogurt, dill and mustard, with salt and pepper to taste.

6 Dress the salad while the potatoes are still warm, tossing lightly.

COOK'S TIP

The salad tastes better if it has had time to sit for an hour or so at room temperature and absorb all the flavours before it is served.

Energy 138Kcal/566kJ; Protein 1.3g; Carbohydrate 1.2g, of which sugars 1.1g; Fat 14.2g, of which saturates 2g; Cholesterol 0mg; Calcium 75mg; Fibre 1.4g; Sodium 40mg.

Halloumi and Grape Salad

Firm and salty halloumi cheese is a great standby ingredient for turning a simple salad into a special dish. In this recipe it is tossed with sweet, juicy grapes, which complement its flavour and texture. Serve with a crusty sun-dried tomato bread for a light lunch.

SERVES FOUR

INGREDIENTS
- 150g/5oz mixed salad leaves and tender fresh herb sprigs
- 175g/6oz mixed seedless green and black grapes
- 250g/9oz halloumi cheese
- 75ml/5 tbsp olive oil and lemon juice or vinegar dressing

VARIATION
Instead of using black grapes, you can try out different types of fruit. Choose fruits that are naturally sweet, such as melon, sweet apples and peaches. Slice them thinly or chop into bite-sized chunks. You can also add dried fruits, such as apricots and figs, and seeds and nuts, such as toasted pine nuts, almonds and pistachios.

1 Wash the salad leaves and herbs thoroughly and drain.

2 Toss together the salad leaves and fresh herb sprigs and the green and black grapes, then transfer to a large serving plate.

3 Thinly slice the halloumi cheese. Heat a large, non-stick frying pan.

4 Fry the sliced halloumi cheese and cook briefly until it just starts to turn golden brown on the underside. Turn the cheese and cook the other side until it is golden brown.

5 Arrange the fried cheese over the salad on the plate. Pour over the oil and lemon juice or vinegar dressing and serve immediately.

Energy 314Kcal/1,302kJ; Protein 12.2g; Carbohydrate 7.4g, of which sugars 7.4g; Fat 22.2g, of which saturates 10.5g; Cholesterol 36mg; Calcium 245mg; Fibre 0.7g; Sodium 423mg.

SPICED AUBERGINE SALAD

THE DELICATE FLAVOURS OF AUBERGINE, TOMATOES AND CUCUMBER ARE LIGHTLY SPICED WITH CUMIN AND CORIANDER IN THIS FRESH-TASTING SALAD THAT IS TOPPED WITH YOGURT. IT IS IDEAL TO ACCOMPANY GRILLED KEBABS OR FRIED FISH, OR A RICE DISH.

SERVES FOUR

INGREDIENTS

- 2 small aubergines (eggplants), sliced
- 75ml/5 tbsp extra virgin olive oil
- 50ml/2fl oz/¼ cup red wine vinegar
- 2 garlic cloves, crushed
- 15ml/1 tbsp lemon juice
- 2.5ml/½ tsp ground cumin
- 2.5ml/½ tsp ground coriander
- ½ cucumber, thinly sliced
- 2 well-flavoured tomatoes, thinly sliced
- 30ml/2 tbsp natural (plain) yogurt
- salt and ground black pepper
- chopped fresh flat leaf parsley, to garnish

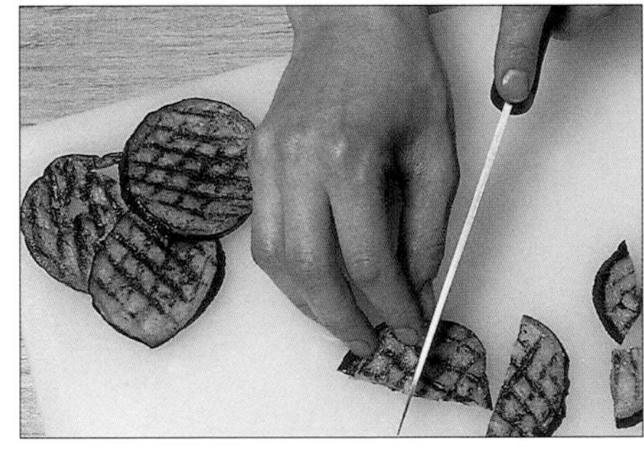

1 Preheat the grill. Lightly brush the aubergine slices with olive oil and cook under a high heat, turning once, until golden and tender. Alternatively, cook them on a griddle pan.

2 When they are done, remove the aubergine slices to a chopping board and cut them into quarters.

3 Mix together the remaining oil, the vinegar, garlic, lemon juice, cumin and coriander. Season with salt and pepper and mix thoroughly. Add the warm aubergines, stir well and chill for at least 2 hours. Add the cucumber and tomatoes. Transfer to a serving dish and spoon the yogurt on top. Sprinkle with parsley and serve.

Energy 155Kcal/642kJ; Protein 1.9g; Carbohydrate 4.9g, of which sugars 4.7g; Fat 14.4g, of which saturates 2.2g; Cholesterol 0mg; Calcium 35mg; Fibre 2.7g; Sodium 14mg.

Grilled Aubergine and Couscous Salad

Packets of flavoured couscous are available in most supermarkets – you can use whichever you like, but garlic and coriander is particularly good for this recipe. Served with a crisp green salad, this dish goes wonderfully with fish and poultry.

SERVES TWO

INGREDIENTS
- 1 large aubergine (eggplant)
- 30ml/2 tbsp olive oil
- 115g/4oz packet garlic-and-coriander (cilantro) flavoured couscous
- 30ml/2 tbsp chopped fresh mint
- salt and ground black pepper
- fresh mint leaves, to garnish

VARIATION

A similar dish, which is also popular around Greece, uses grilled (broiled) courgettes (zucchini) instead of, or as well as, the aubergine. Slice the courgettes into thin rounds or ovals, brush with olive oil, and place under a hot grill (broiler) for a few minutes on each side.

1 Preheat the grill (broiler) to high. Cut the aubergine into large chunky pieces and toss them with the olive oil. Season with salt and ground black pepper to taste and spread the aubergine pieces on a non-stick baking sheet. Grill (broil) for 5–6 minutes, turning occasionally, until golden brown.

2 Meanwhile, prepare the couscous in boiling water, according to the instructions on the packet.

3 Stir the grilled aubergine and chopped mint into the couscous, toss the salad thoroughly to spread the flavours, and serve immediately.

Energy 248Kcal/1,033kJ; Protein 4.4g; Carbohydrate 32.3g, of which sugars 2.5g; Fat 12.1g, of which saturates 1.7g; Cholesterol 0mg; Calcium 24mg; Fibre 2.5g; Sodium 3mg.

WARM BLACK-EYED BEAN SALAD WITH ROCKET

THIS IS AN EASY DISH, AS BLACK-EYED BEANS DO NOT NEED TO BE SOAKED OVERNIGHT. BY ADDING SPRING ONIONS AND LOADS OF AROMATIC DILL, IT IS TRANSFORMED INTO A REFRESHING AND HEALTHY MEAL. IT CAN BE SERVED HOT OR AT ROOM TEMPERATURE.

SERVES FOUR

INGREDIENTS

- 275g/10oz/1½ cups black-eyed beans (peas)
- 5 spring onions (scallions), sliced into rounds
- a large handful of fresh rocket (arugula) leaves, chopped if large
- 45–60ml/3–4 tbsp chopped fresh dill
- 150ml/¼ pint/⅔ cup extra virgin olive oil
- juice of 1 lemon, or to taste
- 10–12 black olives
- salt and ground black pepper
- small cos or romaine lettuce leaves, to serve

1 Thoroughly rinse the beans and drain them well. Tip them into a pan and pour in cold water to just about cover them. Slowly bring them to the boil over a low heat. As soon as the water is boiling, remove the pan from the heat and drain the water off immediately.

2 Put the beans back in the pan with fresh cold water to cover and add a pinch of salt – this will make their skins harder and stop them from disintegrating when they are cooked.

3 Bring the beans to the boil over a medium heat, then lower the heat and cook them until they are soft but not mushy. They will take 20–30 minutes only, so keep an eye on them.

4 Drain the beans, reserving 75–90ml/5–6 tbsp of the cooking liquid. Tip the beans into a large salad bowl. Immediately add the remaining ingredients, including the reserved liquid, and mix well. Serve immediately, piled on the lettuce leaves, or leave to cool slightly and serve later.

Energy 434Kcal/1,811kJ; Protein 16.6g; Carbohydrate 31.4g, of which sugars 2.7g; Fat 27.8g, of which saturates 4g; Cholesterol 0mg; Calcium 149mg; Fibre 12.5g; Sodium 334mg.

Wild Rocket and Cos Lettuce Salad with Herbs

Salads in Greece are clean-tasting and often quite lemony in flavour. The national preference for strong-tasting leaves – sometimes quite bitter ones – is also reflected in fresh salads, especially those that make use of the native cos lettuce. Wild rocket is a favourite ingredient, added to give salads a sharp new edge.

SERVES FOUR

INGREDIENTS

- a large handful of rocket (arugula) leaves
- 2 cos or romaine lettuce hearts
- 3 or 4 fresh flat leaf parsley sprigs, coarsely chopped
- 30–45ml/2–3 tbsp finely chopped fresh dill
- 75ml/5 tbsp extra virgin olive oil
- 15–30ml/1–2 tbsp lemon juice
- salt

COOK'S TIP

It is important to balance the bitterness of the rocket and the sweetness of the cos or romaine lettuce, and the best way to find this out is by taste.

1 If the rocket leaves are young and tender they can be left whole, but older ones should be trimmed of thick stalks and then sliced coarsely. Discard any tough stalks.

2 Slice the cos or romaine lettuce hearts into thin ribbons and place these in a bowl, then add the rocket and the chopped fresh parsley and dill.

3 Make a dressing by whisking the extra virgin olive oil and lemon juice with salt to taste in a bowl until the mixture emulsifies and thickens. Just before serving, pour over the dressing and toss lightly to coat everything in the glistening oil. Serve with crusty bread and a cheese or fish dish.

Energy 348Kcal/1,447kJ; Protein 8.7g; Carbohydrate 22.1g, of which sugars 3.4g; Fat 25.7g, of which saturates 7.3g; Cholesterol 20mg; Calcium 199mg; Fibre 3.2g; Sodium 764mg.

CABBAGE SALAD WITH LEMON DRESSING AND BLACK OLIVES

In winter, LAHANO SALATA *frequently appears on the Greek table. It is made with compact creamy-coloured "white" cabbage. In more northern climates, this type of tight-headed cabbage tends to be a little woody, but in Greece, it always produces a rather sweet-tasting, unusual salad, which has a crisp and refreshing texture.*

SERVES FOUR

INGREDIENTS
- 1 white cabbage
- 12 black olives

For the dressing
- 75–90ml/5–6 tbsp extra virgin olive oil
- 30ml/2 tbsp lemon juice
- 1 garlic clove, crushed
- 30ml/2 tbsp finely chopped fresh flat leaf parsley
- salt

1 Cut the cabbage in quarters, discard the outer leaves and trim off any thick, hard stems as well as the hard base.

2 Lay each quarter in turn on its side and cut long, very thin slices until you reach the central core, which should be discarded. The key to a perfect cabbage salad is to shred the cabbage as finely as possible. Place the shredded cabbage in a bowl and stir in the black olives.

3 Make the dressing by whisking the extra virgin olive oil, lemon juice, garlic, chopped parsley and salt together in a bowl until well blended. Pour the dressing over the cabbage and olives, and toss the salad until everything is evenly coated.

Energy 208Kcal/861kJ; Protein 4g; Carbohydrate 12.9g, of which sugars 12.5g; Fat 15.8g, of which saturates 2.2g; Cholesterol 0mg; Calcium 155mg; Fibre 6.2g; Sodium 303mg.

DESSERTS, TARTS AND CAKES

Dried and fresh fruit, nuts and, of course, the fantastically perfumed Greek honey, combine to make the most heavenly desserts imaginable. Cakes are traditionally eaten throughout the day, and can also be enjoyed as mouthwatering desserts.

HONEY-BAKED FIGS WITH HAZELNUT ICE CREAM

THIS IS A DELECTABLE DESSERT – FRESH FIGS ARE BAKED IN A LIGHTLY SPICED LEMON AND HONEY SYRUP AND SERVED WITH A GORGEOUS HOME-MADE ROASTED-HAZELNUT ICE CREAM.

SERVES FOUR

INGREDIENTS

- 1 lemon grass stalk, finely chopped
- 1 cinnamon stick, roughly broken
- 60ml/4 tbsp clear honey
- 200ml/7fl oz/scant 1 cup water
- 8 large figs

For the hazelnut ice cream

- 450ml/¾ pint/scant 2 cups double (heavy) cream
- 50g/2oz/¼ cup caster (superfine) sugar
- 3 egg yolks
- 1.5ml/¼ tsp vanilla extract
- 75g/3oz/¾ cup hazelnuts

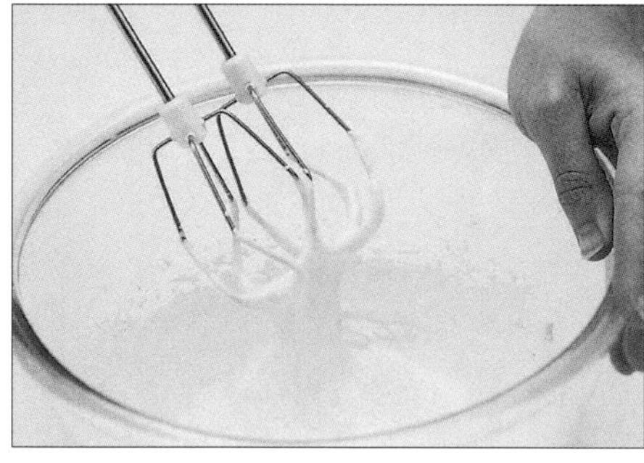

1 To make the ice cream, place the cream in a pan and heat slowly until almost boiling. Place the sugar and egg yolks in a bowl and beat until creamy.

2 Pour a little of the cream on to the egg yolk mixture and stir. Pour into the pan and mix with the rest of the cream. Cook over a low heat, stirring constantly, until the mixture lightly coats a spoon – do not boil. Pour into a bowl, stir in the vanilla extract, and allow to cool.

3 Preheat the oven to 180°C/350°F/Gas 4. Place the hazelnuts on a baking sheet and roast for 10–12 minutes, or until golden. Leave the nuts to cool, then place them in a food processor or blender and process until they are coarsely ground.

4 Transfer the ice cream mixture to a metal or plastic freezer container and freeze for 2 hours, or until the mixture feels firm around the edge. Remove the container from the freezer and whisk the ice cream to break down the ice crystals. Stir in the ground hazelnuts and freeze the mixture again until half-frozen. Whisk again, and then freeze until firm enough to scoop.

COOK'S TIPS

- If you prefer, rather than whisking the semi-frozen ice cream, tip it into a food processor and process until smooth.
- There are several different types of figs available and they can all be used in this recipe. Choose from green-skinned figs that have an amber-coloured flesh, dark purple-skinned fruit with a deep red flesh, green- or yellow-skinned figs with a pinky-coloured flesh.

5 Place the lemon grass, cinnamon stick, honey and water in a small pan and heat slowly until boiling. Simmer the mixture for 5 minutes, then leave the syrup to stand for 15 minutes.

6 Meanwhile, soak a small clay pot in cold water for 15 minutes. Cut the figs into quarters, leaving them joined at the bases. Place the figs in the clay pot and pour over the honey-flavoured syrup.

7 Cover the clay pot and place in an unheated oven. Set the oven to 200°C/400°F/Gas 6 and bake the figs for about 15 minutes, or until tender.

8 Take the ice cream from the freezer about 10 minutes before serving, to soften slightly. Transfer the figs to serving plates. Strain a little of the cooking liquid over the figs and then serve them with a scoop or two of hazelnut ice cream.

VARIATION

This recipe also works well with halved, stoned (pitted) nectarines or peaches – simply cook as from step 6 and serve with the home-made ice cream.

Energy 895Kcal/3,709kJ; Protein 8.2g; Carbohydrate 44.9g, of which sugars 44.5g; Fat 77.1g, of which saturates 39.6g; Cholesterol 305mg; Calcium 206mg; Fibre 4.2g; Sodium 59mg.

Fresh Fig Filo Tart

Figs cook wonderfully well and taste superb in this tart – the riper the figs, the better. Serve it with a sprig of fresh mint and a few spoons of creamy Greek yogurt.

SERVES SIX TO EIGHT

INGREDIENTS
- 5 sheets filo pastry, 35 x 25cm/14 x 10in, thawed if frozen
- 25g/1oz/2 tbsp butter, melted, plus extra for greasing
- 6 fresh figs, cut into wedges
- 75g/3oz/⅔ cup plain (all-purpose) flour
- 75g/3oz/6 tbsp caster (superfine) sugar
- 4 eggs
- 450ml/¾ pint/scant 2 cups creamy milk
- 2.5ml/½ tsp almond extract
- 15ml/1 tbsp icing (confectioners') sugar, for dusting
- whipped cream or Greek (US strained plain) yogurt, to serve

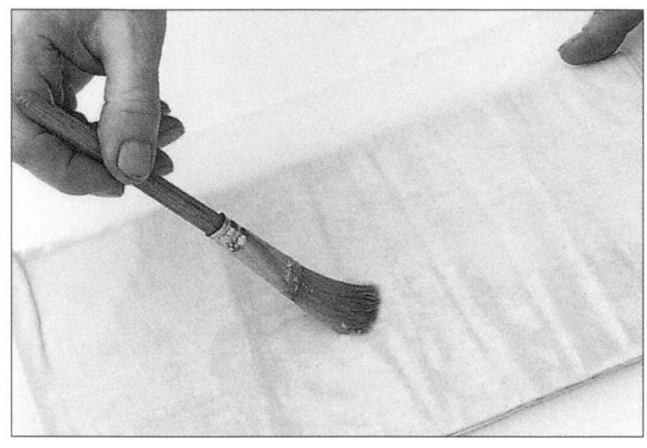

1 Preheat the oven to 190°C/375°F/ Gas 5. Grease a 25 x 16cm/10 x 6¼in baking tin (pan) with butter. Brush each filo sheet in turn with melted butter and use to line the prepared tin.

VARIATION
Nectarines or plums are also delicious cooked this way. Remove their stones (pits) and quarter them as for the figs.

2 Using scissors, cut off any excess pastry, leaving a little overhanging the edge. Arrange the fig wedges skin down in the filo case.

3 Sift the flour into a bowl and stir in the caster sugar. Add the eggs and a little of the milk and whisk until smooth. Gradually whisk in the remaining milk and the almond extract. Pour the mixture over the figs; bake for 1 hour, or until the batter has set and is golden.

4 Remove the tart from the oven and allow it to cool in the tin on a wire rack for 10 minutes. Dust with the icing sugar and serve with whipped cream or Greek yogurt. It will be delicious for a few days if kept refrigerated.

Energy 304Kcal/1,286kJ; Protein 9.9g; Carbohydrate 49.2g, of which sugars 30.2g; Fat 9.1g, of which saturates 4.1g; Cholesterol 140mg; Calcium 203mg; Fibre 2.3g; Sodium 118mg.

DATE AND ALMOND TART

FRESH DATES ARE POPULAR THROUGHOUT GREECE AND MAKE AN UNUSUAL BUT DELICIOUS FILLING FOR A TART. ORANGE FLOWER WATER ADDS A DELICATE SCENT TO THE FILLING.

SERVES SIX

INGREDIENTS
- 175g/6oz/1½ cups plain (all-purpose) flour
- 75g/3oz/6 tbsp butter
- 1 egg

For the filling
- 90g/3½oz/7 tbsp butter
- 90g/3½oz/½ cup caster (superfine) sugar
- 1 egg, beaten
- 90g/3½oz/scant 1 cup ground almonds
- 30ml/2 tbsp plain (all-purpose) flour
- 30ml/2 tbsp orange flower water
- 12–13 fresh dates, halved and stoned (pitted)
- 60ml/4 tbsp apricot jam

1 Preheat the oven to 200°C/400°F/ Gas 6. Place a baking sheet in the oven. Sift the flour into a bowl, add the butter and work with your fingertips until the mixture resembles fine breadcrumbs. Add the egg and 15ml/ 1 tbsp cold water, then work to a smooth dough.

2 Roll out the pastry on a lightly floured surface and use to line a 20cm/8in tart pan. Prick the base with a fork, then chill until needed.

3 To make the filling, cream the butter and sugar until light, then beat in the egg. Stir in the ground almonds, flour and 15ml/1 tbsp of the orange flower water, mixing well.

4 Spread the mixture evenly over the base of the pastry case. Arrange the dates, cut side down, on the almond mixture. Bake on the hot baking sheet for 10–15 minutes, then reduce the heat to 180°C/350°F/Gas 4. Bake for a further 15–20 minutes until light golden and set.

5 Transfer the tart to a rack to cool. Gently heat the apricot jam, then press through a sieve (strainer). Add the remaining orange flower water.

6 Brush the tart with the jam and serve at room temperature.

Energy 478Kcal/2,003kJ; Protein 6.2g; Carbohydrate 61.1g, of which sugars 33.7g; Fat 25g, of which saturates 14.9g; Cholesterol 122mg; Calcium 82mg; Fibre 1.7g; Sodium 199mg.

Sifnos Cheese and Honey Tart

This is a kind of Aegean cheesecake, made with honey and the fresh, unsalted local cheese called MIZITHRA, *which is similar to the Italian ricotta. Cakes like these are an Easter speciality in the Cyclades, particularly on Sifnos and Ios, and Santorini has a similar speciality called* MILITINIA. *In Crete smaller versions are made and these are known as* LYHNARAKIA, *translated as little lanterns.*

SERVES SIX TO EIGHT

INGREDIENTS

- 225g/8oz/2 cups plain (all-purpose) flour sifted with a pinch of salt
- 30ml/2 tbsp caster (superfine) sugar
- 115g/4oz/½ cup unsalted (sweet) butter, cubed
- 45–60ml/3–4 tbsp cold water

For the filling

- 4 eggs
- 50g/2oz/¼ cup caster (superfine) sugar
- 15ml/1 tbsp plain (all-purpose) flour
- 500g/1¼lb/2½ cups fresh *Mizithra* or ricotta cheese
- 60ml/4 tbsp Greek thyme-scented honey
- 2.5ml/½ tsp ground cinnamon

1 Make the pastry by mixing the flour and sugar in a bowl, then carefully rub in the butter with your fingertips until the mixture resembles breadcrumbs.

2 Add the water, a little at a time, until the mixture clings together and forms a dough. It should not be too wet. Draw it into a ball, wrap it in clear film (plastic wrap) and chill for 30 minutes.

3 Preheat the oven to 180°C/350°F/ Gas 4. Put a large baking sheet in the oven to heat.

4 Place the chilled pastry on a lightly floured surface, roll it out thinly and use it to line a 25cm/10in round springform tin (pan). Ease the pastry right into the corners of the tin as this will bring the filling flavours right out to the edge of the cake. Carefully trim off any excess pastry by running a sharp knife around the edge.

5 To make the filling, beat the eggs in a bowl, add the caster sugar and flour, stir in and then beat until fluffy. Add the cheese, honey and half the cinnamon and beat until well mixed.

COOK'S TIP

You could save time by using ready-made fresh or thawed frozen shortcrust pastry instead of making your own. Look for a 500g/1¼lb packet, and remember to leave time for it to thaw completely if you are using frozen pastry.

6 Pour the cheese mixture into the pastry case and level the surface. Place the tin on the hot baking sheet and cook the tart for 50–60 minutes, or until it is light golden.

7 Remove the tart from the oven and sprinkle with the remaining cinnamon while still hot. Serve with prepared fresh fruits, such as peaches, nectarines, oranges and figs.

VARIATIONS

- It is traditional on many of the Greek islands to make smaller and even individual-sized cakes. Use the same recipe but divide the pastry and filling between four or six smaller pies. You may find that you will need more of the pastry and less of the filling.
- Occasionally, the Greeks may cook this dish using a small amount of fruit to decorate the top. Try adding thin slices of peach or apricots to the cake surface 5 minutes before the cake is ready. Pop it back in the oven to finish cooking, and then sprinkle with cinnamon as before.

Energy 626Kcal/2,619kJ; Protein 23.7g; Carbohydrate 53.4g, of which sugars 22.3g; Fat 36.9g, of which saturates 22.6g; Cholesterol 216mg; Calcium 389mg; Fibre 1.3g; Sodium 495mg.

NECTARINES BAKED WITH NUTS

FRESH NECTARINES STUFFED WITH A GROUND ALMOND AND CHOPPED PISTACHIO NUT FILLING ARE BAKED IN A CLAY POT UNTIL MELTINGLY TENDER, THEN SERVED WITH A PASSION FRUIT SAUCE.

SERVES FOUR

INGREDIENTS

- 50g/2oz/½ cup ground almonds
- 15ml/1 tbsp caster (superfine) sugar
- 1 egg yolk
- 50g/2oz/½ cup shelled pistachio nuts, chopped
- 4 nectarines
- 200ml/7fl oz/scant 1 cup orange juice
- 2 ripe passion fruit
- 45ml/3 tbsp Cointreau or other orange liqueur

1 Soak a small clay pot, if using, in cold water for 15 minutes. Mix the ground almonds, sugar and egg yolk to a paste, then stir in the pistachio nuts.

2 Cut the nectarines in half and carefully remove the stones (pits). Pile the ground almond and pistachio filling into the nectarine halves, packing in plenty of filling, and then place them in a single layer in the base of the clay pot or an ovenproof dish.

3 Pour the orange juice around the nectarines, then cover the pot or dish and place in an unheated oven. Set the oven to 200°C/400°F/Gas 6 and cook for 15 minutes.

4 Remove the lid from the pot or dish and bake for a further 5–10 minutes, or until the nectarines are soft. Transfer the nectarines to individual, warmed serving plates and keep warm.

5 Cut the passion fruit in half, scoop out the seeds and stir them into the cooking juices in the clay pot or dish with the liqueur. Place the nectarines on serving plates and spoon the sauce over and around them.

Energy 272Kcal/1,135kJ; Protein 7.6g; Carbohydrate 20.7g, of which sugars 20g; Fat 15.4g, of which saturates 1.9g; Cholesterol 50mg; Calcium 62mg; Fibre 3.5g; Sodium 74mg.

Greek Chocolate Mousse Tartlets

If you are a chocolate fan, you will adore these tarts, with their rich dark chocolate pastry, creamy filling and yet more chocolate drizzled over the top.

SERVES SIX

INGREDIENTS
- 200g/7oz white chocolate, broken up
- 120ml/4fl oz/½ cup milk
- 10ml/2 tsp powdered gelatine
- 30ml/2 tbsp caster (superfine) sugar
- 5ml/1 tsp vanilla extract
- 2 eggs, separated
- 250g/9oz/generous 1 cup Greek (US strained plain) yogurt
- melted dark (bittersweet) chocolate, to decorate

For the pastry
- 115g/4oz/1 cup plain (all-purpose) flour
- 25g/1oz/¼ cup icing (confectioners') sugar
- 25g/1oz/¼ cup cocoa powder (unsweetened)
- 75g/3oz/6 tbsp butter
- 2 eggs
- 2.5ml/½ tsp vanilla extract

1 To make the pastry, sift the flour, sugar and cocoa powder into a mixing bowl. Rub or cut in the butter until the mixture resembles fine breadcrumbs.

2 Mix together the eggs and vanilla extract in a small bowl, then add to the dry ingredients and mix to a soft dough. Tip out on to a lightly floured surface and knead lightly until smooth. Wrap in clear film (plastic wrap) and chill for 20 minutes.

3 Roll out the pastry and use to line six deep 10cm/4in loose-based tartlet tins (muffin pans). Cover and chill for a further 20 minutes. Meanwhile, preheat the oven to 190°C/375°F/Gas 5.

4 Prick the base of each pastry case all over using a fork, then line with baking parchment, fill with baking beans and bake blind for 10 minutes.

5 Remove the paper and beans, return the cases to the oven and bake for a further 15 minutes, or until the pastry is firm. Cool completely in the tins.

6 To make the filling, melt the white chocolate in a heatproof bowl set over a pan of hot water. Pour the milk into a pan, sprinkle over the gelatine and heat gently, stirring, until the gelatine has all dissolved. Remove from the heat and stir in the chocolate.

7 Whisk together the sugar, vanilla extract and egg yolks in a large bowl, then beat in the chocolate mixture. Beat in the yogurt until evenly mixed. Chill until beginning to set.

8 Whisk the egg whites in a grease-free bowl until stiff, then gently fold into the mixture. Divide among the pastry cases and leave to set. Drizzle the melted dark chocolate over the tartlets in a random pattern to decorate.

Energy 490Kcal/2,048kJ; Protein 12.9g; Carbohydrate 46.2g, of which sugars 31.2g; Fat 30g, of which saturates 16.6g; Cholesterol 155mg; Calcium 235mg; Fibre 1.1g; Sodium 238mg.

Honey and Pine Nut Tart

Greek honey is especially fine, with a delicate scent of herbs. Pine nuts also add their unmistakable flavour to this wonderful tart.

SERVES SIX

INGREDIENTS

For the pastry

- 225g/8oz/2 cups plain (all-purpose) flour
- 115g/4oz/½ cup butter
- 30ml/2 tbsp icing (confectioners') sugar
- 1 egg

For the filling

- 115g/4oz/½ cup unsalted (sweet) butter, diced
- 115g/4oz/generous ½ cup caster (superfine) sugar
- 3 eggs, beaten
- 175g/6oz/⅔ cup sunflower or other flower honey
- grated rind and juice of 1 lemon
- 225g/8oz/2 cups pine nuts
- pinch of salt
- icing sugar, for dusting

COOK'S TIP

You could save time by using a 500g/1¼lb packet of ready-made fresh or thawed frozen shortcrust pastry instead.

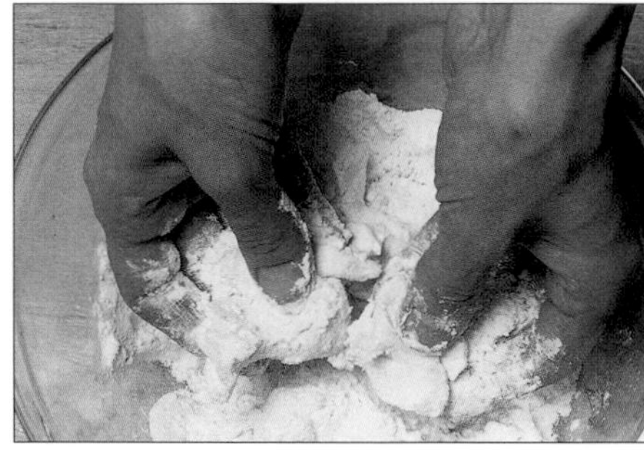

1 Preheat the oven to 180°C/350°F/Gas 4. Sift the flour into a bowl, add the butter and work it in with your fingertips until the mixture resembles fine breadcrumbs.

2 Stir in the icing sugar. Add the egg and 15ml/1 tbsp of lukewarm water and work to a firm dough that leaves the bowl clean.

3 Roll out the pastry on a floured surface until it is thin and large enough to cover a 23cm/9in tart tin (quiche pan), plus extra for fitting into the corners. Line the tin, easing the pastry right into the corners. Prick the base with a fork, and chill for 10 minutes.

4 Line with foil or baking parchment and fill with dried beans or rice, or baking beans if you have them. Bake the tart shell for 10 minutes. Remove the beans.

5 Cream together the butter and caster sugar until light. Beat in the eggs one by one. Gently heat the honey in a small pan over a low heat until it is runny, then add to the butter mixture with the lemon rind and juice. Stir in the pine nuts and salt, then pour the filling into the pastry case.

6 Bake for about 45 minutes, or until the filling is lightly browned and set. Leave to cool slightly in the tin, then dust generously with icing sugar. Serve warm or at room temperature.

Energy 899Kcal/3,750kJ; Protein 13.4g; Carbohydrate 78.4g, of which sugars 49.8g; Fat 61.4g, of which saturates 22.8g; Cholesterol 209mg; Calcium 97mg; Fibre 1.9g; Sodium 285mg.

Walnut Cake

This luscious cake, karythopitta, *is the finest Greek dessert of all. On the islands it is traditionally made for name-day celebrations, when any number of guests may drop in during the evening to convey their good wishes.*

SERVES TEN TO TWELVE

INGREDIENTS

- 150g/5oz/10 tbsp unsalted (sweet) butter
- 115g/4oz/generous ½ cup caster (superfine) sugar
- 4 eggs, separated
- 60ml/4 tbsp brandy
- 2.5ml/½ tsp ground cinnamon
- 300g/11oz/2¾ cups shelled walnuts
- 150g/5oz/1¼ cups self-raising (self-rising) flour
- 5ml/1 tsp baking powder
- salt

For the syrup

- 250g/9oz/1¼ cups caster (superfine) sugar
- 30ml/2 tbsp brandy
- 2 or 3 strips of pared orange rind
- 2 cinnamon sticks

1 Preheat the oven to 190°C/375°F/Gas 5. Grease a 35 x 23cm/14 x 9in roasting pan or baking dish that is at least 5cm/2in deep. Cream the butter in a large mixing bowl until soft, then add the sugar and beat well until the mixture is light and fluffy.

2 Add the egg yolks one by one, beating the mixture after each addition. Stir in the brandy and cinnamon. Coarsely chop the walnuts in a food processor and add them to the mixture. Mix them in using a wooden spoon – do not use an electric mixer at this stage.

COOK'S TIP

The cake will stay moist for 2–3 days, provided it is covered with clear film (plastic wrap), and does not need to go into the refrigerator.

3 Sift the flour with the baking powder and set aside. Whisk the egg whites with a pinch of salt until they are stiff. Fold them into the creamed mixture, alternating with tablespoons of flour until the whites and the flour have all been incorporated.

4 Spread the mixture evenly in the prepared pan or dish. It should be about 4cm/1½in deep. Bake for about 40 minutes, or until the top is golden and a skewer inserted in the cake comes out clean. Take the cake out of the oven and let it rest in the pan.

5 Mix the sugar and 300ml/½ pint/1¼ cups water in a small pan. Heat gently, stirring, until the sugar has dissolved. Bring to the boil, lower the heat and add the brandy, orange rind and cinnamon sticks. Simmer for 10 minutes.

6 Slice the *karythopitta* into 6cm/2½in diamond or square shapes while still hot and strain the syrup slowly over it. Let it stand for 10–20 minutes, or until it has absorbed the syrup and is thoroughly soaked through.

Energy 563Kcal/2,349kJ; Protein 8.5g; Carbohydrate 50.6g, of which sugars 39.2g; Fat 35.3g, of which saturates 10.1g; Cholesterol 108mg; Calcium 114mg; Fibre 1.5g; Sodium 177mg.

SEMOLINA CAKE

THIS IS A UNIVERSAL FAMILY TREAT, LOVED BY EVERYONE IN GREECE. IT TAKES VERY LITTLE TIME TO MAKE – ABOUT 20 MINUTES – AND USES QUITE INEXPENSIVE INGREDIENTS THAT MOST GREEK KITCHENS WILL HAVE IN STOCK. IT MAKES A PERFECT ACCOMPANIMENT TO GREEK COFFEE.

SERVES SIX TO EIGHT

INGREDIENTS

- 500g/1¼lb/2¾ cups caster (superfine) sugar
- 1 litre/1¾ pints/4 cups cold water
- 1 cinnamon stick
- 250ml/8fl oz/1 cup olive oil
- 350g/12oz/2 cups coarse semolina
- 50g/2oz/½ cup blanched almonds
- 30ml/2 tbsp pine nuts
- 5ml/1 tsp ground cinnamon

1 Put the sugar in a heavy pan, pour in the water and add the cinnamon stick. Bring to the boil, stirring until the sugar dissolves, then boil without stirring for about 4 minutes to make a syrup.

2 Meanwhile, heat the oil in a separate, heavy pan. When it is almost smoking, add the semolina gradually and stir continuously until it turns light brown.

3 Lower the heat, add the almonds and pine nuts, and brown together for 2–3 minutes, stirring continuously. Take the semolina mixture off the heat and set aside. Remove the cinnamon stick from the hot syrup using a slotted spoon and discard it.

4 Protecting your hand with an oven glove or dish towel, carefully add the hot syrup to the semolina mixture a little at a time, stirring continuously. The mixture will probably hiss and spit at this point, so stand well away.

5 Return the pan to a gentle heat and stir until all the syrup has been absorbed and the mixture looks smooth.

6 Remove the pan from the heat, cover it with a clean dish towel and let it stand for 10 minutes so that any remaining moisture is absorbed.

7 Scrape the mixture into a 20–23cm/8–9in round cake tin (pan), preferably fluted, and set it aside.

8 When it is cold, unmould it on to a serving platter and dust it evenly all over with the ground cinnamon. Cut into chunky slices and serve with black coffee or tea.

COOK'S TIP

In Greece, this cake would be made with extra virgin olive oil, but you may prefer the less dominant flavour of a light olive oil.

Energy 888Kcal/3,731kJ; Protein 9.1g; Carbohydrate 133.1g, of which sugars 87.6g; Fat 39.1g, of which saturates 4.9g; Cholesterol 0mg; Calcium 75mg; Fibre 1.9g; Sodium 13mg.

LEMON AND LIME SYRUP CAKE

This Greek favourite is perfect for busy cooks as it can be mixed in moments and needs no icing. The simple tangy lime topping transforms it into a fabulously moist cake.

SERVES EIGHT

INGREDIENTS

- 225g/8oz/2 cups self-raising (self-rising) flour
- 5ml/1 tsp baking powder
- 225g/8oz/generous 1 cup caster (superfine) sugar
- 225g/8oz/1 cup butter, softened
- 4 eggs, beaten
- grated rind of 2 lemons
- 30ml/2 tbsp lemon juice

For the topping

- finely pared rind of 1 lime
- juice of 2 limes
- 150g/5oz/⅔ cup caster sugar

1 Preheat the oven to 160°C/325°F/ Gas 3. Grease and line a 20cm/8in round cake tin (pan). Sift the flour and baking powder into a bowl.

2 Add the caster sugar, butter and eggs, and beat thoroughly. Then gradually add and beat in the lemon rind and juice. Spoon the mixture into the prepared tin, then smooth the surface and make a shallow indentation in the top with the back of a spoon.

3 Bake for 1¼–1½ hours, or until the cake is golden and a skewer inserted in the centre comes out clean.

4 Meanwhile, mix the topping ingredients together in a small bowl. As soon as the cake is cooked, remove it from the oven and pour the topping evenly over the surface. Allow the cake to cool in the tin.

VARIATION

Use lemon rind and juice instead of lime for the topping if you prefer. You will need only one large lemon.

Energy 524Kcal/2,197kJ; Protein 6g; Carbohydrate 70.4g, of which sugars 49.5g; Fat 26.2g, of which saturates 15.5g; Cholesterol 155mg; Calcium 143mg; Fibre 0.9g; Sodium 310mg.

CRUNCHY-TOPPED FRESH APRICOT CAKE

ALMONDS ARE PERFECT PARTNERS FOR FRESH APRICOTS, AND THIS IS A GREAT WAY TO USE UP FIRM FRUITS. IN GREECE THIS IS SERVED AS A CAKE OR SNACK TO BE EATEN THROUGHOUT THE DAY.

SERVES EIGHT

INGREDIENTS

- 175g/6oz/1½ cups self-raising (self-rising) flour
- 175g/6oz/¾ cup butter, softened
- 175g/6oz/scant 1 cup caster (superfine) sugar
- 115g/4oz/1 cup ground almonds
- 3 eggs
- 5ml/1 tsp almond extract
- 2.5ml/½ tsp baking powder
- 8 firm apricots, stoned (pitted) and chopped

For the topping

- 30ml/2 tbsp demerara (raw) sugar
- 50g/2oz/½ cup flaked (sliced) almonds

1 Preheat the oven to 160°C/325°F/Gas 3. Grease an 18cm/7in round cake tin (pan). Cut out a round of baking parchment to fit the cake tin and line it carefully into the corners.

2 Put all the cake ingredients, except the apricots, in a large mixing bowl and whisk until creamy. Fold the apricots into the cake mixture.

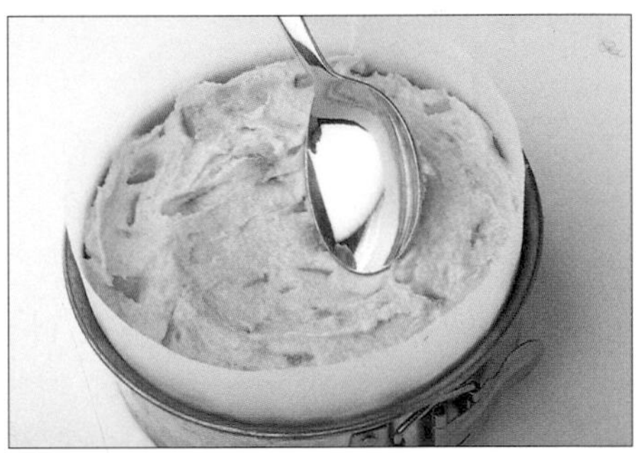

3 Spoon into the tin. Make a hollow in the centre with the back of a spoon. Sprinkle 15ml/1 tbsp of the demerara sugar over with the flaked almonds.

4 Bake for 1½ hours or until an inserted skewer comes out clean. Sprinkle the remaining sugar over and cool for 10 minutes in the tin. Remove from the tin and cool on a wire rack.

Energy 414Kcal/1,734kJ; Protein 6.2g; Carbohydrate 46.8g, of which sugars 30.3g; Fat 23.9g, of which saturates 12.3g; Cholesterol 118mg; Calcium 126mg; Fibre 1.8g; Sodium 241mg.

SWEETS, PASTRIES COOKIES AND BREADS

The Greeks love to celebrate special occasions such as Easter, Christmas and name days, with all kinds of special sweets, cookies and breads, and these will vary from region to region. Many are given as presents or gifts, especially on name days.

Loukoumia

This is the Greek version of Turkish Delight and this versatile recipe is made all over the counrty. Serve a few cubes with coffee after a heavy meal, for a pick-me-up. You can put cocktail sticks in each piece and decorate with a sprinkling of icing sugar.

MAKES 450G/1LB

INGREDIENTS

- 400g/14oz/2 cups sugar
- 300ml/½ pint/1¼ cups water
- 25g/1oz powdered gelatine
- 2.5ml/½ tsp cream of tartar
- 30ml/2 tbsp rose water
- pink food colouring
- 45ml/3 tbsp icing (confectioners') sugar, sifted
- 15ml/1 tbsp cornflour (cornstarch)

VARIATION

Try different flavours in this recipe, such as lemon, crème de menthe and orange and then vary the food colouring accordingly. For a truly authentic touch, add some chopped pistachio nuts to the mixture before pouring it into the tins.

1 Slightly dampen the insides of two 18cm/7in shallow square tins (pans) with lukewarm water – be sure not to wet them too much. Place the sugar and all but 60ml/4 tbsp of the water in a heavy pan. Heat gently over a low heat, stirring occasionally, until the sugar has completely dissolved.

2 Blend the gelatine and remaining water in a small bowl and place the mixture in a small pan. Heat gently over a low heat, stirring frequently, to dissolve the gelatine completely.

3 Bring the sugar syrup to the boil and boil steadily for about 8 minutes until the syrup registers 130°C/260°F on a sugar thermometer.

4 Stir the cream of tartar into the gelatine, then pour into the boiling syrup and stir until well blended. Remove from the heat.

5 Add the rose water and a few drops of pink food colouring to tint the mixture pale pink. Pour the mixture into the tins and allow to set for several hours or overnight, if possible.

6 Dust a sheet of waxed paper or baking parchment with some of the icing sugar and cornflour. Dip the base of the tin in hot water. Invert on to the paper. Cut into 2.5cm/1in squares using an oiled knife.

Energy 1,806Kcal/7,707kJ; Protein 2.3g; Carbohydrate 478.8g, of which sugars 465g; Fat 0.1g, of which saturates 0g; Cholesterol 0mg; Calcium 238mg; Fibre 0g; Sodium 35mg.

ORANGE SPOON PRESERVE

SPOON PRESERVES ARE MADE WITH VARIOUS TYPES OF FRUIT IN A LUSCIOUS SYRUP. FIGS, CHERRIES, GRAPES AND APRICOTS ARE ALL SUITABLE, AS ARE SMALL BITTER ORANGES, WHICH ARE LEFT WHOLE. THERE IS ALSO A BEAUTIFUL PRESERVE WHICH IS MADE FROM ROSE PETALS.

MAKES ABOUT THIRTY PIECES

INGREDIENTS

- 8 or 9 thick-skinned oranges, total weight about 1kg/2¼lb, rinsed and dried
- 1kg/2¼lb/5¼ cups caster (superfine) sugar
- juice of 1 lemon

1 Grate the oranges lightly and discard the zest. Slice each one vertically into 4–6 pieces (depending on the size of the oranges), remove the peel from each segment, keeping it in one piece, and drop it into a bowl of cold water. Use the flesh in another recipe.

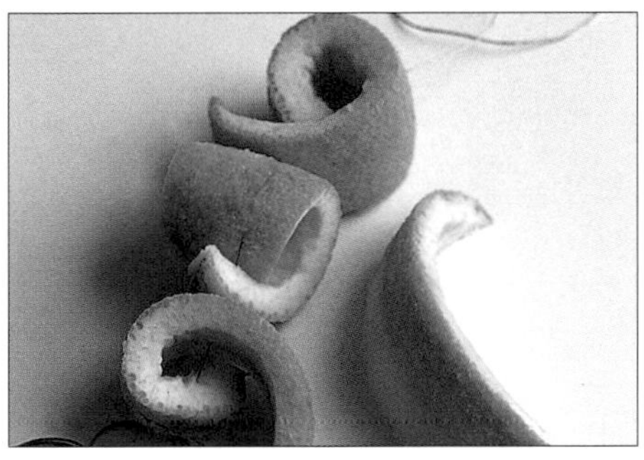

2 Have ready a tapestry needle threaded with strong cotton string. Roll up a piece of peel and push the needle through it so that it is threaded on the string. Continue this process until there are 10–12 pieces on the string, then tie the two ends together.

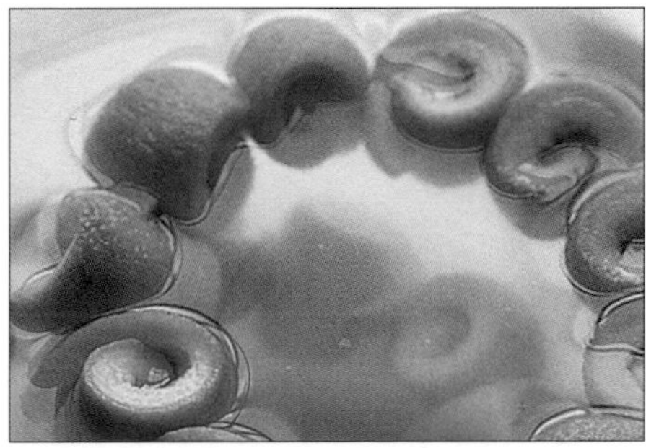

3 Put the strings in a bowl of fresh cold water and leave for 24 hours, changing the water 3–4 times.

4 Next day, drain the strings of peel and put them in a large pan. Pour in about 2.8 litres/5 pints/12½ cups water. Bring to the boil, partially cover the pan and continue to boil for 15 minutes. Drain well. Return the strings of peel to the pan, cover with the same amount of water and boil for a further 10 minutes, or until the peel feels soft but is not overcooked or disintegrating. Tip them into a colander and leave to drain for at least 1 hour.

5 Put the sugar in a large, heavy pan and add 150ml/¼ pint/⅔ cup water. Stir over a gentle heat until the sugar dissolves, then boil gently without stirring for about 4 minutes until it forms a thick syrup.

6 Release the fruit into the syrup by cutting the threads. Simmer for 5 minutes, then remove the pan from the heat and leave the cooked peel to stand in the syrup overnight.

7 Next day, boil the syrup very gently for 4–5 minutes, until it starts to set. Stir in the lemon juice, take the pan off the heat and let the preserve cool. Pack the curled peel and syrup into sterilized jars. Seal and label, then store in a cool, dry place.

HOW TO SERVE

This type of spoon preserve – glyko tou *koutaliou* – is often served to visitors. Offer one piece on a spoon, resting in a saucer, along with a glass of cold water.

Energy 131Kcal/560kJ; Protein 0.3g; Carbohydrate 34.8g, of which sugars 34.8g; Fat 0g, of which saturates 0g; Cholesterol 0mg; Calcium 31mg; Fibre 0g; Sodium 3mg.

SEMOLINA AND NUT HALVA

Semolina is a popular ingredient in many desserts and pastries in Greece, especially on the Greek islands. Here it provides a spongy base for soaking up a deliciously fragrant spicy syrup and orange flavours. The nuts used here are hazelnuts and almonds, although other nuts can be used. Pistachio nuts, for example, are very popular additions to these syrupy dessert dishes, as are walnuts and toasted pine nuts.

MAKES TWENTY-FOUR PIECES

INGREDIENTS

For the halva

- 115g/4oz/½ cup unsalted (sweet) butter, softened
- 115g/4oz/generous ½ cup caster (superfine) sugar
- finely grated rind of 1 orange, plus 30ml/2 tbsp juice
- 3 eggs
- 175g/6oz/1 cup semolina
- 10ml/2 tsp baking powder
- 115g/4oz/1 cup ground hazelnuts

To finish

- 350g/12oz/1¾ cups caster (superfine) sugar
- 2 cinnamon sticks, halved
- juice of 1 lemon
- 60ml/4 tbsp orange flower water
- 50g/2oz/½ cup unblanched hazelnuts, toasted and chopped
- 50g/2oz/½ cup blanched almonds, toasted and chopped
- shredded rind of 1 orange

1 Preheat the oven to 220°C/425°F/Gas 7. Grease and line the base of a 23cm/9in square deep solid-based cake tin (pan).

2 Lightly cream the butter in a bowl. Add the sugar, orange rind and juice, eggs, semolina, baking powder and hazelnuts and beat the ingredients together until smooth.

3 Turn into the prepared tin and level the surface. Bake for 20–25 minutes until just firm and golden. Leave to cool in the tin.

4 To make the syrup, put the caster sugar in a small, heavy pan with 575ml/19fl oz/2¼ cups water and the halved cinnamon sticks. Heat gently over a low heat, stirring frequently but carefully to ensure that the cinnamon sticks do not break up. Continue heating the mixture until the sugar has dissolved completely.

COOK'S TIP

The wonderfully spicy syrup is the great feature of this dish, so be sure to use a deep, solid-based cake tin, rather than one with a loose base, otherwise the syrup will seep out.

5 Bring to the boil and boil fast, without stirring, for 5 minutes. Measure half the boiling syrup and add the lemon juice and orange flower water to it. Pour over the halva. Reserve the remainder of the syrup in the pan.

6 Leave the halva in the tin until the syrup is absorbed, then turn it out on to a plate and cut diagonally into diamond-shaped portions. Sprinkle with the nuts.

7 Boil the remaining syrup until slightly thickened, then pour it over the halva. Sprinkle the shredded orange rind over the cake and serve with lightly whipped or clotted cream, or a few spoonfuls of Greek (US strained plain) yogurt.

Energy 4,910Kcal/20,601kJ; Protein 74.5g; Carbohydrate 638.2g, of which sugars 498g; Fat 247g, of which saturates 74.5g; Cholesterol 816mg; Calcium 738mg; Fibre 18.1g; Sodium 976mg.

BAKLAVA

THE ORIGINS OF THIS RECIPE ARE IN GREECE AND TURKEY, BUT IT HAS BEEN WILLINGLY ADOPTED THROUGHOUT SOUTH-EASTERN EUROPE AND THE MIDDLE EAST. IT IS A VERY SWEET DESSERT AND BLACK COFFEE IS THE PERFECT ACCOMPANIMENT.

MAKES 24 PIECES

INGREDIENTS

- 175g/6oz/¾ cup butter, melted
- 400g/14oz packet filo pastry, thawed if frozen
- 30ml/2 tbsp lemon juice
- 60ml/4 tbsp clear thick honey
- 50g/2oz/¼ cup caster (superfine) sugar
- finely grated rind of 1 lemon
- 10ml/2 tsp cinnamon
- 200g/7oz/1¾ cups blanched almonds, chopped
- 200g/7oz/1¾ cups walnuts, chopped
- 75g/3oz/¾ cup pistachio nuts or hazelnuts, chopped
- chopped pistachio nuts, to decorate

For the syrup

- 350g/12oz/1¾ cups caster (superfine) sugar
- 115g/4oz/½ cup clear honey
- 600ml/1 pint/2½ cups water
- 2 strips of thinly pared lemon rind

1 Preheat the oven to 160°C/325°F/Gas 3. Brush the base of a shallow 30 x 20cm/12 x 8in loose-bottomed or Swiss roll tin (jelly roll pan) with butter.

2 Using the tin as a guide, cut the sheets of filo pastry with a sharp knife to fit the tin exactly.

VARIATION

In Greece, rose water is often used as a glaze. If you can find it in a specialist shop, use it lavishly instead of the syrup or add some to the syrup for flavour.

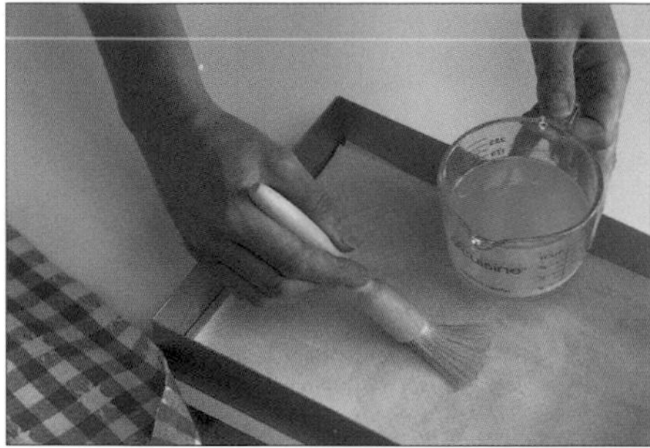

3 Place one sheet of pastry in the base of the tin, brush with a little melted butter, then repeat until you have used half of the pastry sheets. Cover the remaining pastry with a clean dish towel and set aside.

4 To make the filling, place the lemon juice, honey and sugar in a pan and heat gently, stirring continuously until it has completely dissolved. Stir in the lemon rind, cinnamon and nuts.

5 Spread half the filling over the pastry and cover with three layers of the filo pastry, brushing butter on each layer as you go. Then spread the remaining filling over the pastry.

6 Finish by using up the remaining sheets of filo pastry and butter on top, brushing butter over each sheet as you go. Finally brush the top of the pastry liberally with butter, ensuring that you cover the whole surface.

7 Using a sharp knife, carefully mark the pastry into squares, almost cutting through the filling. Bake in the preheated oven for 1 hour, or until crisp and golden brown.

8 Meanwhile, make the syrup. Place the caster sugar, honey, water and lemon rind in a pan, and stir over a low heat until the sugar and honey have dissolved. Bring to the boil, then boil for a further 10 minutes until the mixture has thickened slightly.

9 Take the syrup off the heat and leave to cool slightly. Remove the baklava from the oven. Remove and discard the lemon rind from the syrup then pour over the pastry. Leave to soak for 6 hours or overnight. Cut into squares and serve, decorated with chopped pistachio nuts.

Energy 282Kcal/1,179kJ; Protein 4.1g; Carbohydrate 27.4g, of which sugars 23.8g; Fat 18.1g, of which saturates 4.9g; Cholesterol 16mg; Calcium 48mg; Fibre 1.2g; Sodium 64mg.

Christmas Honey Cookies

Delicious, honey-coated melomakarona *are a treat specially made during the Christmas period. They are easy to make and taste simply marvellous.*

MAKES TWENTY

INGREDIENTS
- 2.5ml/½ tsp bicarbonate of soda (baking soda)
- grated rind and juice of 1 large orange
- 150ml/¼ pint/⅔ cup extra virgin olive oil
- 75g/3oz/6 tbsp caster (superfine) sugar
- 60ml/4 tbsp brandy
- 7.5ml/1½ tsp ground cinnamon
- 400g/14oz/3½ cups self-raising (self-rising) flour sifted with a pinch of salt
- 115g/4oz/1 cup shelled walnuts, chopped

For the syrup
- 225g/8oz/1 cup clear honey
- 115g/4oz/½ cup caster (superfine) sugar

1 Mix together the baking soda and orange juice. Beat the oil and sugar with an electric mixer until blended. Beat in the brandy and 2.5ml/½ tsp of the cinnamon, then add and beat in the orange juice and soda.

2 Using your hand, gradually work the flour and salt into the mixture. As soon as it becomes possible to do so, knead it. Add the orange rind and knead for 10 minutes or until the dough is pliable.

3 Preheat the oven to 180°C/350°F/ Gas 4. Flour your hands and pinch off small pieces of the dough. Shape them into 6cm/2½in long ovals and place on ungreased baking sheets.

4 Using a fork dipped in water, flatten each oval of dough a little. Bake for 25 minutes, or until golden. Cool slightly, then transfer to a wire rack to harden.

5 Meanwhile, make the syrup. Place the honey, sugar and 150ml/¼ pint/⅔ cup water in a small pan. Bring gently to the boil, stirring continuously. Then skim any surface foam, lower the heat and simmer for 5 minutes.

6 Immerse the cold *melomakarona* about six at a time into the hot syrup and leave them cooking for about 1–2 minutes.

7 Lift them out with a slotted spoon and place on a platter in a single layer. Sprinkle with the chopped walnuts and remaining cinnamon.

Energy 173Kcal/724kJ; Protein 2.7g; Carbohydrate 19.5g, of which sugars 4.6g; Fat 9.2g, of which saturates 1.1g; Cholesterol 0mg; Calcium 78mg; Fibre 0.8g; Sodium 73mg.

BUTTER AND ALMOND SHORTBREADS

DAZZLING WHITE KOURABIEDES *ARE TRADITIONALLY MADE AT CHRISTMAS AND EASTER, BUT ARE ALSO AN IMPORTANT FEATURE OF MANY OTHER GREEK CELEBRATIONS.*

MAKES TWENTY TO TWENTY-TWO

INGREDIENTS
- 225g/8oz/1 cup unsalted butter
- 150g/5oz/⅔ cup caster (superfine) sugar
- 2 egg yolks
- 5ml/1 tsp vanilla extract
- 2.5ml/½ tsp bicarbonate of soda (baking soda)
- 45ml/3 tbsp brandy
- 500g/1¼lb/5 cups plain (all-purpose) flour sifted with a pinch of salt
- 150g/5oz/1¼ cups blanched almonds, toasted and coarsely chopped
- 350g/12oz/3 cups icing (confectioners') sugar

1 Cream the butter and beat in the caster sugar gradually, until light and fluffy. Beat in the egg yolks one at a time, then the vanilla.

2 Mix the soda with the brandy and stir into the mixture. Add the flour and salt and mix to a firm dough. Knead lightly, add the almonds and knead again.

3 Preheat the oven to 180°C/350°F/ Gas 4. Cover half the dough with clear film (plastic wrap) and set aside. Roll out the remaining dough until about 2.5cm/1in thick. Press out star or half-moon shapes, using pastry cutters. Repeat with the remaining dough.

4 Place the shapes on the baking sheets and bake for 20–25 minutes, or until pale golden. Do not let them brown.

5 Meanwhile, sift a quarter of the icing sugar on to a platter. As soon as the *kourabiethes* come out of the oven, dust them generously with icing sugar. Let them cool for a few minutes, then place them on the sugar-coated platter. Sift the remaining icing sugar over them, making them pure white.

Energy 324Kcal/1,363kJ; Protein 4.4g; Carbohydrate 46.1g, of which sugars 26.9g; Fat 14.3g, of which saturates 6.4g; Cholesterol 44mg; Calcium 71mg; Fibre 1.3g; Sodium 72mg.

FRUIT AND NUT PASTRIES

AROMATIC SWEET PASTRY CRESCENTS, KNOWN AS MOSHOPOUNGIA *IN GREECE, ARE PACKED WITH CANDIED CITRUS PEEL AND WALNUTS, WHICH HAVE BEEN SOAKED IN A COFFEE SYRUP.*

MAKES SIXTEEN

INGREDIENTS

- 60ml/4 tbsp clear honey
- 60ml/4 tbsp strong brewed coffee
- 75g/3oz/½ cup mixed candied citrus peel, finely chopped
- 175g/6oz/1½ cups walnuts, chopped
- 1.5ml/¼ tsp freshly grated nutmeg
- milk, to glaze
- caster (superfine) sugar, for sprinkling

For the pastry

- 450g/1lb/4 cups plain (all purpose) flour
- 2.5ml/½ tsp ground cinnamon
- 2.5ml/½ tsp baking powder
- pinch of salt
- 150g/5oz/10 tbsp butter
- 30ml/2 tbsp caster (superfine) sugar
- 1 egg
- 120ml/4fl oz/½ cup chilled milk

1 Preheat the oven to 180°C/350°F/ Gas 4. To make the pastry, sift the flour, cinnamon, baking powder and salt into a bowl. Rub or cut in the butter until the mixture resembles breadcrumbs. Stir in the sugar. Make a well.

2 Beat the egg and milk together and pour into the well in the dry ingredients. Mix to a soft dough. Divide the dough into two and wrap each piece in clear film (plastic wrap). Chill for 30 minutes.

3 Meanwhile, mix the honey and coffee in a mixing bowl. Add the candied peel, walnuts and nutmeg. Stir well, cover and leave for 20 minutes.

4 Roll out one portion of the dough on a lightly floured surface to a thickness of 3mm/⅛in. Stamp out rounds, using a 10cm/4in plain pastry cutter.

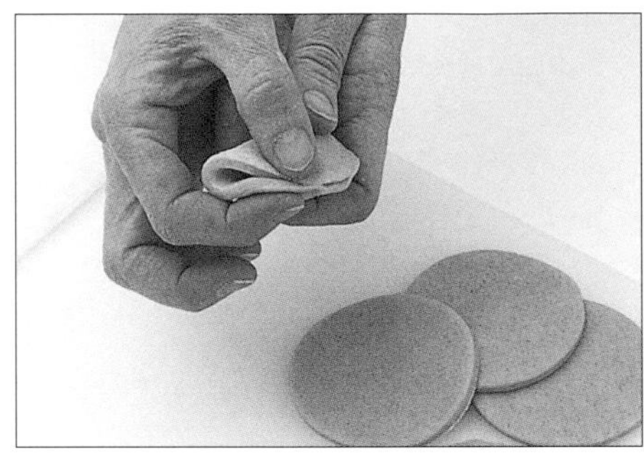

5 Place a heaped teaspoonful of filling on one side of each round. Brush the edges with a little milk, then fold over and press together to seal. Repeat with the second piece of pastry until all the filling has been used.

6 Place the pastries on lightly greased baking sheets, brush lightly over the whole top surface of each pastry with a little milk, and then sprinkle with a little caster sugar. Make a steam hole in the centre of each pastry with a skewer. Bake for 35 minutes, or until slightly puffy and lightly browned. Cool on a wire rack, and serve with coffee or tea.

VARIATION

Instead of the walnuts, use pecan nuts or almonds, if you prefer.

Energy 278Kcal/1,162kJ; Protein 5g; Carbohydrate 30.2g, of which sugars 8.7g; Fat 16.1g, of which saturates 5.7g; Cholesterol 32mg; Calcium 69mg; Fibre 1.5g; Sodium 80mg.

Olive Bread

Rich olive breads are popular all over the Mediterranean. For this Greek recipe use rich oily olives or those marinated in herbs, rather than canned ones.

MAKES TWO 675G/1½LB LOAVES

INGREDIENTS
- 2 red onions, thinly sliced
- 30ml/2 tbsp extra virgin olive oil
- 225g/8oz/2 cups pitted black or green olives
- 800g/1¾lb/7 cups strong white bread flour
- 7.5ml/1½ tsp salt
- 20ml/4 tsp easy-blend (rapid-rise) dried yeast
- 45ml/3 tbsp each roughly chopped fresh flat leaf parsley, coriander (cilantro) or mint

1 Fry the onions in the oil until soft. Roughly chop the olives.

2 Put the flour, salt, yeast and parsley, coriander or mint in a large bowl with the olives and fried onions and pour in 475ml/16fl oz/2 cups hand-hot water.

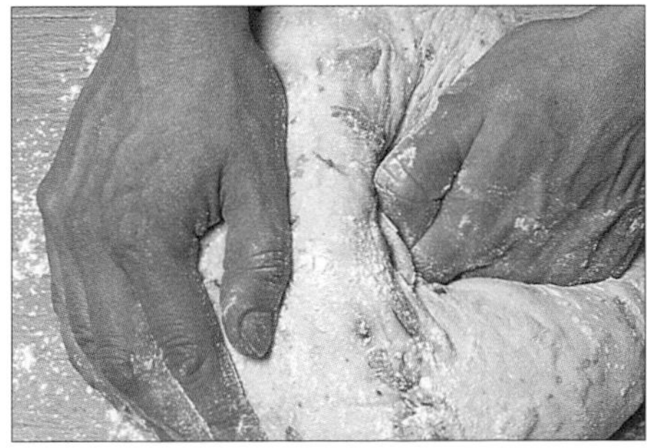

3 Mix to a dough using a round-bladed knife, adding a little more water if the mixture feels dry. Turn out on to a lightly floured surface and knead for about 10 minutes.

4 Put in a clean bowl, cover with clear film (plastic wrap) and leave in a warm place until doubled in bulk.

5 Preheat the oven to 220°C/425°F/Gas 7. Lightly grease two baking sheets. Turn the dough on to a floured surface and cut in half. Shape each half into a round and place both on the baking sheets. Cover loosely with lightly oiled clear film and leave in a warm place until doubled in size.

VARIATION

You can make individual rolls. Shape the dough into 16 small rolls. Slash the tops as above and reduce the cooking time to 25 minutes.

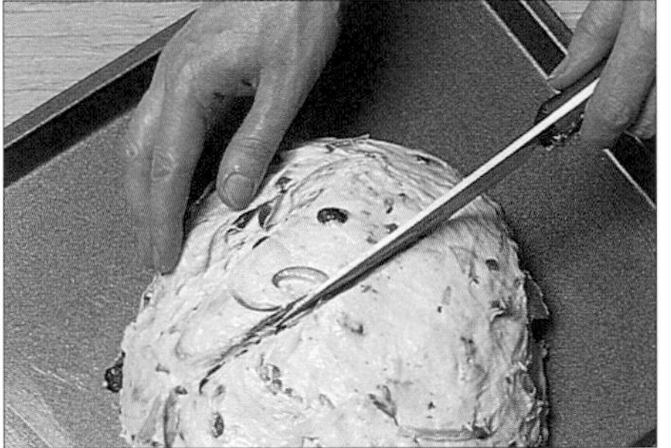

6 Slash the tops of the loaves with a knife and then bake in the oven for about 40 minutes, or until the loaves are golden brown and sound hollow when tapped on the bottom. Transfer to a wire rack to cool. Serve with fresh unsalted Greek butter or as part of a meze table with a Greek salad.

Energy 1,546Kcal/6,538kJ; Protein 38.5g; Carbohydrate 301.9g, of which sugars 13.2g; Fat 28.8g, of which saturates 4.3g; Cholesterol 0mg; Calcium 671mg; Fibre 17.8g; Sodium 4,028mg.

CHRISTOPSOMO

A Byzantine cross flavoured with aniseed tops this Greek Christmas bread, which is also decorated with walnuts for good fortune. The fluffy, light, butter-enriched bread contains orange rind, cinnamon and cloves – all the lovely warm tastes associated with Christmas.

MAKES ONE LOAF

INGREDIENTS

- 15g/½oz fresh yeast
- 140ml/scant ¼ pint/scant ⅔ cup lukewarm milk
- 450g/1lb/4 cups unbleached strong white bread flour
- 2 eggs
- 75g/3oz/6 tbsp caster (superfine) sugar
- 2.5ml/½ tsp salt
- 75g/3oz/6 tbsp butter, softened
- grated rind of ½ orange
- 5ml/1 tsp ground cinnamon
- 1.5ml/¼ tsp ground cloves
- pinch of crushed aniseed
- 8 walnut halves
- beaten egg white, for glazing

1 Lightly grease a large baking sheet. In a large bowl, mix the yeast with the milk until the yeast is dissolved, then stir in 115g/4oz/1 cup of the flour to make a thin batter. Cover with lightly oiled clear film (plastic wrap) and leave to "sponge" in a warm place for 30 minutes.

2 Beat the eggs and sugar until light and fluffy. Beat into the yeast mixture. Gradually mix in the remaining flour and salt. Beat in the softened butter and knead to a soft but not sticky dough. Knead on a lightly floured surface for 8–10 minutes until smooth and elastic. Place in a lightly oiled bowl, cover with lightly oiled clear film and leave to rise in a warm place for 1½ hours, or until doubled in bulk.

3 Turn out on to a lightly floured surface and gently knock back (punch down). Cut off about 50g/2oz of dough; cover and set aside. Gently knead the orange rind, cinnamon and cloves into the large piece of dough and shape into a round loaf. Place on the baking sheet.

4 Knead the aniseed into the remaining dough. Cut the dough in half and shape each piece into a 30cm/12in-long rope. Cut through each rope at either end by one-third of its length. Place the two ropes in a cross on top of the loaf, then curl each cut end into a circle, in opposite directions.

5 Place a walnut half inside each circle. Cover the loaf with lightly oiled clear film and leave to rise for 45 minutes, or until doubled in size.

6 Preheat the oven to 190°C/375°F/Gas 5. Brush the bread with the egg white and bake for 40–45 minutes, or until golden. Cool on a wire rack and then refrigerate. You can keep it refrigerated for up to a week.

Energy 2,840Kcal/11,958kJ; Protein 65.5g; Carbohydrate 436.2g, of which sugars 93.1g; Fat 105g, of which saturates 46.5g; Cholesterol 549mg; Calcium 941mg; Fibre 15.2g; Sodium 1,658mg.

Greek Easter Bread

In Greece, Easter celebrations are very important, and involve much preparation in the kitchen. This bread is sold in all the bakers' shops, and also made at home. It is traditionally decorated with red-dyed eggs.

MAKES ONE LOAF

INGREDIENTS
- 25g/1oz fresh yeast
- 120ml/4fl oz/½ cup warm milk
- 675g/1½lb/6 cups strong white bread flour
- 2 eggs, beaten
- 2.5ml/½ tsp caraway seeds
- 15ml/1 tbsp caster (superfine) sugar
- 15ml/1 tbsp brandy
- 50g/2oz/¼ cup butter, melted
- 1 egg white, beaten
- 2 or 3 hard-boiled eggs, dyed red
- 50g/2oz/½ cup split almonds

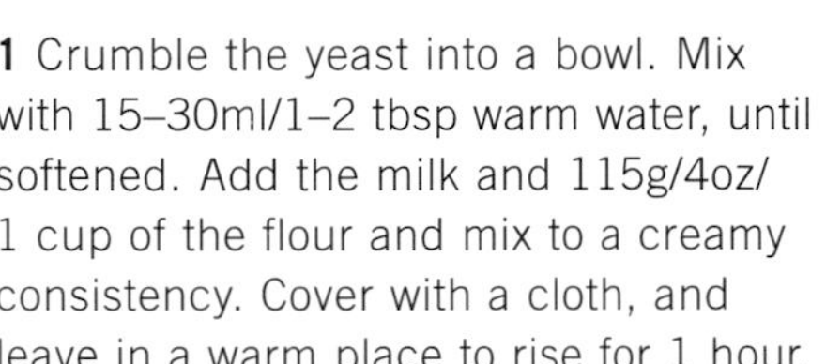

1 Crumble the yeast into a bowl. Mix with 15–30ml/1–2 tbsp warm water, until softened. Add the milk and 115g/4oz/ 1 cup of the flour and mix to a creamy consistency. Cover with a cloth, and leave in a warm place to rise for 1 hour.

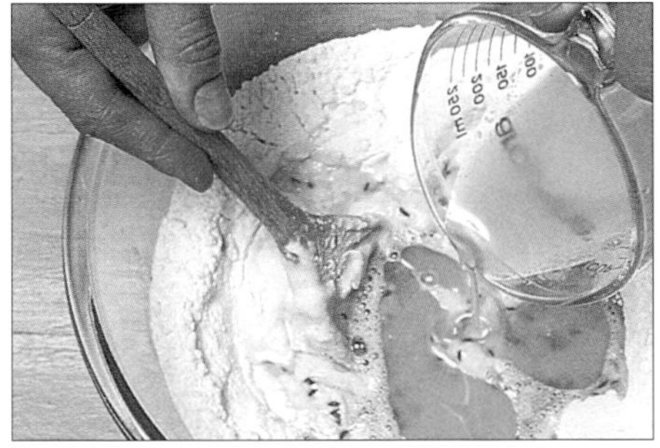

2 Sift the remaining flour into a large bowl and make a well in the centre. Pour the risen yeast into the well, and draw in a little of the flour from the sides. Add the eggs, caraway seeds, sugar and brandy. Incorporate the remaining flour, until the mixture begins to form a dough.

3 Mix in the melted butter. Turn on to a floured surface, and knead for about 10 minutes, or until the dough becomes smooth. Return to the bowl, and cover with a cloth. Leave in a warm place to rise for 3 hours.

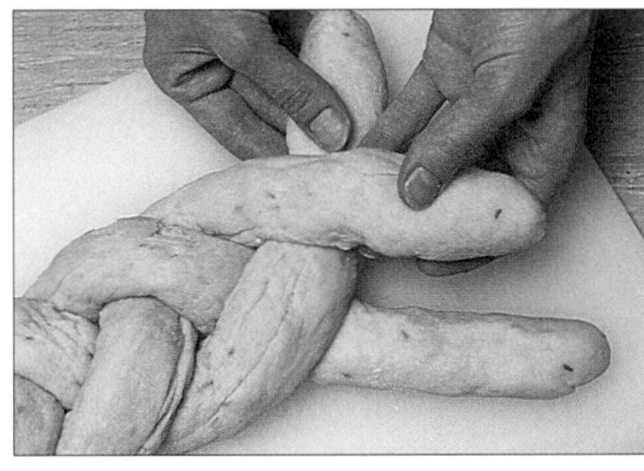

4 Preheat the oven to 180°C/350°F/ Gas 4. Knock back (punch down) the dough and knead on a floured surface for a minute or two. Divide it into three, and roll each piece into a long sausage. Make a braid as shown above.

5 Place the loaf on a greased baking sheet. Tuck the ends under, brush with the egg white and decorate with the dyed eggs and split almonds.

6 Bake for about 1 hour, until the loaf sounds hollow when tapped on the bottom. Serve while it is still hot, or cool on a wire rack and serve cold with butter, Greek (US strained plain) yoghurt, assorted nuts and fresh and dried fruits.

COOK'S TIP

You can often buy fresh yeast from bakers' shops. It should be pale cream in colour with a firm but crumbly texture.

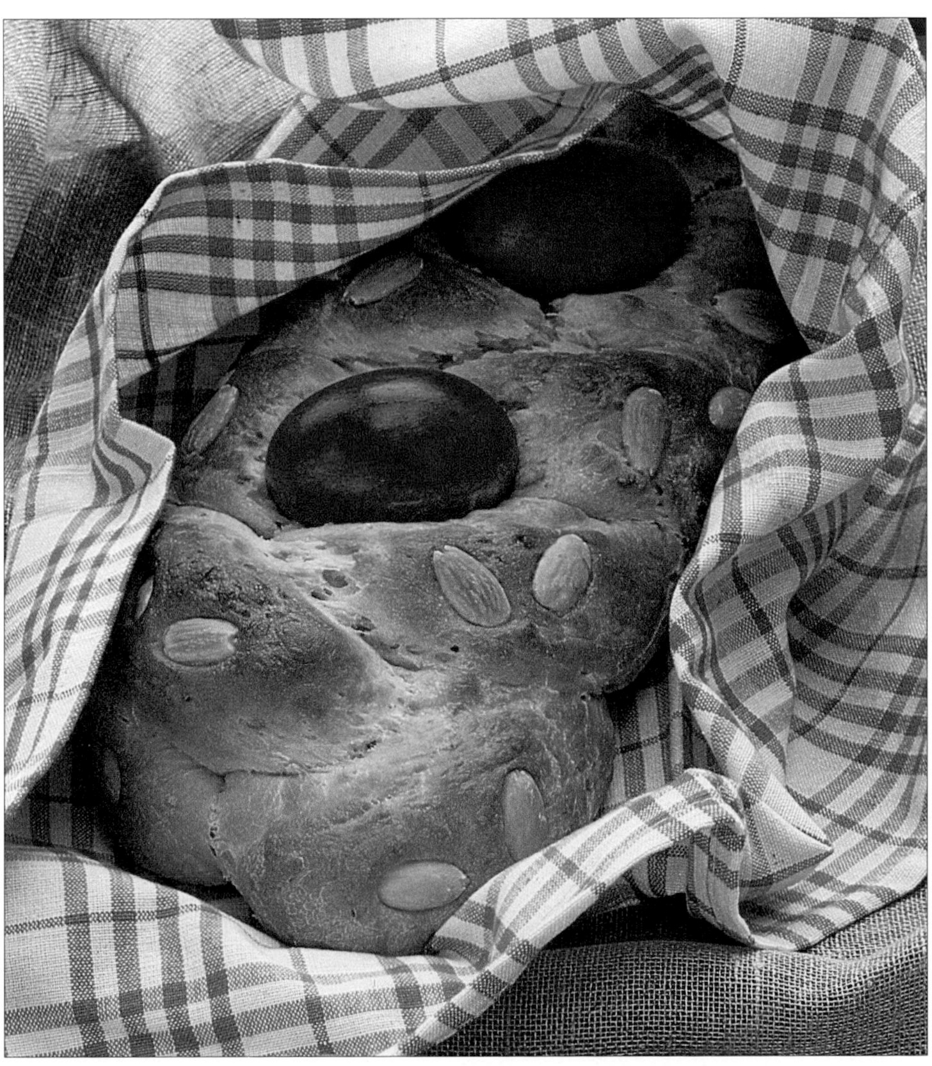

Energy 3,286Kcal/13,869kJ; Protein 93.8g; Carbohydrate 549.5g, of which sugars 33.8g; Fat 90.9g, of which saturates 34g; Cholesterol 494mg; Calcium 1,285mg; Fibre 24.6g; Sodium 584mg.

PITTA BREAD

SOFT, SLIGHTLY BUBBLY PITTA BREAD IS A PLEASURE TO MAKE. IT CAN BE EATEN IN A VARIETY OF WAYS, SUCH AS FILLED WITH SALAD OR LITTLE CHUNKS OF BARBECUED MEAT.

MAKES TWELVE

INGREDIENTS

- 500g/1¼lb/5 cups strong white bread flour, or half white and half wholemeal (whole-wheat)
- 12.5ml/2½ tsp easy-blend (rapid-rise) dried yeast
- 15ml/1 tbsp salt
- 15ml/1 tbsp olive oil

1 Combine the flour, yeast and salt. Combine the olive oil and 250ml/8fl oz/1 cup water, then add the flour mixture, stirring in the same direction, and then working with your hands until the dough is stiff. Place the dough in a clean bowl, cover with a clean dish towel and leave in a warm place for at least 30 minutes and up to 2 hours.

2 Knead the dough for 10 minutes, or until smooth. Lightly oil the bowl, place the dough in it, cover again and leave to rise in a warm place for about 1 hour, or until doubled in size.

3 Divide the dough into 12 equal pieces. With lightly floured hands, flatten each piece, then roll out into a round measuring about 20cm/8in and about ½–1cm/¼–½in thick.

4 Heat a heavy frying pan over a medium-high heat. When hot, lay one piece of flattened dough in the pan and cook for 15–20 seconds. Turn it over and cook the second side for about 1 minute.

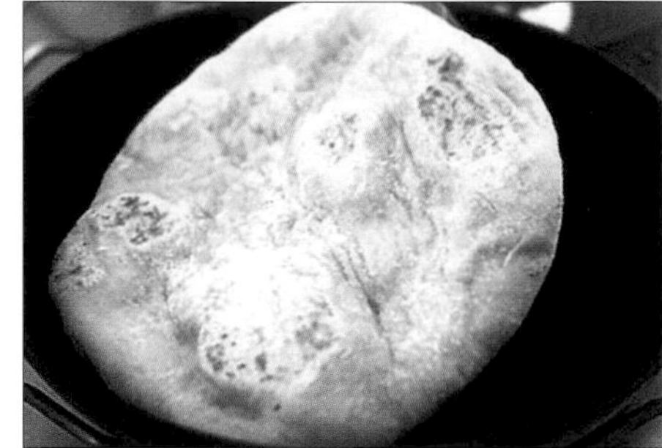

5 When large bubbles start to form on the bread, which should be after about 1–2 minutes or so, turn it over again. It should puff up. Using a clean dish towel, gently press on the bread where the bubbles have formed. Cook the bread for a total of 3 minutes, then remove the pitta from the pan. Repeat with the remaining dough.

6 Wrap the pitta breads in a clean dish towel, stacking them as each one is cooked. Serve the pittas hot while they are soft and moist, with a main meal, such as lamb kebabs, or as part of a meze table.

VARIATION

To bake the breads, preheat the oven to 220°C/425°F/Gas 7. Fill an unglazed or partially glazed dish with hot water and place in the bottom of the hot oven. Alternatively, arrange a handful of unglazed tiles in the base of the oven. Use either a non-stick baking sheet or a lightly oiled baking sheet and heat in the oven for a few minutes. Place two or three pieces of flattened dough on to the hot baking sheet and place in the hottest part of the oven. Bake for 2–3 minutes, or until puffed up. Repeat with the remaining dough.

Energy 150Kcal/638kJ; Protein 3.9g; Carbohydrate 32.4g, of which sugars 0.6g; Fat 1.5g, of which saturates 0.2g; Cholesterol 0mg; Calcium 58mg; Fibre 1.3g; Sodium 165mg.

SPRING ONION FLATBREADS

USE THESE FLATBREADS TO WRAP AROUND BARBECUE-COOKED MEAT AND CHUNKY VEGETABLE SALADS, OR SERVE WITH TASTY DIPS SUCH AS HUMMUS. THEY'RE AT THEIR BEST AS SOON AS THEY'RE COOKED.

MAKES SIXTEEN

INGREDIENTS

- 450g/1lb/4 cups strong white bread flour, plus extra for dusting
- 5ml/1 tsp salt
- 7g/¼oz packet easy-blend (rapid-rise) dried yeast
- 4 spring onions (scallions), finely chopped

1 Place the flour in a large mixing bowl and stir in the salt, yeast and spring onions. Make a well in the centre and pour in 300ml/½ pint/1¼ cups hand-hot water. Mix to form a soft, but not sticky, dough.

2 Turn out the dough on to a floured work surface and knead for about 5 minutes, until smooth.

3 Put the dough back in the bowl, cover with a damp dish towel and leave in a warm place until doubled in size.

4 Knock back (punch down) the dough to get rid of any excess air, and turn it out on to a floured work surface or board. Divide the dough into 16 pieces and roll each piece into a smooth ball. Roll out each ball to flatten it to a 13cm/5in round.

5 Heat a large frying pan until hot. Dust off any excess flour from one dough round and cook for 1 minute, until slightly browned in parts, then flip over and cook for 30 seconds. Repeat with the remaining dough rounds.

VARIATION

To make garlic flatbreads, use 2 finely chopped garlic cloves in place of the spring onions (scallions).

Energy 97Kcal/410kJ; Protein 2.7g; Carbohydrate 21.9g, of which sugars 0.5g; Fat 0.4g, of which saturates 0.1g; Cholesterol 0mg; Calcium 40mg; Fibre 0.9g; Sodium 124mg.

INDEX

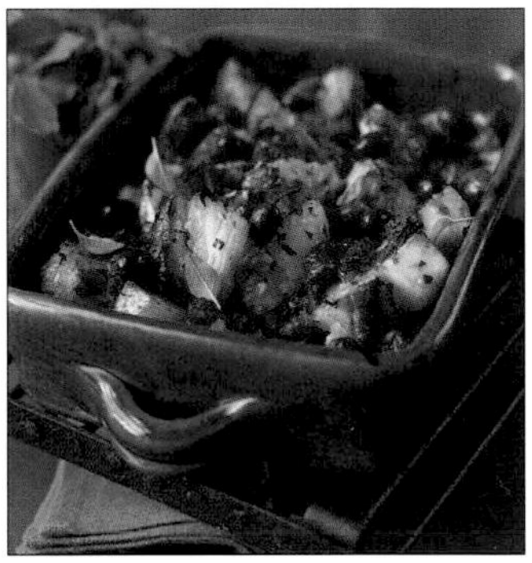

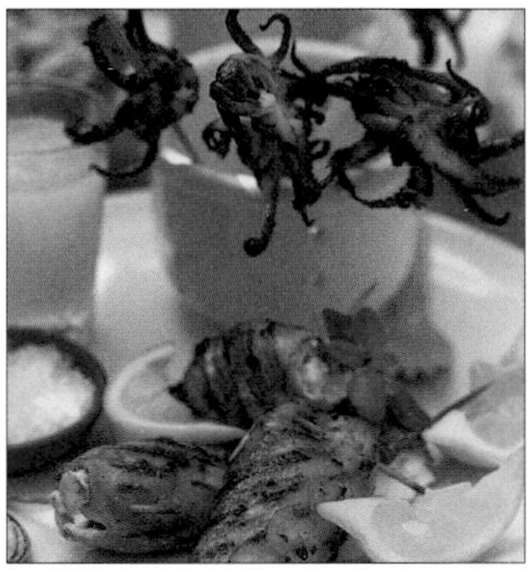

Publisher's Acknowledgements
The publisher would like to thank the following picture agencies and photographers for use of their images: Alamy Images: p6 (top), p7 (top and bottom), p9 (top), p10 (top), p12 (top), p15 (top), p19 (bottom), p20 (top and bottom), p21 (top), p22 (top), p23 (top and bottom), p24 (bottom), p25 (bottom), p26 (top), and p27 (top and bottom). Karita Lightfoot and Mark Wright: p16 (bottom), and p17 (top). Joanna Lorenz: p11 (bottom), p14 (bottom) and p17 (bottom).